The Illustrated History of
THE PIPE

ALEXIS LIEBAERT and ALAIN MAYA

Translated and adapted by
JACQUES P. COLE

HAROLD
S
STARKE
PUBLISHERS

Harold Starke Publishers Limited

This English-language edition
first published 1994
© Harold Starke Publishers Limited 1994,
adapted from *La grande histoire de la pipe*
© Flammarion Paris 1993
Editorial direction: Ghislaine Bavoillot
Graphic design: Marc Walter
Picture research: Sabine Greenberg
Colour reproduction: Colourscan France
Typesetting: The Five Castles Press Limited

ISBN 1 872457 20 7
Harold Starke Publishers Limited
Pixey Green, Stradbroke, Eye,
Suffolk IP21 5NG, England
and 203 Bunyan Court, Barbican,
London EC2Y 8DH, England
Printed in Germany

CONTENTS

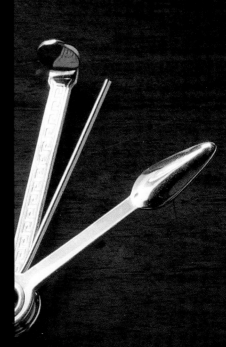

PREFACE

I must admit that I smoked my first pipe in order to impress a girlfriend whom I had taken to the cinema. I was seventeen at the time and I felt a little queasy afterwards! I remember the tobacco I smoked; although it was a very good one, it would not be recommended today by an experienced tobacconist as one suitable for a beginner. But then, someone once kindly said of me: "He was born with briar dust in his mouth."

What do pipes mean to me? I was born in the French town of Saint-Claude to which my father had come as a young man when working with an English pipe company shortly after the end of the First World War. Growing up in a place where pipe-making was the main occupation decided my future. I knew and loved the smell of a pipe factory at a tender age and, although I spent the war years in England and served in the British forces, I was lured back to pipes in 1948. Then, when I returned to England in 1957, I worked . . . in the pipe trade. And eventually I entered the journalistic side of the pipe and tobacco industry.

Pipe shapes and finishes were always my main interests. While some smokers, like the authors of this fine book, talk about the sensual attractions of a pipe, I believe that it is the combination of quality, expertise and attention to detail on the part of the pipe-maker which puts the finished article into an artistic class of its own.

I read this book with a great deal of fascination, enjoying the confirmation of what I already knew and sometimes smiling at the deeper attributes ascribed to pipes by the authors. But the fact remains that they also have a fine sense of the historical, social and artistic value of pipes created by craftsmen who fully understand the material they are working with.

The relaxing power of pipe-smoking is something to be experienced and enjoyed. True, it requires patience and time. So does reading, which is similarly relaxing, and therefore the two are a great combination, especially when the book in question is a book about pipes. In addition, this particular volume gathers together such a variety of relevant illustrations – something which has rarely, if ever, been achieved before.

Pipe-smokers the world over have a very strong bond. A pipe is a barrier breaker; an interest in pipes can also communicate to those who have not had the good fortune to experience the calm of lighting up and puffing away quietly while daydreaming or pondering more serious thoughts.

I often wonder if the countryman who said: "Sometimes I sits and thinks, and sometimes I just sits" was a pipe-smoker. Maybe he was.

Jacques Cole

Editor – *Tobacco*
Member of the *Academie Internationale de la Pipe*

For the photographer Jacques-Henri Lartigue, a pipe is a child's toy . . . (facing page *Dani at Aix-les-Bains, 1925*)

SWIRLING
WISPS OF
SERENITY

Fill your pipe, light it and then, with all your senses and your intellect suddenly sharpened in the spirals of the blue smoke, look at length for the answer to this question which appears easy, both for you and for non-smokers: Is there any object which like a pipe evokes subtle pleasure, sure comfort and perfect serenity? One can be sure that when you have finished your pipe, the answer will be "No". There is nothing like a "good pipe" . . .

What image could show those who do not have the slightest idea of it, the meaning of this precious formula, this overwhelming experience of pleasure? Perhaps one should set the scene in a quiet room with shaded lights. Then place a man comfortably in his armchair in front of a wood fire in the grate. In one hand he holds a glass of old brandy and in the other a pipe from which escapes a wisp of smoke. This gives some idea of the atmosphere. For whether it is in the narrow space of a comfortable sitting-room or elsewhere – at work, in a train or in the street – the climate "distilled" in a pipe is the same. The pipe-smoker, unlike the cigarette-smoker, savours his pleasure slowly, one short puff at a time, and enjoys more than just the smoke: he enjoys serenity. But this background does not do justice to the richness and the "generosity" of his pipe. The pipe-smoker lovingly caresses the object of his pleasure. His eyes are charmed by the harmony of its shape and colour from the first encounter; and his hand can feel the fine texture of the briar or meerschaum and the peculiarly pleasant warmth of the pipe. The aroma of the tobacco delicately tickles his nostrils even before lighting up; and this aroma changes its nature when the tobacco is being smoked. For example, there are the aromas of cocoa, rum or vanilla, of a wood in autumn, of damp earth and of oriental spices. And when the smoker's taste-buds are in contact with this mild and soft smoke, with its incomparable subtle flavours, the sensation is equal to those created by fine wines, delicate teas or the most delicious chocolates.

For those who have never smoked a pipe,

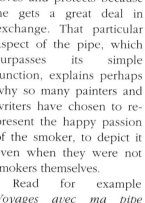

or worse still have never really learnt how to smoke one, this gives a faint insight into what they are missing: an overall pleasure which gratifies at least four of the five senses, and the spirit.

While many factors make a pipe an absolutely unique object in the social history of mankind, the other words which come to mind go beyond the daily activities of smokers: mystery and magic. Only a dictionary can pretend that a pipe is just an instrument used for the smoking of tobacco. In spite of appearances, it has remained, since its origin, an object connected with the hidden face of the universe, that of the sacred, the magical and the religious. It is an object of earth, air, fire and water, that the smoker touches, sucks, loves and protects because he gets a great deal in exchange. That particular aspect of the pipe, which surpasses its simple function, explains perhaps why so many painters and writers have chosen to represent the happy passion of the smoker, to depict it even when they were not smokers themselves.

Read for example *Voyages avec ma pipe* (*Travels With My Pipe*) a collection of tales from the 1920s, whose author Leon Werth has only recently been rediscovered. He was a free spirit, so deeply amazed by small things that the French author Saint-Exupery dedicated his fantasy *Le petit prince* to him. In this collection of a hundred pages, Werth takes the reader, sometimes in a dream, from Brittany to Honduras, from Paris to Holland, without once mentioning his pipe. This seeming absence of the pipe in the body of the book, contrasting with its presence in the title, give us a precious lesson. Just as he refuses to talk about himself - "see all without being seen", he writes - Werth decided not to show his pipe. This is because he considers his pipe to be such a close travelling companion that they are as one. It is also the case of Derzou Ouzala, in the tale by Arseniev, in which the pipe appears only rarely, as for example when the hunter goes to sleep and his pipe drops out of his mouth. So why should Werth mention his pipe, which is part of

The serenity of a "good pipe" ... (preceding pages). The pipe has always been the familiar companion of artists, poets and writers, encouraging their creativity. Gustave Courbet used it as an essential element in his self-portraits (right, The Man with a Pipe).

In the calm of his manor house in Normandy, Jean de la Varende was inspired by his pipe to write his novels, glorifying the past of his homeland with its Catholic and royalist traditions (facing page, photographed by Robert Doisneau in 1943).

Guillaume Apollinaire (left) - seen here in about 1911 in the studio of his friend Picasso. And Ossip Zadkine (right) - photographed in his studio by A Kertesz in 1926. These two resolutely modern artists (a poet and a sculptor) reflected their time.

the secret of his travels, his magic formula, his key? The pipe then is more than a pleasure for the senses, it is a familiar companion with mysterious powers, one that opens windows on the world for the astonished reader.

Look at the painting of *Le souffleur à la pipe* (*The Pipe-smoker*); Georges de La Tour probably painted the original in 1648, but there are now only copies in existence. It is known that La Tour used to represent secular scenes in the daylight, while he set those showing religious inspiration at night in a contrasting light. Thus a pipe-smoker should have been painted in daytime, in the same way as a musician, a card-player or a story-teller. But La Tour chose the night. What he wanted to show was not the pleasure of "tobacco drinking" as it was then called; this would not have distinguished the subject from a simple connoisseur of good food. It was as though, with this pipe and the ritual it imposed, the smoker was part of the "sacred" world. Thus the pipe was not just a simple clay object, perhaps made in Gouda, held in the smoker's hand; it was intrinsically connected with breathing life into the embers, with the flame and the light of the flame. There is also the calm and silence of the night, the seriousness of the smoker devoted to his rite and, above all, the intimacy of the scene. The light of the flame only illuminates the young man and his pipe. They are at that moment completely alone and surrounded by mystery. The light in which they are united is a universe of peaceful pleasure inaccessible to any outsider.

Thus La Tour pictured the essence of his subject, summarized in a few words: magic, ritual, intimacy and pleasure. Note also *Courbet au chien noir* (*Courbet with a Black Dog*), the self-portrait of a genius who was then only twenty-three years old. Two centuries had passed, the approach to painting was not the same and Courbet did not have the mystical *élan* of La Tour. And yet . . . the proud young man was exposing, not without a degree of arrogance, the intimate scene of his pleasure from which we are manifestly excluded.

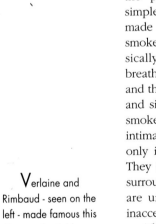

Courbet seems to say: "See all that I love, and which is enough for me. In the foreground I have put myself, as I am a handsome romantic young man, gifted and with a good future. Then, in no particular order, the countryside and its flowers, my walking-stick to help me travel in it, my drawing-book to sketch it, my dog as a companion, and my pipe . . ." His pipe, of course. But of what use is it? It has gone out and, as with La Tour's, it is far from the smoker's mouth. Once again the simple function of the object is not important. Look at it carefully, at that moment when the painter confronts us through the mirror of his self-portrait, at the moment when he paints: he holds his pipe like a brush. But its value is more than that of a brush. Its role is not to consume tobacco and give pleasure. More than a brush, and by some unknown magic, it serves as a medium between the painter and his painting. Suddenly the universe of La Tour and that of Courbet are the same, a universe where the magical power of a pipe gives birth to mysteries within the exclusive framework of intimacy. In the same way, the displayed objects and the dog are possessions that can be neither loaned nor exchanged, belonging to a single man. And the pipe, lit or not, transmuted into a brush by a strange "chemistry", gives the painter the power to create.

Many artists, philosophers and scientists have thus described the creative function of their pipes. "Smoking a pipe does away with thinking", wrote Schopenhauer, summing up in a simple sentence this indisputable phenomenon. He merely meant that, while smoking a pipe, thoughts come without effort, which was also implicitly suggested by Courbet in the context of shapes and colours. A little later, towards the end of the nineteenth century, when cigarettes were becoming popular, the French poet, Mallarmé, who had already adopted the habit of smoking (as seen in the fine portrait by Manet), praised his neglected pipe which was the only thing that made him work and, at the same time, a function indispensable to a poet, fed him with memories

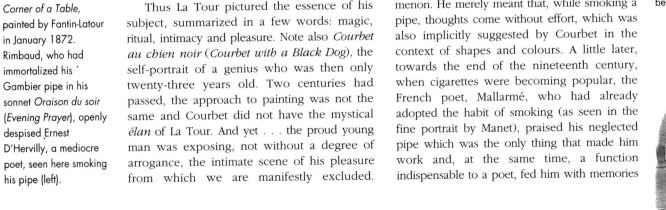

and dreams: "Yesterday, I found my pipe while dreaming of a long winter evening of work. Threw away the cigarettes associated with childish summer joy, with the leaves made blue-green by the sun, and returned to my pipe which needs to be smoked without interruption, so as to draw better; but I was not ready for the surprise prepared by my neglect of it; I had only just pulled the first puffs when I forgot the long books I planned to write. Amazed and moved, I took a breath of winter which was returning . . ."

Mallarmé was serious and solemn when he took up his pipe, as was La Tour's pipe-smoker, but after the first puff he was as astonished by its magic as Proust was by a *madeleine,* and also as moved as we can imagine the pipe-smoker to be. This is because a pipe will only give pleasure if it is respected.

Where does this mysterious power come from, this power that invites creativity? A creativity to which Apollinaire and Rimbaud, Mark Twain and Günter Grass, Van Gogh and Manet, Newton and Einstein all bear witness? At the very least it is a power which can free the mind to solve problems, as portrayed by the brilliance of the three most famous detectives of literature and cinema: Sherlock Holmes, Philip Marlowe and Commissaire Maigret? How, in a word, does a pipe encourage the activity of the mind, without the doubtful properties of tobacco being responsible? This time, it is another French poet Baudelaire, whose portrait by Courbet shows him with a pipe between his teeth, who leads us to the answer. In his famous sonnet he makes the pipe speak: "I am the pipe of an author; (. . .) When he is full of pains (. . .) I embrace and soothe his soul (. . .) And I distil a

powerful remedy / Which charms his heart and cures / His mind from tiredness." A tender speech from a pipe which was later answered by Tristan Corbière: "I am the pipe of a poet / his nurse who soothes him and puts his black mood to sleep."

Baudelaire and Corbière give us the description of the phenomenon: if a pipe favours the activity of the mind, it is because it cures the mind of its fatigue, while relieving the smoker of his pain and soothing his soul. "A pipe is to the troubled soul what the caresses of a mother are for her suffering child," says an Indian proverb. The pipe is a balm, a treatment which feeds the mind, so that revived, re-established and full of new vigour it can then expand.

But where do these therapeutic and energy-giving properties of a pipe come from? The answer to this question must have been evident to Sigmund Freud, who was both a pipe- and cigar-smoker. Another French poet, Francis Jammes, had felt it in confiding: "I smoke a brown pipe like the breast of a little negress." It would have been more correct to write that he smoked it like the maternal breast. Because the pipe - according to the poets – rocks, pacifies and nourishes exactly as he says. It is a dummy which calms, in the same way as the dummy in the mouth of a baby produces peace and quiet; or for that matter the one that a child may use, its thumb. Each of us, even Bismarck and MacArthur who planned battles with a pipe in their mouths, even Stalin, who never cleaned his pipes, which disturbed his terrified "advisers", misses the sensual contact with our mother. Desmond Morris evoked this with humour in *Man-watching*: "It would be difficult to convince a businessman, sucking his unlit

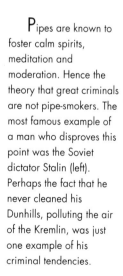

Who can tell what part the pipe played in Carl Gustav Jung's elaboration of his theory of "collective subconscious"? The Swiss psychiatrist was for a long time a disciple of Freud. But a breach grew between the two: unlike Jung, one fine day Freud came to prefer cigars to pipes (above right)

Mark Twain – seen here in his house at Hartford (Connecticut) in 1903 – had definite ideas of comfort: a pipe (he liked Petersons) and a rocking-chair. It was perhaps in this chair that he decided to make the young Tom Sawyer a pipe-smoker (facing page).

Pipes are known to foster calm spirits, meditation and moderation. Hence the theory that great criminals are not pipe-smokers. The most famous example of a man who disproves this point was the Soviet dictator Stalin (left). Perhaps the fact that he never cleaned his Dunhills, polluting the air of the Kremlin, was just one example of his criminal tendencies.

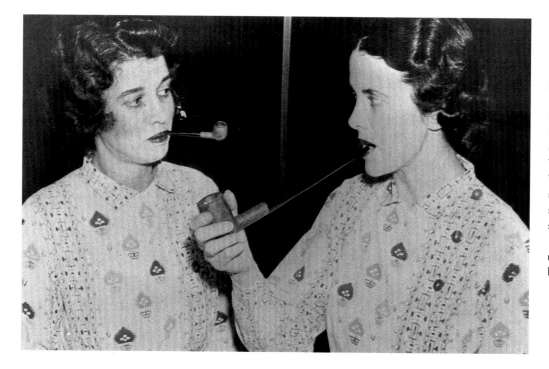

There appears to be a prejudice against women smoking pipes, which leads some women smokers to pretend that they buy them for their husbands. This prejudice was fought by George Sand who smoked a pipe before taking up cigarettes. It was thus that Musset drew her in around 1835 (below).

Women who dare to take up pipe-smoking become as keen and expert as men. They prefer more graceful models, specially designed to be feminine. This is what Louisa Wilke – daughter of a manufacturer of the same name – told her sister Anna in the 1930s. Anna, in response, took up a large model . . . (left)

pipe or pulling on his cigar, that he is in reality looking for a little comfort in a sophisticated version of a baby's dummy."

This interpretation leads naturally to another question: why then, apart from rare exceptions, do women not smoke pipes? It seems that women are satisfied with cigarettes, as a substitute for a dummy, for reasons both symbolic and historical. Unlike snuff, which became very popular in the sixteenth century among men and women of high society, the pipe remained at that time an instrument used mostly by sailors and soldiers. Very early – as witnessed by all the Dutch popular imagery of the seventeenth century – the pipe appeared as a phallic symbol and was a constant source of broad even lewd insinuations. Hence its association with virile conviviality in army barracks and inns, so that few women dared indulge; those who did, as some still do, wanted to present a certain image of femininity. The writer George Sand was one of the most famous examples. She smoked a pipe until she discovered cigarettes, giving herself up

to that pleasure, as shown in a small drawing by Musset, in about 1835. Nobody will ever know if this particular motive animated the very energetic Marquise de Pompadour, favourite of Louis XV. She owned three hundred pipes which she smoked with passion. And what of the delicate Elizabeth Vigée-Lebrun, who showed herself in a self-portrait smoking a clay pipe against a background of all the necessary accessories of a dedicated smoker. It is perhaps only in the countryside, where women have always shared the hardest tasks equally with men, that this preconceived idea of the virile aspects of the pipe is less widespread. Not so long ago, in Brittany, a region populated by sailors and peasants, it was not unusual to meet women smoking pipes. Even today, many women do not hesitate to smoke pipes in the Swiss canton of the Valais. In Germany, Goethe's cook, who was certainly a robust peasant woman, was not forgiven by her master for being an inveterate smoker: "She was constantly stubborn, vulgar, unmanageable and sly and led me an

Ancient clay models are quite elegant with their slim and graceful stems, and slightly inclined bowls. They are well adapted for women smokers (facing page). Sailors or peasants, the Bretons have always been great pipe-smokers, without sex distinction, until the middle of the twentieth century (below left).

A great traveller, art connoisseur and collector of paintings, the German photographer Herbert List, who disappeared in 1975, could only have been a pipe-smoker (left).

As the cane and bowler hat were indispensable to Charlie Chaplin, a pipe is part of the silhouette of Jacques Tati, in the film *Mr Hulot's Holiday*, in 1953 (below).

If Hemingway, who was a pipe-smoker, had allowed his most famous hero a little leisure during his struggle against the swordfish, he would have looked like this "Old Man of the Sea" photographed by Edouard Boubat (facing page).

impossible life . . .", wrote this enemy of tobacco smoke in a letter of "recommendation" just before she left his service. The cook tore up the letter and, as soon as her master had left for his daily walk, she took her revenge by smoking in his study . . . Whatever the truth of the story, let those in the country and the towns be reassured: for modern ladies who would not like their femininity to be doubted, various makers such as Dunhill and Butz-Choquin still offer suitably elegant pipes.

There you have the benevolent magic of the pipe reduced to the logic of the unconscious. This also takes into account the virtues of the cigarette and the cigar. A pipe, of course, offers extra advantages, linked to the beauty of its form and material, and with the complex manoeuvres called for by its infinite variety.

As opposed to the cigar-smoker and particularly the cigarette-smoker where the "dummy factor" is conclusive, a connoisseur of pipes gets almost as much pleasure from touching and looking at them as from smoking. A pipe comforts even when empty or not lit. Even its shape, combining the compact volume of the bowl and the slender line of the stem and

mouthpiece, suggests a satisfying balance of the mind. For those pipe-smokers with even a slightly artistic soul, the object becomes a small gracious masterpiece which gladdens the heart. The material itself contributes to that pleasure, particularly when it is natural, like briar which portrays with the beauty of its grain the whole story of its life.

But what distinguishes the pipe from its rivals is the important ritual that surrounds it. To smoke a pipe demands knowledge, a knowledge that every beginner must acquire. Certain pipe-makers have understood the practical and symbolic importance of this apprenticeship and they include instructions with their products. Between the teat and the pipe, is everything that separates man from animal, adult from infant, to wit, culture and civilization. A pipe is proper for a man.

Should we worry therefore, about its decline in popularity? This started after the First World War, when cigarettes became predominant. It has accelerated during the past

This is winter 1819 in Denmark: *Der Richter Jacob Wilder (Judge Jacob Wilder)* finishes his days quietly like an "old baby" sucking his pipe that he does not smoke . . . Painted by Johann August Kraft, German school, 1798–1829 (facing page).

Pipes with long stems were relatively common up to the nineteenth century. Apart from providing a sweet and light smoke, they had the advantage of conviviality, as it was often difficult to light them oneself, as shown in *Danish Artists in Rome*, by Constantin Hansen in 1837 (right).
"When all is said and done, love is trite compared with the spirituality of a tobacco pipe" – radical thought of the Goncourt brothers, written in their *Journal*. And who knows to what height Jules de Goncourt aspired, in this sublime moment illustrated in the *Journal de l'art*? (below).

twenty years, as if our way of living was stopping us from taking time to indulge in the rites of pipe-smoking. And while the representation of pipes abounded in all the arts, it has now virtually disappeared from paintings, literature and the cinema. We could question ourselves at length on that disaffection, comparable to the current threat to reading. In many ways, the two activities are similar: pipes make way for cigarettes as reading makes way for television, because both demand an active participation, and therefore effort. Perhaps they also need some of La Tour's light – if that light suggests mystery and silence, calm and solitude, it is a "flame", in other words, passion and fervour.

We can see some reasons for optimism. In the same way as books, pipes will not disappear during this era which is as temporary as the objects that it venerates. They are neither ephemeral nor disposable, but they leave a lasting trace in the mind, not least because they offer another singular property which is useful in our society: to those who feel bruised by the incertitude and violence of the world, they give the comfort of being able to withdraw within oneself, perhaps as if in a dream; if, on the contrary, one feels the pain of being alone, they provide, thanks to the knowledge and ritual that one can always share, the comfort of conviviality. All round the world, dedicated pipe-smokers love to meet to share their passion.

These two needs that pipes may meet – the desire to be open to the world or to be protected from it – may, in reality, be united within the same person. Each of us looks at these alternatives in a search for his or her own lifestyle. And on the threshold of the third millenium, nothing points to a great change in that respect . . .

HISTORY

At the beginning, there was fire. No one will ever know where or when the first pipe in history was smoked, but it is certain that it goes back to an ancient, even pre-historic, idea stimulated by the inhalation of the smoke of a fire. Greek mythology gives a short-cut to that story: Epimetheus, enchanted by the aroma of the smoke coming from the fire that his brother Prometheus had just stolen from the gods, started to inhale it with a straw. The two titans were punished and the whole of humanity with them, for having appropriated something that only the gods felt entitled to.

One can imagine these early pipes, lost in time. Nature is not short of convenient elements which, with little alteration, are suitable: a straw, a simple rolled leaf, a bone that can be emptied, a reed pushed into an opened nut . . . But one has to wait until "historic" times to find the first written evidence, and archaeological discoveries, and to know more about our smoking ancestors.

BEFORE TOBACCO

Historians agree at least on one point: that in most old civilizations, smoke – rising to the heavens, as a mediation between men and the gods – was always associated with religious rituals. It was thus that certain divine messages, oracles such as that of Delphi, were interpreted. Ritual smoke, often intoxicating, was first of all the preserve of priests, then sorcerers and magicians, who thought themselves invested with divine power and so capable of forecasting the future, to guide, to purify and to cure. These practices are still in use today in isolated regions, such as Amazonia. But they are also found nowadays in the purification rituals associated with incense in Christian churches. The first evidence of such uses of smoke comes from Heroditus who, in 500 BC, reported the use of hemp by the Scythians. The smoke coming from seeds thrown on burning hot stones used to make them shout with pleasure. Archaeological discoveries in Scythian tombs confirmed this but the experts came to

the conclusion that it was part of a funeral ritual rather than just drunken pleasure: enraptured by the fumes of the hemp, the priest would lead the soul of the deceased to the hereafter.

For the ancient Greeks, it was only a short step from the use of the smoke (given off by burning plants) for religious rites to its use in a therapeutic context. In the fifth century BC, Hippocrates, the first master of medical science, prescribed fumigations to treat certain gynaecological conditions. To cure the most common ailments – from a simple cold to impotence – the Romans inhaled the smoke of many plants such as hemp, colt's foot, lavender, henbane, marjoram, thyme, mint, vervain and others. We know that these inhalations were sometimes carried out with an instrument. Very often, it was only a simple reed, but to be cured or just intoxicated, the Romans also used hollowed-out marrow bones and, according to some, real pipes with clay bowls. These two smoking instruments are the oldest "historical" pipes discovered by archaeologists. The first come from a dig in Yorkshire, where Roman legionaires appear to have taught the Celts how to use bones for smoking. The second come from finds in Scotland and Ireland early this century of pipes called "elfin pipes", so named because of their small size and bowls similar to Chinese opium-pipes.

But some archaeologists now disagree with this dating, as for other pipes found in the French Jura and Côte d'Or regions, made of iron and said to be from the Gallo-Roman era. Clay pipes, seemingly from Roman times, have also been found in Spain. Finally, several oil lamps were dug from a site at Senemes, near Vaison-la-Romaine (south of France) showing a rather grotesque figure, holding in his hand what appears to be a long pipe.

Of all the ancient European pipes unearthed at the beginning of the twentieth century, none has officially been judged authentic. Many have been found to have signs of techniques which appeared in Europe much later than their purported dates. Furthermore, there are no traces,

The French naturalist and traveller Sonnini relates, in around 1789, that in Egypt, the pastime is to smoke and drink coffee. "The pipe is always in the mouth from morning till night, whether at home, visiting, in the street or on horseback . . . The pipes' stems are very long in various woods, often aromatic. I have kept one in jasmine . . . The most common wooden pipes are wrapped in a silk cloth surrounded by gold thread... The part that one puts in the mouth is a piece of yellow amber with a sweet and fragrant aroma, which when heated and pressed relieves the bitter taste of the tobacco." Left: *The Seller of Tobacco Pipes in an Oriental Café*, by Georg Ferdinand Waldmuller (1793-1865).

Delicious miraculous herb, or degrading vice? In invading the Old World, tobacco triggered contradictory passions opposing hedonists and virtuous hypocrites. This *Allegory of Smokers* (Holland seventeenth century) did not reconcile them . . . (below)

In this peaceful *A Courtyard at Delft*, painted by Peter de Hooch (1629-1688), a burgher enjoys a moment of relaxation. Only a little way from there, the manufacturers of Gouda were producing millions of clay pipes, exported to the rest of Europe (pages 24 and 25).

written or otherwise, of the use of pipes in Europe during the whole of the Middle Ages. This lack of evidence has led today's historians to believe that the use of pipes was unknown in the Old World before the sixteenth century, except – and it is not possible to verify the hypothesis – at very local level.

We also know that other civilizations, further afield, pre-dated Europe in the use of pipes. Early explorers brought some back from Africa, often finely carved in copper, wood or metal, indicating ancient customs in that continent. But even then, nothing shows that they were earlier than the sixteenth century, when tobacco was introduced to western Africa, in relation to the slave trade. In India, certain tribes practised a curious method of inhalation, that one could call a "communal pipe with a static combustion chamber". A number of smokers used to dig a hole and fill it with aromatic leaves; the leaves were stirred up with burning embers, then covered with earth; the smokers then inhaled the trapped smoke with a reed. This method continued for centuries, to the astonishment of European soldiers in the First World War who saw the Indian soldiers in the trenches dig a hole and smoke according to this ancestral method.

THE FIRST TOBACCO PIPES

The real ancestors of pipe-smokers were undoubtedly the American Indians. Until the end of the fifteenth century, they were the only ones in the world who appreciated regularly the virtues of a plant unknown elsewhere; some called it "petun" and others "tabaco". We will deal later with the origins of the plant, today grown in all continents. Its use had been current among the natives of North America for perhaps several thousand years. Archaeological digs discovered, in the Yucatan peninsula, some tobacco

It is on the American continent that the oldest pipes have been found. These pre-Columbian pipes were of baked clay, decorated with religious motifs from Mexico (above) and Colombia (right). The Eskimo pipe (below) shows its ancient use in North America. It is made up of a tin bowl and a long stem formed by two wooden pieces tied with strips of seal leather.

pollen together with objects dating back some four thousand years. The use of pipes in pre-Columbian America seems to have been proven by one of the oldest known representations of the pipe, although some historians hesitate to give it formal identification. One can see, in a fresco of a Mayan temple built in the fifth century AD, at Palenque in Mexico, a priest in ceremonial dress holding in his mouth a "long mouthpiece" from which thick smoke is emitted. Several pre-Columbian pipes have also been discovered in central America and in the valley of the Mississippi. They are made of red steatite or catlinite (a type of slate), either carved or painted with various motifs: such as birds or reptile heads. There again, the motivation of the smokers seemed to be essentially religious. The Mayan priests used, during certain ceremonies, to blow smoke to the four corners of the earth. Among the North American Indians, the tobacco smoke inhaled from wooden or stone pipes was supposed to have magic powers. It was through the smoke that the gods cured, and gave the necessary strength to overcome enemies, while guaranteeing peace. But we may wonder whether, over periods of time, the American Indians did not put aside the religious and magical practice of smoking for something more human and prosaic: their own pleasure. It seems that the first European explorers met many simple recreational smokers at the end of the fifteenth century.

THE CONQUEST OF THE OLD WORLD

Christopher Columbus discovered tobacco when he discovered the New World on October 15, 1492, three days after anchoring his caravelle, the *Pinta* at the island of Gunahani in the Bahamas. That day, in his log, the Genoese noted that one of his men had met a native who was transporting a quantity of large leaves in his canoe, leaves to which the native attached great

"With this sacred pipe, you will walk on Earth . . . The bowl is in red stone, it of the Earth. The young bison carved in the stone, and looking to the centre, represents the quadrupeds that live on Mother-Earth. The wooden stem represents all that grows on the Earth. The twelve feathers which hang from where the stem penetrates the bowl, belong to the Spotted Eagle and represent the eagle and all the creatures in the sky. All creatures are contained in the pipe, and they smoke with you to send a voice to Wakan Tanka, the Great Spirit.

When you pray with this pipe, you pray for everything in the universe, and everything in the universe prays with you." Black Elk, holy man of the Oglalas Sioux, quoted by Serge Bramly in *Sacred Earth* (right, Rocky Bear, Sioux, Omaha, 1899).

importance. For the first time in history, white men had come face to face with tobacco. When the fleet landed on San Fernando, now Cuba, Columbus sent some of his sailors on a tour of inspection. They reported that they had seen Indians of both sexes strolling about with lighted rolled leaves from which they inhaled a perfume according to their custom.

One of these observers was Rodrigo de Jerez, who, astonished by this strange practice which seemed to have no reason, tried it and must have liked it since he brought back some leaves to Spain in due course. De Jerez was probably the first smoker in Europe and its first victim. Back in Spain in 1498, he was arrested in Barcelona while quietly smoking what was in fact a cigar. He was hauled in front of the Inquisition and denounced as a sorcerer indulging in a heathen practice and he spent ten years in jail. Others say that he was released from prison after a shorter sentence.

This sentence did not discourage the growing number of connoisseurs of tobacco, who were initiated into the habit by Spanish and Portuguese sailors. It seems that few cared about the pronouncements of some fanatical clerics against this "scandalous" pleasure, this "vice" resulting from pagan superstitions. In fact, the use of tobacco became rapidly widespread in Europe during the first years of the sixteenth century. It does not really matter who was the first "official" importer of tobacco into the Old World, whether it was the Spanish monk Ramon Pane, Cortez, Hernandez of Toledo, the Flemish Damien de Goes or the English John Rolfe – the honour has been attributed to each of them by various historians. The most important fact is that each ship returning from the New World carried a few bales of tobacco, and in particular seeds of the precious plant, which was cultivated at first in Spain and Portugal.

In France, tradition attributes to Jean Nicot, François II's ambassador to the Portuguese Court, the distinction of being the first to introduce tobacco into his country in 1560. Having discovered the plant in Lisbon and appreciated its curative properties when taken

as "snuff", he sent a small quantity to the King's mother, Catherine of Medici, who suffered from migraine. A letter sent by Jean Nicot to the Cardinal of Loraine, dated April 16, 1560, appears to reveal the true role of Nicot in the history of tobacco in France. He reports the existence and the qualities of a plant which was supposed to cure certain skin ulcers. He continues, in the quaint French of the time, to say that it was quite effective against a type of ulcer which he calls *Noli me tangere* which medical men of the time could not cure. He then suggests that he will send some seeds to the cardinal's gardener at Marmoutier, to be planted in a barrel, together with instructions on how to transplant and tend them.

Whatever the story, Catherine of Medici had the opportunity to try this "grass from the Indies", found it relieved her migraine and shared the recipe with her friends. Shortly after, the whole Court was taking snuff. A new trend was launched and the remedy was called the "Queen's herb". Ten years later, the botanist Jean Liebault associated the name of Nicot with the newly-found plant, by calling it *Nicotiana*. At the beginning of the nineteenth century, "nicotine", a dangerous alkaloid in its pure state, was extracted from the plant.

In truth, whatever the origin of the infatuation with tobacco in France, the first importer was probably the Franciscan monk André Thevet. He was a traveller and botanist of note, who was impressed by the flowers of the tobacco plant that he found in Brazil. He brought some back to France in 1556 and grew it in his garden, calling the plant *Angoulmoisine* in honour of his native town But other Frenchmen had anticipated him. A French text, written in 1525 by Pierre Grignon, a chart-maker and seafarer from Dieppe, author of *Pearl of Cosmography*, states: "Yesterday, I met an old sailor with whom I shared a pitcher of Breton wine. While drinking, he suddenly brought out of his bag an object of white clay which I thought was a writing accessory – it looked like an ink-well with a long stem, and a small container. He filled the large end with brown leaves that he crushed in the palm of his hand, lit it with a lighter (sic) and having put the stem in his mouth emitted smoke from the mouth, which impressed me a great deal. He told me that he had learned that from the Portuguese who had picked it up from Mexican Indians. He called it "to petune" and said that it cleared the mind and induced happy thoughts. (The "container" in question must have been an early tobacco pouch.) Interestingly, a similar report exists in relation to a sailor in Scotland at about the same time.

From the second half of the sixteenth century onwards, the reputation of the therapeutic and almost magical properties of tobacco was the driving force in its spread. The speed at which it conquered France after relieving Catherine de Medici's migraine is very significant. Medical men saw it as a medicinal plant capable of curing almost all illnesses, from vertigo to the plague via skin infections. After Paris, this expensive trend – importation and local production could not meet the demand – reached all the European Courts, and the palaces of the Middle and Far East.

There is no evidence of the extent of the use of pipes at the time. Tobacco was used in many ways: in powder as snuff, inhaled through a tube or pipe, chewed or made up in horrible pharmaceutical concoctions. It seems that the use of pipes – the name comes from the low Latin *pipa*, a reed or stem – did not take root until the beginning of the seventeenth century, when pipe-making started. It was in England that the first pipes were made in the Old World.

We do not really know why pipes were so successful in England. Their use was spread rapidly at the end of the sixteenth century by English sailors. During their voyages, they became familiar with the clay pipes of the North American Indians. Among those who explored the New World, Sir Walter Raleigh, poet, seafarer and favourite of Elizabeth I, was one of the leading promoters of tobacco and pipes in Britain. An inveterate pipe-smoker, he introduced the use of tobacco at Court initially among the aristocracy. Within a few years, "drinking tobacco", as it was called then, became part of the lifestyle of the period, and knowledge-

able "teachers" started giving pipe-smoking lessons to the English elite. There were then rumours that Raleigh, businessman and courtier, had encouraged the trend in order to take profits from a tobacco plantation that he had created in Ireland in 1580. It was a lucrative activity which he wished to extend five years later by setting up a colony of tobacco planters in North America in the colony that he called Virginia. The name, which has become the best known in the tobacco business, was chosen by Raleigh in honour of his Queen, known as the "Virgin Queen".

Whatever the truth, the pioneer met incomprehension on the part of those around him: legend has it that one day while he was quietly smoking his clay pipe at his doorstep, a worried servant thought he was on fire and threw a bucket of water over him. But Sir Walter Raleigh's problems had only just started. He fell from grace when James I succeeded to the throne and, following an alleged plot, he was imprisoned in the Tower of London from 1603 to 1616. When set free, he headed an expedition to the Americas, but his attacks on Spanish settlers created a diplomatic incident between England and Spain. He was arrested on his return and condemned to death. As all Englishmen know, he went to the scaffold in 1618 smoking his favourite "Indian" pipe. His pipe, or one similar, is now part of the Dunhill collection.

By that time, all English people of social standing were smoking pipes, regardless of sex or age, and if one is to believe the story of a French traveller some years later, quoted by Alfred Dunhill in his *Pipe Book*:

"When the children went to school they carried in their satchel a pipe, which their mother took care to fill in the morning, it serving them instead of breakfast; and at the accustomed hour everyone laid aside his book to light his pipe, the master smoking with them and teaching them how to hold their pipe and draw in the tobacco, thus habituating them to it from their youth, believing it absolutely necessary for a man's health."

In addition to the increase of the trend from the end of the sixteenth century, Lon-

To honour the memory of Sir Walter Raleigh, an English tobacco manufacturer called one of his brands *Myrtle Grove*. It was at Myrtle Grove that the founder of Virginia, while quietly smoking his pipe, was drenched by his servant who thought that he was on fire! (right).

In Germanic countries, a violent anti-smoking campaign was launched during the seventeenth century. In 1653, smoking was banned in Dresden, in 1656 in all Bavaria and in 1661 at Berne. In this caricature condemning tobacco, one notes that it was sold as twist. Twist remained popular until the nineteenth century (above right). Often only tobacco excess was condemned, as shown in this etching of 1630, illustrating a pamphlet called *The German Tobacco Drinker* (below right).

Crafft, Tugent und würckung des hochnutzbarlichen Tabac, durchs A. B. C. gezogen, fein gröblich.

Der best Tabac der ist hie feil,
Kompt herbey kaufft ieder ein theil.

Ich brauch Tabac und befinds gut,
Trücknet die flüß reinigt das blut.

Wann ich gleich hab Bier oder Wein,
Muß Tabac doch getruncken sein.

Mann sagt zu viel sey ungesund,
Das merck ich itzt zu dieser stund.

Mein Naß die ist verstopffet seer,
Brauch Schnupff-Tabac dass ich sie leer.

Der Schnupff Tabac purgiret gut,
Darzeit wann was entfahren thut.

Auszkündige Alamodo Bauchpürgation, Causirt Durchlauff, Effectuirt Fartzen, Groltzen, Husten, Jurren, Kotzen, Lufft in hosen, Murmeln im leibe, Niesten, Operirt, Purgirt, Qualificirt, Rotz, Schnupffen, Speyen, Tabac Vertreibt Wütigkeit, Xantho Yn Zähnen.

doners took part in smoking parties, where they were taught how to smoke, but the faith in the medical properties of tobacco led to excesses which were exploited by its opponents.

The most famous opponent was James I. In his *Counterblaste to Tobacco*, published anonymously in 1604, the King attacked the practice as barbaric, a menace to society, harmful to health, and in the final count profiting the Spanish trade. A growing number of "experts" and medical men joined in the campaign, such as a doctor who declared in 1611 that "tobacco makes man a smelly animal, weakened and ready for all depravations".

In this argument, one perceives moral considerations against this "Indian vice" which encourages nonchalance and day-dreaming at a time when military prowess was exalted. But it was a lost fight, such was the spread of the use of tobacco in the Old World. In 1609, in Japan where the Portuguese had introduced tobacco some twenty years earlier, the Shoguns decided, in vain, to forbid the practice, which had caused an increasing number of fires.

In Turkey, from 1605, the Sultan decreed a total ban. The penalties were severe: from piercing the nose to the disgrace of being exhibited through the streets on the back of a donkey, and death in cases of recidivism. Smokers in Russia risked dire torture, including having their nose cut off. In spite of all these threats, the pleasure of tasting the delights of tobacco was too great, and nothing and nobody stopped its spread.

In England, the King gave in. But he soon found consolation in putting a tax on the tobacco that settlers in America were shipping in increasing quantities, amounting to 40,000 lb (over 18,000 kilograms) in 1620. The State budget could now afford to ignore "morality". A few years later, Richelieu imitated King James by taxing tobacco in France, by an ordinance of November 17, 1626, at 30 sols per pound weight. This measure encouraged smuggling which flourished in France until the end of the nineteenth century.

THE REIGN OF GOUDA

The growing consumption of tobacco in England from the end of the sixteenth century, coupled with the reduction in price due to increased production, created a shortage of pipes. The Indian clay pipes used at the time were produced in small quantities and were quite fragile. Imports did not satisfy demand. Conditions were therefore ripe for the establishment of pipe manufacture in the Old World.

Some of the first English clay pipes were made at Broseley in Shropshire, c.1575. They were small and had a flat "heel" so that they

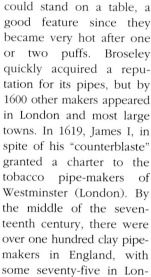

could stand on a table, a good feature since they became very hot after one or two puffs. Broseley quickly acquired a reputation for its pipes, but by 1600 other makers appeared in London and most large towns. In 1619, James I, in spite of his "counterblaste" granted a charter to the tobacco pipe-makers of Westminster (London). By the middle of the seventeenth century, there were over one hundred clay pipe-makers in England, with some seventy-five in London, and their number had more than doubled by 1700.

But the initial hostility of James, as well as political and religious persecution coupled with growing international competition, drove some pipe-makers out of England. Some refugees settled in Holland at Gouda, near Rotterdam and Delft, centres renowned since the Middle Ages for their potteries, due to the fine quality of the clay found in the river Ijssel. The beginning of Dutch clay pipe-making is attributed to William Baernelts, a dissenter, who became Barentsz in Holland, and who set up the first manufacture of pipes in Gouda in 1617. He named it the Crowned Rose, in honour of the Tudors, and gained an immediate success. This success increased from 1630, when tobacco cultivation started in the regions of Utrecht and Gelderland.

In less than ten years, Gouda became a main centre of pipe production in Europe and the principal competitor of the English pipe-

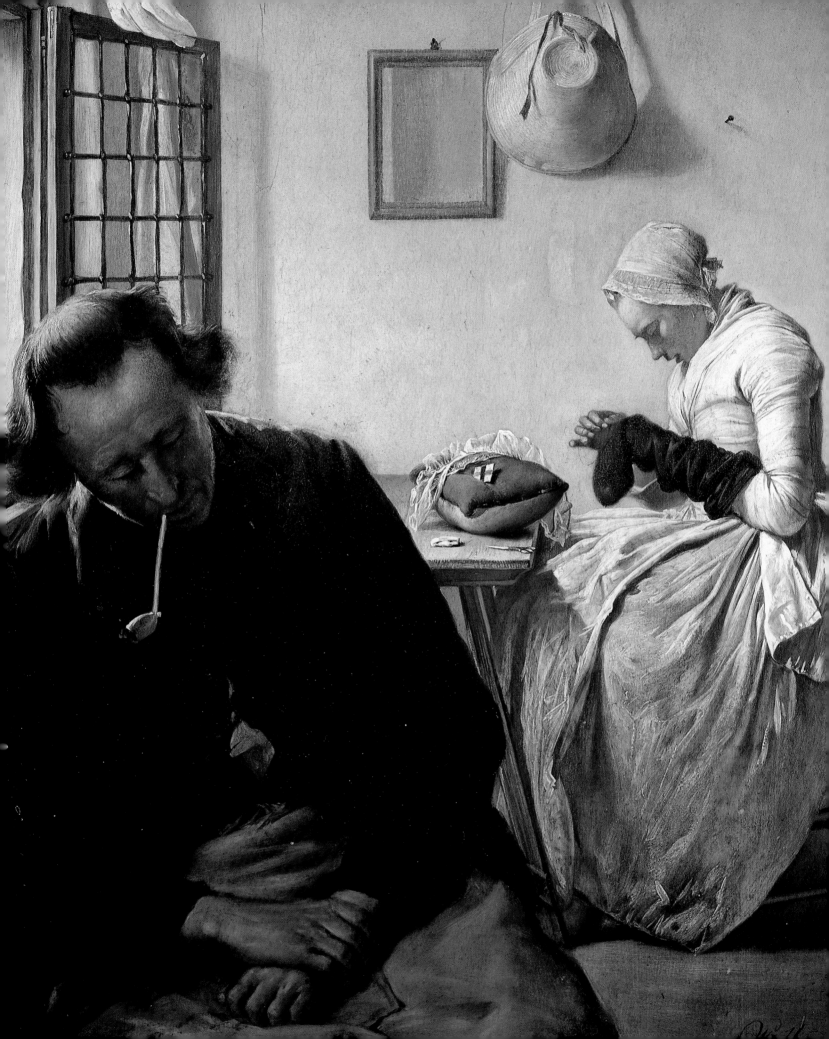

Since its introduction to Europe, the pipe, with the sexual symbol which its shape and stem evoke, often gave rise to coarse jokes. The interiors of taverns were ideal settings that the painter Jan Steen (1626-1679) liked to portray. Left: *Bad Company.*

In this *Interior of an Inn*, Jan Steen, himself an inn-keeper, represented himself as the jovial character in the centre. As for the smoker on the right, his unspoken gesture and look suggest a next scene . . . (left).

makers. A tacit agreement existed between the pipe-makers of English origin and the local potters. These latter were going through a period of recession and welcomed the immigrants who could use their kilns. An unwritten contract emerged by which the pipe-makers kept the "secrets" of pipe-making learnt in England but had to use the Dutch kilns. This situation lasted until about 1630, when the Dutch realised the potential of pipe-making. Having acquired the English expertise, they did not hesitate in setting up their own workshops and flooding the market with copies. In 1641, Dutch pipe-makers insisted that the Gouda Town Council set up a Guild and a monopoly which excluded foreign competition. Legend has it that the wives of English makers protested with such vigour that the Town Council had to act with moderation. The decision concerning the new guild was adjourned, and a regulation was passed decreeing, without other obligations, that all makers should put their name or mark on each pipe. Twenty years later, the Guild of Gouda pipe-makers was established, grouping all manufacturers without distinction of origin. The industry at the time employed more than 15,000 workers, which was about half the working population.

By the middle of the seventeenth century, the clay pipes from Gouda and its region were

Since the eighteenth century, Dutch pipes, hitherto sober, have acquired various decorations: flowers, mythological scenes, eroticism. Some carried images and slogans in praise of the House of Orange (above, right). Many contemporary painters knew how to use the fine and elegant lines of Dutch pipes, which were familiar everyday objects. In this still-life, by Chardin, *Pipes and Jug,* the balance of the composition is underlined by the diagonals of the pipes (below)

shipped throughout Europe where they were often copied. They were generally plain, the artisans being content to produce simple shapes with few variations: small bowls at right angles or laid back to the stems, with or without heels and of various lengths from ten to eighty centimetres; the *Gouwenaar,* one of the longest was a favourite among the Dutch. From the middle of the eighteenth century, the pipe-makers of Gouda devised more elaborate products. Each created his own designs and motifs, which were protected by the Guild, to avoid imitations. Thus were created pipes which were glazed or polished after drying, with a variety of motifs, ranging from simple flowers to "daring" subjects, or with simple slogans or political affiliation. This was achieved by the use of copper moulds, sometimes finely engraved. With the *doorrooker* pipes, popular for a long time, the decorations were applied with enamel: they remained white during firing while the rest of the pipe darkened.

The growth in importation and local production reduced the price of tobacco and created a demand for larger pipes. This meant that attention had to be given to the quality of the material, to make the pipes look better and more solid. The craftsmen solved the problem by extra rinsing of the clay which made it purer, and enhanced further the reputation of Gouda. Certain models became luxury items, sometimes lasting a lifetime, such as the "wedding pipes", the objects of a charming custom in which one cannot help but see a rather crude symbol, as portrayed in a number of Dutch paintings and engravings, associating pipes and smoke with rather bawdy scenes. Some examples are given in Simon Schama's book *Embarrassment of Richness.* When a man wanted to propose to his lady-love, he would go and visit her with a pipe in his mouth and ask for a light; if she agreed to light his pipe, the outcome seemed promising; if the next time she asked to take a few puffs, she indicated her

Pupil of Rambrandt and lover of contrasting shades, the Dutch painter Gerald Dou (1613-1675), placed his pipe in the centre of this self-portrait (facing page).

Until the eighteenth century, extraordinary ceramic pipes were produced in Staffordshire (England), called "serpentines". Virtually unsmokable, they were used as decorations (below). Different Dutch clay pipes, at Hajenius in Amsterdam, in an Art-Deco setting, have remained intact since 1914 (below centre).

acceptance and the betrothal could be officially announced.

During the same period, in England where the tradition of the early craftsmen was being maintained, real artists in the Staffordshire potteries created some extraordinary models: their long snake-like stems, measuring several metres, were vividly decorated and entwined. In creating these pipes, more often than not difficult to smoke, the Staffordshire potters thought more in terms of shape than of function. Being destined to become decorative ornaments, they were the first pipes made as works of art. Some are believed to have been apprentices' pieces to mark their graduation.

Gouda's zenith was reached by the middle of the eighteenth century. The range of Dutch pipes had increased and the products improved, and they were exported to the rest of Europe and to America. To counter the Dutch and foreign competition, the makers of Gouda made a play of the argument about quality by guaranteeing their products with a double

logo: each pipe bore not only the maker's mark but also Gouda's coat of arms. Unfortunately, the competition organized itself. In 1740 other Dutch pipe-makers obtained permission to use the Gouda coat of arms to facilitate exports. But it was the growth of foreign production which slowly reduced Gouda's domination.

THE GOLDEN AGE OF ENGLISH CLAY PIPES

Gouda became the important centre of clay pipe-making in Europe, first because of the initiative of William Baernelts (who changed his name to Barentsz) in the early years of the seventeenth century, but also because Dutch traders, at the time, were the most important wholesalers in tobacco and related goods in Europe.

While there may have been a shortage of pipes in England in the early 1600s, the seventeenth century has long been regarded by experts as the "Golden Age" of clay pipe-making in Britain. In spite of his dislike of tobacco, King James I had

The smoking habit is "a costume lothsome to the eye, hateful to the nose, harmful to the brain, daungerous to the lungs, and in the black stinking fume thereof, nearest resembling the horrible Stigian smoke of the pit that is bottomless." James I's *Counterblaste to Tobacco*, published in 1604, had no effect on his subjects. Pipe-smoking rapidly spread through all levels of society, to women and even children. English painting bears witness to that expansion, showing clergymen as well as aristocrats happily smoking: *To Crown the Feast*, by George Godwin Kilburne (top left) and *A Quiet Drink*, by Jean Hegesippe Vetter (facing page).

Only the *King's corsair*, Jean Bart, could smoke his pipe in front of Louis XIV, who detested the smell of tobacco (right). The Grande Dauphine and her ladies-in-waiting did not have the same privilege, which caused the king's anger when he caught them smoking; an etching by N Arnould *Charming Smoking Party* probably evokes this incident. It is accompanied by a quatrain: In a delicious alcove / Alive with so much charm / Who would not give up arms / Elated by good wine, tobacco and love (below, right)

granted a charter to the pipe-makers of Westminster (London) in 1619, one of the reasons for this being that they had, by then, become quite influential and powerful in London. This charter was renewed by Charles II in 1663. Between 1600 and 1650, there were some seventy-five pipe-makers in London. Their number increased in the second half of the century, so that by around 1700, there were 136 principal pipe-makers. Adrian Oswald of the Department of Archaeology, Birmingham City Museum, is the author of *Clay Pipes for the Archaeologist* (British Archaeology Report 14 – 1975). This work dates clay pipes and gives students and collectors very clear details of sizes and styles from what were, in effect, early pipes. He also identifies the main makers and reckons that, by 1700, there were over 360 important clay pipe-makers in London, Bristol, Chester and Hull. According to Oswald, over 3,400 clay pipe-makers have been traced in England alone.

In fact, very little is known of pre-1600 English clay pipes. The first description of them is found in William Harrison's *Great Chronologie* of 1573; he describes a pipe as "an instrument [for smoking] formed like a ladell". Until around 1610, the pipes were plain and small, the bowls having an inside diameter of a quarter of an inch (7 mm.). These pipes were seldom longer than four to six inches (100 to 150 mm.) Sizes began to rise as tobacco became cheaper, so that by about 1640 or 1650, there were pipes up to 12 to 14 inches long (200 to 360 mm.) The bowls were generally laid back and the top of the bowls were "rouleted", milled or grooved. Most had some sort of heel under the bowl, originally flat and heart-shaped, but eventually pointed. Some of the pipes

also showed early attempts at decoration, such as masonic emblems, designs representing names of inns, taverns and regiments.

One of the problems for British clay pipe-makers was transport, first of the clay and then of the finished articles. As a result, many of the makers were producing pipes for local needs, but at the same time the industry also spread to Bristol, Broseley, Chester, Gateshead, York and Hull. It is thought that some London makers migrated to eastern ports, such as Hull, where there was a good coastal trade. Bristol, in the west, was also an obvious place for trading. Tobacco came from America, and clay-pipes could be shipped there. Broseley has, of course, become well-known, but the names of individual makers are difficult to identify. Clay pipe-making in Britain – to include Scotland, Wales and Ireland – remained essentially a cottage industry until the nineteenth century.

The increase in popularity of snuff-taking in the early eighteenth century, and the loss of the American colonies after 1783, marked a decline in clay pipe-making in Britain, but there was some revival in the nineteenth century, in parallel with the French industry. Although there had also been a decline in standards of design in the early eighteenth century, these had subsequently improved, as had the quality. Long pipes, originally called "aldermen", but generally called "straw", were made up to 24 inches (600 mm.) long. Motifs came back with heraldic designs including Royal and City coats of arms; the Prince of Wales feathers were also popular. The long pipes popularly known as Churchwardens were sometimes made during this period but they were relatively rare; for markcting purposes, shorter versions were the norm.

In the nineteenth

In the nineteenth century, the Fiolet and Gambier catalogues illustrated thousands of models of clay pipes, from the simple straight model to more sophisticated models. These precious documents show the advertising creativity of the time; one sees here the degree of fantasy in promoting "endosmoide" (sic) clay pipes which were tougher than ordinary clays (facing page).

L: FIOLET, à S:Omer.

MODÈLES NOUVEAUX

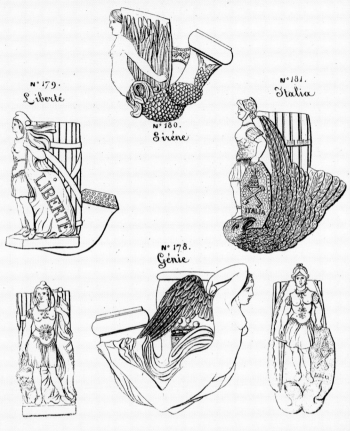

N° 179.
Liberté

N° 180.
Sirène

N° 181.
Italia

N° 178.
Génie

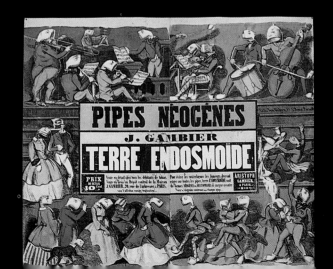

century makers' names begin to appear. To quote but a few: Henry Leigh (Porchester, until 1932), Charles Crop (London, until 1924), Southorn (Broseley, only closed in the 1960s). Stephen Bell is the earliest pipe-maker, recorded in Edinburgh (c. 1649). The last twentieth-century clay pipe-maker was John Pollock, established in 1879, whose son only retired a few years ago and sold the business as a going concern to Wilsons of Sharrow Mill, Sheffield. The latter still list the clay pipe-making activity of the company in the 1994 directory of the trade journal *Tobacco*.

THE FRENCH CLAY PIPES

The first French clay pipe-makers established themselves at the beginning of the seventeenth century in Flanders, close to Holland and Gouda, and started copying the Dutch products. Dunkirk, then a free port of transit for the importation of American tobacco, became the first important centre of production. Other pipe factories appeared later in a number of French towns, from Saint-Malo to Marseilles, and including Nimes, Onnaing, Saint-Omer, Rennes and Montereau. But slowly the production of clay pipes, the only type used in France until the nineteenth century, was concentrated in the north. Two important factories shared the bulk of the nineteenth-century market: the Fiolet factory, at Saint-Omer in the Pas-de-Calais département, which produced tens of millions of pipes a year, and particularly the famous firm of Gambier, founded in 1780 at Givet, in the Ardennes, which became the best known among European smokers.

The writer Arthur Rimbaud immortalized these famous pipes (made just outside Charleville, his native town) in the first quatrain of *Oraison du soir*

(*Evening Prayers*) written in 1871. He depicts himself at seventeen years old, sitting at a table in a smoked-filled tavern: "I spend my life sitting . . . Holding a well-fluted beer mug,/ With arched belly and neck, a Gambier/ Between my teeth, like an impalpable sail in the wind."

Gambier, which produced a hundred thousand pipes a day, and had a catalogue showing more than two thousand models, specialized in the reproduction of effigies of famous people and a wide variety of objects. In this, the Gambier catalogue presented a remarkable digest of French popular culture of the nineteenth century: it featured historical and contemporary figures such as Victor Hugo, Napoleon and Gambetta, and also fictitious characters such as Gervaise or a Paimpol (Brittany) woman, next to various sizes of skulls, a frog, a fish and even a chamber pot. Pipe-smokers could also obtain for a cheap price subjects, such as nudes and ladies' legs with alluring high laced boots, "reserved" for a men's get-together. But the most successful model was the Jacob. It was often copied and called either the Grand Jacob or the Good Jacob. It represented the head of a long-bearded, turbaned Oriental. Nobody really knows whether it was the head of the zouave Henri Jacob, a well-known person at the time, who had – it was claimed – healing powers, or the Jacob of the Bible. The long beard of this mysterious Jacob probably accounted for its popularity. The length of the beard meant that this part of the pipe remained cool and the smoker could hold it without getting his fingers burnt.

When France was in a semi-permanent state of war, pipes appeared to be the main comfort of soldiers. Louis XIV detested the smell of tobacco which he forbade at Court, but he made sure that his troops were provided with pipes and tinderboxes to sustain their morale while waiting for battle or in barracks. There was one

While Napoleon did not smoke, he made sure that his soldiers were supplied with tobacco and pipes. Pipes not only brought them a simple comfort, but were also thought to keep them awake, as sleepiness was one of the main enemies during a campaign. Facing page, left: *The Imperial Grenadier*, by N T Charlet.
"My 'nom de guerre' is 'La Tulippe' / I am as you see a fine lad / When in one hand I hold my pipe / And in the other a bottle / And I have a pocket well filled / I am sure to drink to oblivion." *La Tulippe*, seventeenth century print (above)

The Napoleonic wars created a great number of disabled, living with difficulty on half-pay, happy however not to have "broken their pipe", meaning not to have been killed. This French expression – still common – is said to have come from the battlefields: if a wounded soldier had to have an amputation, when his pipe, clenched in his teeth, fell to the ground and broke, he was recognized as dead!
Below, a publicity poster for Jean Nicot pipes aimed at army veterans (c. 1850).

A number of French clay pipes of the nineteenth century, among them the extremely popular Jacob. The long beard enabled the bowl to be held without burning the fingers. The skull was also current (left)

Frederick William I founded the *Tabaks-kollegium*, where daily debates covered important political subjects, to the extent that it was called the "Tobacco Parliament". A painting from 1737, attributed to Georg Lisiewski, depicts one of these meetings before it degenerates under the influence of beer (right)!

A "bouquet" of pipes was part of the sign of a tobacco outlet in France in the mid-nineteenth century (below).

exception to the smoking ban at Court. The famous admiral and privateer Jean Bart (his name has been given to a tobacco) while waiting for an audience with the King decided to "light up"; the King saw him, but did not see in this a mark of insolence as he would have done in others. The "Grande Dauphine" and her ladies-in-waiting were caught smoking pipes which they had borrowed from the Swiss Guards, to the great anger of the Sun King.

Two centuries later, under the Empire, pipes had become common objects in the daily life of the French. Many women did not hesitate to take up the habit, including the Princess of Metternich, a great friend of the Empress Eugenie, who smoked while playing the piano. Innkeepers provided pipes and tobacco and regulars had theirs on racks on the walls. Enterprising unemployed found that they could earn some money by breaking in pipes for other smokers; for a very small price the owners could dispense with the first harsh puffs of a new pipe.

Many of Napoleon I's marshals – Murat, Kleber, Lassalle, Oudinot – were inveterate smokers. The French used to call a pipe a *bouf-farde*; this may go back to Jean Nepomucene

Bouffardi, a corporal in the Imperial Guard, who never relinquished his pipe even during the fiercest battle. He died at Friedland having lost both arms; his faithful pipe was still in one of his hands. Others, however, believe that the name comes, not from the corporal, but from the old French *bouffer* (to blow). In the same way as Louis XIV had done, the Emperor also made certain that his soldiers were provided with pipes and tobacco, although he took snuff himself. His flirtation with the pipe was brief, according his faithful valet, Constant, quoted by Pierre Sabbagh in his *Pipe Guide*. It seems that the Persian ambassador had presented him with a fine-looking pipe. One day the Emperor felt like trying it, but he could not light it. Constant did it for him but when Napoleon took a puff it made him choke. When he got his breath back he cried : "Take this thing away, what a horror ! Oh the **** ! My heart is thumping." It affected him for an hour or so, and he renounced for ever this pleasure "which," he said, "was good for idlers to pass the time." On the British side, Wellington was also concerned about the supply of pipes and tobacco for his troops. His officers also took to cigars in Spain but, in later years, the Duke wanted to ban smoking in the army.

Paintings have followed the evolution of pipes during their history. The introduction of porcelain pipes, c. 1700, enabled artistic pipe-makers and also painters to develop their talents. This *Still Life with Porcelain Pipe* was painted by the German artist August Holmberg, in 1890 (left).

In the eighteenth century, wealthy officers had silver pipes that they could carry without risk of breakage. These were often fitted with covers which also had the advantage of slowing down combustion (below and right)

FROM THE TABAKSKOLLEGIUM . . .

The French clay pipes were not the only ones to put an end to Gouda's supremacy. To a lesser degree, England (where production had never ceased), and Prussia (where, from 1744 the factories at Stettin and Konigsberg were protected by a Customs duty on Dutch pipes) contributed to the decline.

Prussia knew then an infatuation, even a passion for pipe-smoking, which was nurtured, for the conviviality it created, by its first two kings. Before becoming King of Prussia in 1701, Frederick I, Elector of Brandenburg, was something of a spendthrift, lover of luxurious festivities and inveterate smoker. He had instituted at his court, "real pipe evenings". Frederick-William I, also a smoker like his father, was more sober, thrifty and military-minded – they called him the "Sergeant-King". He continued these evenings by founding the famous *Tabakskollegium* (Tobacco college). Every evening his courtiers, officers, ministers, councillors, and other occasional guests, chosen for their good humour, their knowledge and their aptitude for conversation, gathered together. The smoking-rooms in the palaces of Berlin, Potsdam and Königswusterhausen were furnished in keeping with the king's parsimony. The guests sat on simple wooden chairs around a long table laid with only the bare necessities: a stock of tobacco and some beer tankards. Should they

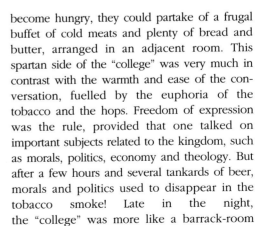

become hungry, they could partake of a frugal buffet of cold meats and plenty of bread and butter, arranged in an adjacent room. This spartan side of the "college" was very much in contrast with the warmth and ease of the conversation, fuelled by the euphoria of the tobacco and the hops. Freedom of expression was the rule, provided that one talked on important subjects related to the kingdom, such as morals, politics, economy and theology. But after a few hours and several tankards of beer, morals and politics used to disappear in the tobacco smoke! Late in the night, the "college" was more like a barrack-room than the guest-room of grand nobility: with gross humour, the letting off of fireworks under the chairs and the breakage of dozens of overheated pipes. More refined than his father, to whom he was often opposed, Frederick II preferred snuff to "tobacco drinking" and closed the *Tabakskollegium* on his accession to the throne in 1740.

. . . TO THE PIPES OF ULM

To the competition from Prussia, must be added that of the dynamic merchants of Cologne. Clay pipes were first made in the region in 1628. These merchants obtained supplies from the small neighbouring town of Hohr, whose craftsmen specialized in ceramics, and could copy Dutch pipes very cheaply. Very soon, cheaper pipes that looked like Gouda pipes, but were made in Cologne, were found on most European markets. These same makers from Hohr revolutionized pipe manufacture by inventing, during the seventeenth century, the separate mouthpiece; only the bowls were made of clay and one could add a cherrywood mouthpiece. But the decline of Gouda corresponded to the decline of clay pipes in general. The exception was France, where these cheap but fragile pipes resisted competition until the

First World War, by which time, stronger pipes in other materials had established themselves.

It appears that from the beginning of the seventeenth century, the soldiery looked for more solid substitutes for clay pipes which could be slipped in the tops of riding boots during a cavalry charge. Thus were created metal pipes, sometimes called "musketeers pipes", forged by army blacksmiths and copied from current clay pipes. Unfortunately, they would heat up quickly and burn the fingers! This defect was partly corrected by more sophisticated pipes, sometimes in silver, that wealthy officers had specially made; the bowl was fitted with a cover with holes which slowed down combustion. These silver pipes became for a time popular with the more affluent classes in civilian society. Some highly decorated examples, and even some encrusted with precious stones, were real works of art.

Pipe-smokers thought that they had found the ideal material when porcelain, a product hitherto imported from China, was developed in Europe. The Saxon alchemist Johann Friedrich Boettger discovered the secret in 1700 and this was applied by the first porcelain factory at Meissen (Royal Saxon Porcelain) ten years later. From the start, porcelain pipe bowls were produced at Meissen. The makers assimi-

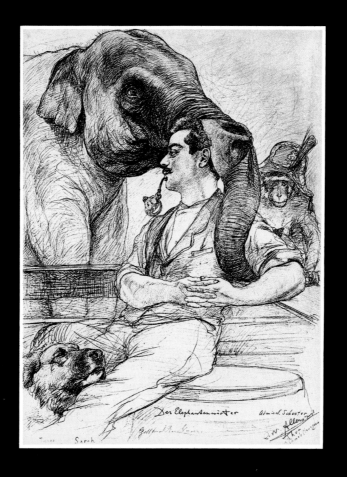

lated the invention of the pipe-makers of Hohr – the separate and removable mouthpiece – having come to the conclusion that mouthpieces of other materials were preferable to keep the heat of the smoke down. After several trials, the choice fell on several types of wood (including cherrywood), and on horn (from stags and other animals) and also on amber.

Porcelain pipes became the rage, except in France and England, although some were made in both countries, at Sèvres and Worcester for instance. They were more heat-resistant than clays, but their main fault was the lack of porosity, which was compensated by the fitting of a reservoir. Porcelain pipes had the advantage of a variety of shapes and designs. The porcelain clay, very easy to work, gave the craftsmen

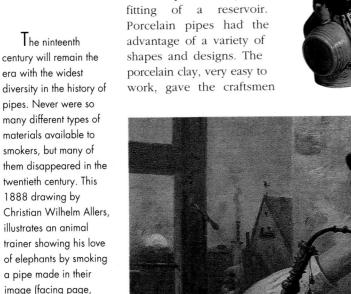

the opportunity to exploit their imagination and craft. There was a profusion of simple models, but some were richly decorated and formed real sculptures which are works of art in ceramic. The factory at Meissen became famous from the start, with the most original and inventive artist in Gottlieb Ehder, from about 1740. His imagination and dexterity knew no bounds and he produced, among others, heads of Arabs, Japanese, women, etc. . . Other porcelain factories were created after Meissen, in particular in the eighteenth century, such as those of Vienna, Berlin and Kassel, all of which included pipes in their catalogues.

Porcelain pipes had an extraordinary success in Germany at the beginning of the nineteenth century. No soldier, student

In France the Napoleonic era inspired many designs on porcelain pipes, made by the Sèvres factory (above left). Porcelain pipes benefited from a German invention of the eighteenth century, the separate stem. These stems, often made of cherrywood, softened the sharpness of the non-porous porcelain bowls.

Small German trinkets, dating from 1860, that could be smoked (centre). In Germany, pipes from Ulm were the only ones to compete with porcelain. They were made of elm or alder, delicately carved and fitted with covers, sometimes in silver. *At the Window*, by H G Jentzsch (1862) (below).

The ninteenth century will remain the era with the widest diversity in the history of pipes. Never were so many different types of materials available to smokers, but many of them disappeared in the twentieth century. This 1888 drawing by Christian Wilhelm Allers, illustrates an animal trainer showing his love of elephants by smoking a pipe made in their image (facing page, above). During the same epoch, glass pipes were created in England and Italy, for decorative purposes. This one was blown at Nailsea, England in around 1800 (facing page, below)

Traditions are not lost in Switzerland. Wood pipes made in "the old way" are still produced (left) . . . and are still appreciated by Alpine shepherds (facing page).

A small pipe for a big smoker: this carved wood pipe, only seven centimetres high, has two bowls with copper covers; probably Hungarian from the nineteenth century (right).

or burgher was without a highly decorated pipe. Alongside the large manufacturers, a large number of artisans specialized in artistic pipe decoration; these *Hausmaler* sprang up in all towns to meet the growing demand for customized pipes. Every smoker could obtain at little cost a pipe with his chosen decoration or illustration. Some chose their own image, others their own professions illustrated by an emblem, while others honoured contemporary celebrities. The scenes painted by the *Hausmaler* were greatly varied and of course included scenes that were best kept away from the children! The German vogue spread to the rest of Europe as porcelain factories were set up. In France, Sèvres offered several models including many variants on the effigy of Napoleon. In England, Wedgwood produced many striking Jasperware models.

Before the appearance of "the ideal material", clay,

metal and porcelain did not apparently fully satisfy the imagination of European pipemakers. More original models saw the light of day: ivory pipes were carved in Dieppe, where the material had been used since the sixteenth century; Venice, renowned for its glass, produced extremely fragile unsmokable pipes; Italian artisans also tried green marble. However, among these other materials, it was wood, easily obtainable and comparatively cheap, which was used in the greatest number of attempts.

Given the fact that anyone with a minimum of ability and patience can make a pipe out of wood, it is likely that such pipes appeared in the Old World as soon as tobacco arrived. One of the oldest pipes discovered in Germany, made from oak, showing the profile of a man, has been dated to around 1600. Nearly all types of woods were tried, but only the hardest, which did not burn

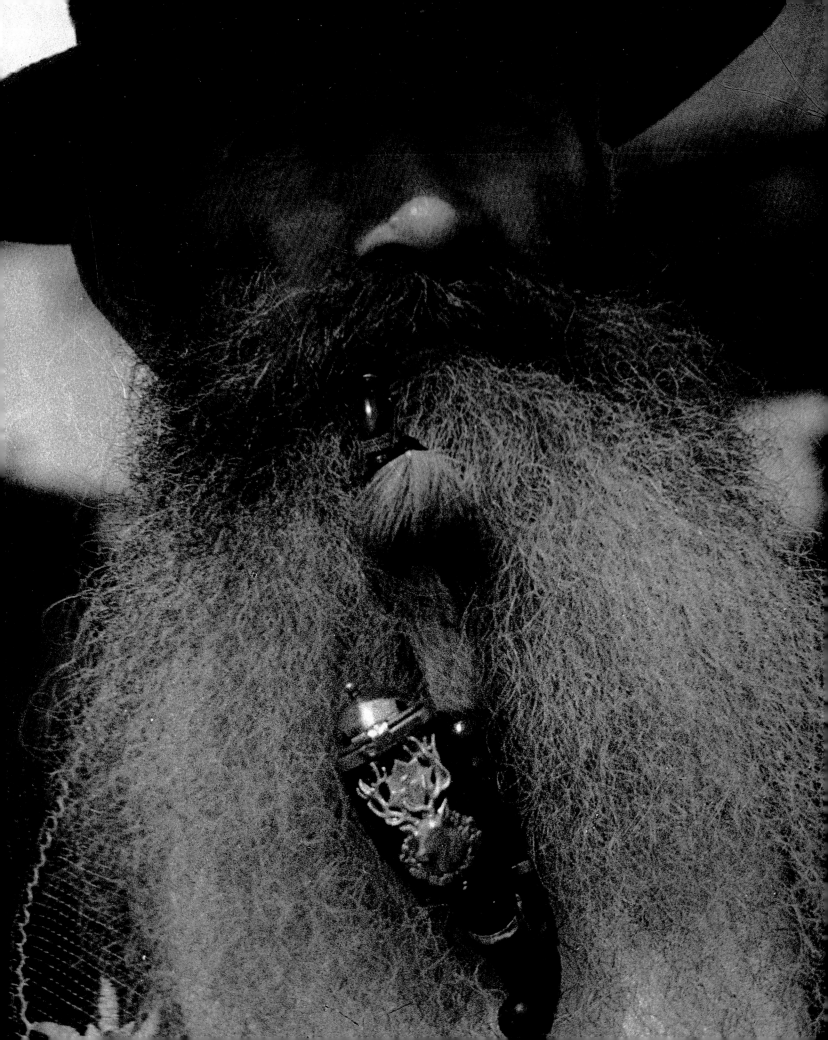

out too quickly, gave some satisfaction, although some were difficult to work on. Among the woods were beech and cherry-wood, in particular the wild variety still used in Hungary and Austria. To avoid the bitter taste that some woods give to tobacco, some bowls were lined with plaster or clay. But there was little industrial development in wooden pipes. The exception was the manufacture at Ulm and in the surrounding region from 1650 of pipes which had some success in Europe due to the elegance of the shapes. The bowls were made of elm, alder, and more rarely walnut or boxwood which have a fine grain to which the artisans added silver fittings. "Ulmer" pipes were fitted with covers and a small chain fastened the mouthpieces to the bowls. The covers had the advantage of slowing down combustion, offering protection from wind and rain if smoked outdoors and acting as a fire prevention measure. Only pipes with covers were allowed in the Bavarian forests where smoking was normally forbidden at the time.

Pipe-staining in a New York factory, in the 1930s (right). The use of briar marked a turning point in the history of pipes. By the end of the nineteenth century, the majority of pipes were made in this wood, which was relatively abundant, light and heat-resistant.

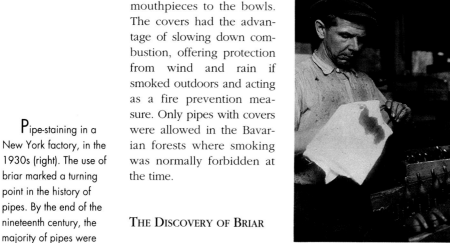

THE DISCOVERY OF BRIAR

All wooden pipes suffered from the same defect: they all burnt more or less with the tobacco, which altered the taste of the smoke. It was not until the invention of the briar pipe that smokers could be satisfied with wood. The quality of briar root – or more specifically that of the "growth" between the trunk and the actual root, but called root for convenience – is summed up by its resistance to heat, its long-lasting life, and its preservation of the aroma of tobacco.

The "inventor" of the ideal wood for pipes never took out a patent and has never been officially identified. The mystery of the origin of the briar pipe has therefore created a number of theories and stories, more or less believable, which have one thing in common: the discovery was made in the south of France and was developed in the town of Saint-Claude, in the heart of the Jura mountains. The most amusing story, the least plausible, relates that a

French pipe-maker, who had not got over the loss of Napoleon, went on a pilgrimage to Corsica in the same year that the Emperor died, 1821; having broken his pipe during a walk, he met a shepherd who fashioned a replacement, a head of Napoleon, out of a block of briar. Surprised at the quality of the wood and the taste of the smoke, the pipe-maker took back a quantity of blocks with him to his native Jura, to the delight of other smokers. Other theories are rather more serious, such as the one that attributes the discovery to a certain David, a wood-turner at Chaumont-les-Saint-Claude (a nearby village), who learnt about the qualities of briar from a merchant at the Beaucaire fair in the south of France. In his book, *La Pipe*, André-Paul Bastien, quotes the story from a contemporary businessman, Jules Ligier, whose precision adds credence. In Saint-Claude, "during the first days of October 1858, a salesman with exuberant manners and also a pronounced southern accent, presented himself one morning at the offices of Mr Gay. He had come to offer blocks of boxwood, commonly called *broussins* that the firm purchased in large quantities to make snuff boxes. After having taken an order for ten thousand kilos of these blocks for delivery in mid-November, and passed the time of day, Mr Taffanel (that was his name) brought out of his pocket a small piece of wood; this had six saw-cut panels, in the shape of a candle snuffer, the larger part being roughly bored out and the smaller part fitted with a bamboo stem. 'This is,' he said, 'the pipe in which a shepherd friend of mine, has assured me he has smoked tobacco for over a year and, as you can see, it is neither burnt nor damaged. It is made out of a briar block, similar to boxwood, that one finds in plenty in our district.' By the end of October, Mr Gay had assessed the incomparable qualities of briar, and had some pipes made in his factory which were sold in Paris, northern France and Belgium."

Note also the story that attributes the manufacture of the first batch of briar pipes to the ancestor of a pipe-maker of Cogolin, in the Var

The workforce of the Courrieu company, in Cogolin at the turn of the century. Ulysse Courrieu may have been the first maker to use briar in 1802. The "invention" is generally attributed to the makers of Saint-Claude, in around 1860 (facing page, above). Pipe-makers have always wanted to produce a cooler smoke. In around 1910, Vincent Genod, in Saint Claude, perfected a divisible mouthpiece (twin bore), marking the pipes with a name with an international flavour, "Brindisi" (facing page, below).

Meerschaum pipes, which are finely carved, are not within everyone's reach. Some real works of art were not meant to be smoked, such as this fabulous pipe, made in 1871, to commemorate the wedding of the Princess Louise, daughter of Queen Victoria to the Marquis of Lorne. It is currently exhibited in the Dunhill museum in London (above). In 1971, in London, Prime Minister Harold Wilson (now Lord Wilson) inaugurated the "Smoking through the ages" exhibition. He had no difficulty in holding the main exhibit which could have floated on water (below).

département. Ulysse Courrieu, a farmer, had already been making these "miraculous" pipes since 1802, having been introduced to briar by a local shepherd. His reputation went beyond the boundaries of the district, encouraging other farmers to follow suit.

The fact that briar, which is found in the lands around the Mediterranean Sea was developed in Saint-Claude is no accident. Wood-turning and its products had been a major part of Saint-Claude's economy since the seventh century. Saint-Claude is built around the old abbey of Saint-Oyand, where Claude, bishop of Besançon decided to end his days. From that time, the monks, who had harnessed the energy of two fast-flowing rivers, became turners and taught artisans who settled around the abbey. In the twelfth century, four hundred years after the death of Bishop Claude, his remains were discovered and found to have been miraculously preserved. The small town of Saint-Oyand became Saint-Claude and became a halting-place for pilgrims on the road to Compostella.

This was the beginning of Saint-Claude's prosperity. It attracted the Jura peasants whose poor land was reducing them to poverty. The number of workshops multiplied, offering pilgrims a range of religious objects. After the introduction of tobacco in France and the spread of its popularity, the artisans began to make snuffboxes in the second half of the sixteenth century. A hundred years later, with a growing reputation, they were supplying Ger-

man and Austrian pipe-manufacturers with mouthpieces made of boxwood, horn, amber and even ivory. Around 1750, they started making their own pipes, generally in boxwood. Through centuries of labour, the expertise that had been passed on from one generation to the next permitted that small Jura town to become the most important centre of pipe-making in the world. Briar pipes quickly overcame competition from other materials, relegating them to mere objects of curiosity. Production grew until the 1920s when it reached some several million pipes a year. Economic crises and the growth of popularity of cigarettes marked the decline. In 1970 Saint-Claude manufactured only about two million pipes and the current production is below one million.

THE LUXURY OF MEERSCHAUM

More than a century before the birth of briar pipes in France, a pipe appeared in Hungary with which all smokers were to become enamoured: the meerschaum pipe was never eclipsed by briar. According to legend, the meerschaum pipe was created by accident in 1723, in the small shop of a Budapest cobbler called Karel Kovacs. That year, an aristocrat, Count Andrassy, had returned from Turkey with a type of stone which was both light and white. Intrigued by this strange mineral, the count had

Divine but fragile. Meerschaum pipes have always been presented in cases to protect them. Pipe-makers made the cases with precision to avoid rubbing (facing page).

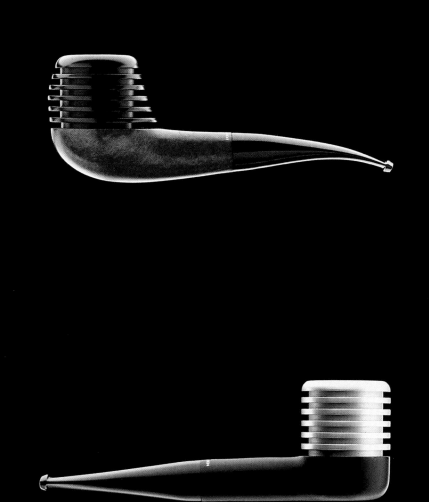

the idea of making it into a pipe. He asked Kovacs, who carved fine wooden pipes in his spare time, to carry out the task. Kovacs made two out of the "stone" and shamelessly decided to keep one. He thought that it was spoilt, since he had handled it with fingers still impregnated with cobbler's wax that had stained it yellow. He made the count's after having carefully cleaned his hands. Smoking his own, he noticed that the wax gave it a fine golden patina. He eventually made many more, replacing the cobbler's wax with beeswax to give a better effect. As for Count Andrassy, he was extremely satisfied and delighted, he showed off his pipe in the best salons of Budapest, and even, it is said, at the Court of Vienna. For the freshness and mildness of the smoke, right from the first puffs, meerschaums put in the shade anything that clay, porcelain or even wood could offer; meerschaum pipes were launched.

The mineral in question is a silicate of magnesium, called *meerschaum* (sea foam) because of its colour and particularly its lightness, since it floats on water. The main source is Anatolia where it has been mined since about 1675, so that it is thought that the Turks were the real inventors of meerschaum pipes. Following the success among the European aristocracy, this material was in great demand but it was not found in huge quantities, took a long time to form and was therefore expensive. It was exported wholesale by the Turks. Meerschaum pipes were made in France, Germany, England and Austria, with Vienna becoming the most famous centre for them.

Initially, meerschaum pipes were limited to copies of the shapes then current in clay or porcelain. But meerschaum is a material which is fairly easy to work and it allowed creativity which came into its own from the beginning of the nineteenth century, when the best works of art were created. Often fitted with silver covers and amber mouthpieces, these miniature sculptures, showing extraordinary finesse and representing a wide variety of subjects – busts or heads of personalities and animals, scenes from

mythology, or hunting scenes – were not within reach of all smokers. Generally reserved for the aristocracy and the more affluent middle classes, they were often given as presents on special occasions.

Their success, and also their cost, encouraged the Viennese makers to gather all the waste from the carved blocks. By adding binding agents to the waste, they were able to press new blocks and have the material for new pipes. The result was a little heavier than "real" meerschaum, but less fragile and certainly cheaper, while having all the same smoking qualities. These pipes, called "Vienna meerschaums" enabled many smokers to enjoy the pleasure of a meerschaum.

IN SPITE OF THE CRISIS, THERE IS HOPE

The reign of the briar pipe began in the second half of the nineteenth century and still continues. Today, briar pipes represent virtually all the pipes made around the world. While a major part of the production is still concentrated in Saint-Claude, a number of pipe-makers are trying to revive the tradition in Italy, Germany, Denmark, England and even America. Let us note in passing a famous pipe design by Alexander Porsche – better known for his cars – which was manufactured by Oldenkott in Germany, now unfortunately closed down. Aluminium cooling rings were fitted around the bowl, in the manner of some car cylinders. As for quantity, meerschaum pipes follow briar, but far behind, as the material is comparatively rare and much more expensive. The art of meerschaum pipe-making has been threatened by a decision of the Turkish government in 1961, banning the exporting of raw blocks in order to encourage domestic production. But meerschaum pipes are made in England by two firms with a material obtained from Africa; this meerschaum is not quite as pure, it is heavier but less fragile that the Turkish variety, but it competes well with briar on price.

The Porsche pipe was designed in the 1980s by Siegfried Ebner in the Ferdinand Alexander Porsche design studio, inspired by the automobile technology. The aluminium flanges were supposed to cool the bowls and give a fresher smoke. It created a lot of talk, but few were sold; production has now ceased (facing page). Below: Ferdinand Alexander Porsche.

Corncob pipes are very popular in the United States. General Douglas MacArthur was a devotee, as seen here during the offensive against the Japanese in January 1945; his was an unusual size (left).

In a park in Peking, an old man with his pipe and his bird, photographed in 1985 by Thomas Hoepker (facing page).

A descendant of the first inhabitants of Hong Kong, this Hakka woman has kept to traditions. But the metal bowl did not appear in China until the end of the nineteenth century; until then, most pipes were made of bamboo.
Gerard D'Abboville, was France's pipe-smoker of the year 1992, an award granted by the Master Pipe Makers of Saint-Claude. He was drawn (below) by caricaturist Jacques Faizant. The lone rower would not have crossed the Atlantic without his pipe!

Other pipes are available to smokers wishing to change their pipes from time to time. Traditional clay pipes are still made in Gouda, in Germany, Belgium, France and England. Corncobs, which were invented by a Missouri farmer in 1869, are popular in the USA, and have been imported regularly into Europe since the Second World War. They were already listed in English catalogues before 1914.

For the past twenty years, pipe-smoking has been in recession and production has fallen. But this has affected mostly the cheaper mass-produced ranges, whilst quality pipes are finding a growing market. At the same time, the average age of pipe-smokers has increased. A recent French study revealed that ninety per cent of pipe-smokers were over thirty-five years of age. In England, it is reckoned that the average age is about fifty-five. Anti-smoking campaigns do not appear to be the cause of that decline. Their target has been mostly the cigarette, which still is a gigantic market. Logically, these campaigns should be in favour of pipe-smoking, as the risk to health is far smaller. But this advantage never seems to have been exploited by the pipe-manufacturers. Pipe-makers and lovers of pipes should be re-assured. Economists and sociologists agree today that the inevitable development of our post-industrial society is leading towards less work and more leisure time for each of us. If the manufacturers and dealers know how to respond to this, the future of the pipe is assured.

Mon J. SOMMER
LOUIS SOMMER
11, 13, 15, Passage des Princes
PARIS
REGISTRE DU COMMERCE SEINE 357.704
TÉLÉPH. : CENTRAL 78-72
5428

THE BIRTH OF A PIPE

Whether it is a fine briar, which still lives in your hand, a light and sweet meerschaum dug from the depth of the earth, or a simple clay, you cannot easily guess the number of distinct operations and the meticulous attention required to produce a pipe. Its manufacture reveals a number of specific artisan's techniques, developed and improved over the years by generations of craftsmen. Being masters of their crafts, pipe-makers have to meet increasing demands not only for quality, but also for diversification. Today, pipe-smokers own many pipes, sometimes dozens, in all materials, shapes, finishes and quality.

THE BRIAR PIPE

In France, tucked into a Jura valley at the junction of the Bienne and the Tacon – two rivers which have for centuries provided motive power to the local artisans – the small town of Saint-Claude has, for almost a hundred and fifty years, been established as the world capital of pipes. There is no other place in the world where so much is concentrated on their manufacture. It was around 1850 that the craftsmen of Saint-Claude, wood-turners for generations, started making briar pipes. Today, seven firms in the Confrérie des Maîtres Pipiers (literally the Brotherhood of Master Pipe-makers) manufacture over 700,000 pipes a year, bearing a dozen different brand names: Bontemps, Butz-Choquin, Chacom, Chap, Ewa, Genod, Graco, Jeantet, Jean Lacroix, Claude Romain, Ropp and Vuillard. They supply virtually the whole French market and export more than half their production around the world, from Canada to Japan.

All visitors to Saint-Claude should take the opportunity to view from above, in the evening, from a curve on the D69 road coming from Morez, the effect of the lights of the town – encircled by the dark Jura mountains – which will remind them of the glow of a lit pipe. Then, during the day, walk along its commercial streets, down its alleys leading to the rivers, across its bridges and observe its adjoining houses, to discover the signs of its vocation. Some of these signs are already fading, such as the largely unused briar drying sheds, the large peeling signs bearing the names of past manufacturers, prosperous in the 1920s, when eighty firms produced thirty million pipes a year. But there is also evidence, beyond the passion and know-how of the makers, of the real quality of the Jura people: patience and tenacity. There is also the veneration given to the pipe, as shown by the large wooden example carved by local Scouts, which presides over one of the town's squares. In contemplating the shop windows, the visitor is soon convinced that pipes in Saint-Claude are still very much alive, in spite of the current recession, which is not the first, and in spite of the spread of cigarette-smoking.

Apart from the work of three pipe master carvers still active in Saint-Claude, whose specialities are animals and portraits of famous personalities, and the top-quality "freehand" models created by Pierre Morel and Alain Albuisson for the Cuty Fort and Butz-Choquin companies, it is the bulk production of briar pipe series which is carried out in the factories. This fact has to be qualified. On the one hand the factories have retained the modest proportions of the early years of the century, old buildings of one or two floors, where hardly modernized machines are manned by a limited number of workers. Most of them are still situated near the rivers, which provided the motive power until the 1930s.

The most important firm, the Berrod-Regad Group, which produces five brands among which is the famous Butz Choquin, employs just under a hundred work people to make four hundred thousand pipes a year. Most of today's master pipe-makers are the sons or grandsons of previous master makers, and their ancestral methods, proven techniques and family traditions characterize the current Saint-Claude production. The range of

At the workshop of Philippe Bargiel, we see the tools of the meer-schaum craftsman including some relics of the firm of Sommer; from top to bottom, a centre-punch, an auger, a carving knife, a chisel, a gouger and a tapping screw (preceding double spread).

A workman of the Courrieu company, at the end of the last century. The lathe is powered by a foot lever. A similar lathe, made entirely of wood, is still in use in the workshop of Charles Courrieu, at Cogolin in the Var département of southern France (right)

The majority of pipes are industrially produced in series, based on definite models. In a factory of the Cuty Fort group in Saint-Claude (right), as elsewhere, the faithful reproduction of the classic models will produce a range of prices which varies according to the quality of the briar.

Seven leading companies which produce some 700,000 pipes a year, make Saint-Claude, in the heart of the French Jura mountains, the pipe world capital (top right).

At the end of the last century, sixty-six pipe-makers employed 1,600 men, five hundred women and two hundred juveniles. The polishing of pipes, a delicate operation, has always been the prerogative of the women, taking a year in training (below).

models produced is so wide and varied that a single series rarely exceeds a few hundred pieces. Smokers must know that the pipes from Saint-Claude, still reasonably priced, are born more from traditional craftsmanship than from a modern robot-controlled industry. Briar is a delicate natural material which demands this guarantee of quality.

It is therefore in this cold and often snow-covered Jura region, that the largest numbers of briar pipes are made. But it is much further south, as the crow flies, that the story starts. The briar used for briar bowls, the ideal material discovered in about 1850, grows only around the Mediterranean. It is a variety of Ericaceae (heath), named *Erica arborea* by botanists, found in heathlands, and which can grow up to five or six metres high; it is seldom found above 1000 metres or below 500 metres in altitude. Neither the trunk nor the branches of the tree are used, but a bulging woody growth of varying size, situated between the actual root and the trunk. It is in fact normally called "root"

for convenience, but also known as a "burl". The tree needs to be at least thirty years old so that the burl can grow to a required minimum size, about the size of a football. It weighs on average about three kilos (six pounds). The largest burl so far discovered, was found in Italy, at the beginning of the century, and weighed 110 kilogrammes!

Among the woods used for pipes, the briar-root offers incomparable qualities: hardness, inalterability and constant resistance to heat; it is nonetheless easy to work. In addition, it is a beautiful wood. Well turned, briar shows up harmonious veins which will yield the "flame" and "bird's eye" grains that purists will seek on the pipe bowl and which are elements that will determine its cost.

The *Erica arborea* grows wild. Intensive exploitation has led to the exhaustion of some sources, which has meant that there may be a non-productive period in some countries. In the first half of the century, Algeria, then a French colony, was the main supplier of briar to

The models of current shapes at the firm of Courrieu (right).

A natural anomaly, the "briar root". It is that burl, situated between the actual roots and the trunk of the tree, that will produce the briar blocks, or *ébauchons*. The "roots" must be at least thirty years old to yield good quality briar (left).

Saint-Claude and others. However, it was not the exhaustion of its "briar forests", but the political situation leading to the country's independence which led the manufacturers to find other sources in Morocco. Most of the briar used in Saint-Claude now comes from there. Greece supplies fine briar particularly appreciated by British quality pipe-makers; Italy and Spain also produce briar, but now in lesser quantities and sometimes of lower quality. Corsican briar, which is very fine and soft, is unfortunately now rare. The firm of Courrieu, at Cogolin in the Var département of southern France, uses briar found in the Maures and Esterel mountain ranges near by. The Moroccan supplies, which have been exploited for some thirty-five years, may be coming to an end. On the other hand, the total stoppage for thirty years in Algeria, has enabled the forests to grow again and some real briar treasures are waiting to be dug up. But the first transformation of the briar roots, carried out at source, requires a knowledge that the French settlers took away with them. Therefore, the return of Algeria as a

primary source would be difficult to achieve.

The harvest of briar is generally carried out between November and May. As soon as they are dug out, the roots are stored under cover, away from the dry air and the sun, to prevent splitting, and kept constantly in damp conditions for several months. This involves covering them with earth or jute bags regularly watered. When still very wet, the roots are cleaned, stones and all foreign elements are discarded, and they are then split in two. The core of the roots, which is useless, is cut out. The next operation – sawing – requires the hands of experts. Each half is cut on a circular saw in order to produce one or more small blocks, called *ébauchons*, the basis of a pipe bowl. Depending on the manufacturer's requirements and the presence of faults in the wood, the sawyers extract three basic sizes of *ébauchon*, each consisting of given dimensions and qualities. The outside "crust" of the briar is kept on the *plateaux*, which are fairly rare; *plateaux* are thick slices of extreme beauty which will eventually be used for the production of "free-

A arborescent briar (*Erica arborea*) used for pipe-making, grows wild around the Mediterranean. The tree flowers in April in Africa, and from March to May in Europe (above).

At Courrieu's, at the beginning of the century, the second of the sixty operations required to make a pipe: the cleaning of the the roots, which consists of eliminating earth and stones with a bill-hook. This operation is still carried out today (left below).

The Courrieu company still uses briars found locally in the Massif des Maures, which are as fine as they are rare (right).

hands", unique models which occasionally keep the "crust" at the top of the bowls. Some pipe-makers call them "flowers". The other types of *ébauchon* are for normal production: the *marseillaises* for turning straight models and the *relevées* for bent models.

One can then understand the importance of the sawing process. The more the sawyer knows how to utilize the nature of the wood to best advantage, taking the grain into account, the better the future pipe will be. But he must also take into account the economic aspect of his work: while the *plateaux* are sold singly at high prices, the regular *ébauchons* (blocks) are sold in bags by weight, according to three standards of quality. It is in the interest of the producer to extract the maximum with the minimum of waste. It should be noted, however, that for each kilogramme of *ébauchons*, there are three which cannot be used, except as fuel for the next operation.

After having sorted the models, their sizes and qualities, the *ébauchons* are boiled in large copper vats, heated with waste briar. This has the function of eliminating the sap and other impurities from the briar, which might split in drying, and also to coat it with tannin giving it a brown colour. The operation is in two phases:

the *ébauchons* are immersed in tepid water which is gradually heated, and then boiled for six hours. After that time, the heat is turned off but the *ébauchons* cool in the water for another twelve hours, at least. They are then dried at normal temperature, on racks in covered sheds for about a month. When considered "half dried", they are once more sorted. In spite of the boiling process, a number will split during this first drying and must be discarded. *Ebauchons* without faults are rare. Only those with minor faults which can be rectified during the manufacturing processes, and which will not compromise the quality of the pipes, will be bagged and shipped to the manufacturers.

The unit of shipment and value of *ébauchons* is the "bale" of 100 kilos. But currently, shipments of "half-bales", weighing 50 kilos of the same size are made. Since the sizes of *ébauchons* vary, each half-bale contains different quantities. The quantity is stencilled on the bales in dozens, which may vary from 24 to 108dz. This will explain why the size of a pipe may affect its price: each bale costs the same whatever the quantity of *ébauchons*, the largest sizes being therefore the most expensive. Whatever the quality of the manufacture, this price which varies in ratio from 1 to 5, will affect the cost of the final product.

Ebauchon selection at Dunhill in London; it needs the eyes of an expert (right).

Series production. Let us return to Saint-Claude, to a vast building situated on the bank of the Tacon river. There, Gérard Chapel, heir to a long line of pipe-makers and president of the local pipe club, leads us into the factory of the Berrod-Regad Group, in which he is one of the experts. In these vast mansard rooms, which have unglazed windows so as to allow a regular draught, half-bales from a number of sources are stored, awaiting the pre-production phase, the final drying. According to quality, meaning in effect source, drying is carried out naturally or artificially. Fine Corsican briar, for instance, is allowed to dry naturally in "free" air, laid out on racks and the *ébauchons* are regularly turned over with a pitchfork. This drying process, which may last as long as four to six months, guarantees the preservation of all qualities. But, in view of the manipulation required, this method is more expensive than artificial drying, recently introduced in Saint-Claude, which uses costly energy. On the ground floor of the factory, most of the Moroccan *ébauchons* are dried artificially in closed rooms in which machines blowing hot air ensure constant air circulation. This second method reduces drying time to four to five weeks, and needs far less handling as the *ébauchons* are kept in their original bales.

Let us now enter the heart of the factory.

Everywhere there is a smell of sulphur, coming from the vulcanite mouthpieces. Once dry, the *ébauchons* are once more sorted. Some eight per cent develop cracks during drying and have to be eliminated. The rest are selected by size to suit given bowls. The work is done by an experienced selector who drops them in bags down a short chute to which is fitted a counter calibrated in dozens. When the time comes for the turning of a certain batch, the manufacturer will know exactly how many he has in any size.

From now on, the actual manufacture can start, against the background of the sounds of the machines: the hum of the motors, the shrill contacts of the saws or the fraises on the wood, the high pitch of the air extractors which take away the dust of the briar. Until packed and shipped, a pipe will gradually be transformed from the raw material, assembled and "decorated". The whole process involves a great number of successive operations, often mechanized, in proper order and with specialized names.

Each block is first of all calibrated to rectify the irregular shapes of the *ébauchons*. This is carried out by hand with a circular saw, and the sawyer squares the block and eliminates unnecessary wood, so that the block will fit with some precision on the machines.

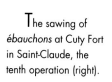

The sawing of *ébauchons* at Cuty Fort in Saint-Claude, the tenth operation (right).

Dominique Jeantet who is responsible for production at Cuty Fort in Saint-Claude, inspects Moroccan *ébauchons* before drying. Air-drying on open floors lasts from four to six months; this method is only used for good-quality briar (right).

A craftsman at W Ø Larsen, in Copenhagen, plans a bowl on a plateau to obtain the maximum advantage of the grain. This method is not feasible for series production and is only used for freehand pipe-making (right).

At Contù, near Como in Italy, Franco Coppo of the Castello firm, selects a plateau. The almost perfect roots, keeping the exterior bark, are destined to produce unique pieces entirely made by hand (below):

Bowl turning reveals the shape of the bowl and bores the combustion hole, the base of the *ébauchon* being held in the jaws of a chuck (which the French makers call *gueule de loup* – snapdragon). The *ébauchon* is turned against set cutters which produce the outside, the top and the combustion chamber of the bowl.

Stem-turning (called *varlopage*) is self-explanatory. The base of the block is still held in a chuck, but is presented horizontally against a set of steel cutters (the *varlope*) which turns extremely fast.

The *ébauchon* has now become a roughhew. The stem (also called a shank) is formed, but the bowl is not complete, the base having been held in the chuck. Fraising will clear most of the bottom of the bowl. The combustion hole is placed onto a conical mandrel and the bottom of the pipe is presented to the fraise which has the contour of the required shape.

The fraise cannot take away all the surplus wood, and this is eliminated by rasping, which for special pieces is carried out by hand with a heavy rasp. For a long time, this operation was carried out by independent workers who lived in a nearby village. They were poor peasants,

often cut off by winter snow, who used to collect the bowls for rasping in the autumn and bring them back in the spring, although as roads improved and road transport became available, the turn-round became much quicker, some raspers working all the year. Today the bowls are rasped six at a time on a reproduction machine, similar to the one used for cutting keys.

Then comes the piercing or drilling of the draught bore, which is the most delicate of the operations. The bowl is put on a boxwood peg, and the stem is drilled horizontally. The turning drill is constantly oiled and must emerge correctly at the bottom of the combustion hole. If not "dead-centre" it might create smoking problems.

The shape of the bowl is almost finished. The previous operations may reveal minor faults in the wood, and a new selection is required. It is the first selection which consists of separating the bowls without faults from the rest, which may have pin-holes or small splits. Some are not good enough and have to be discarded. The others can be rectified by smoothing with emery paper. Then follows a second selection which divides the bowls into five qualities. Including certain variations, all

A workshop at the Genod company, Saint-Claude, where Jacques Craen and his three assistants produce sixteen thousand pipes a year. The best are only sold in Saint-Claude (facing page, top). The twelfth operation, bowl turning; the bowl is turned outside and inside (facing page, two lower photos).

The group Cuty Fort produces a thousand pipes a day. Here we see two phases of bowl turning : bowl boring (above), size checking (centre). After turning the stem, the fraising gives a bowl its final shape (below).

the pipe bowls are sorted into nine different qualities.

The filling or puttying is carried out by hand to correct bowls with small flaws in the briar. The faults are "cleaned" with a small hand gouge, and the putty (or filling) is applied with a spatula. In most pipe-making countries, certainly in England, the trade calls it "mastic", which is made up with a composition of alabaster and fish-glue, to which a small amount of stain is added, to match the final colour. The fillings have to be left "proud" and the surplus is later eliminated with emery paper.

After turning the bowls, the combustion holes may not be fully smooth. They are polished with a piece of felt on a suitable peg with oil and pumice. The French makers call this operation *bobéchonnage*.

The maker now returns to the stem (or shank) which is not quite ready. The second drilling consists of opening the end to a suitable size to fit the peg or push, the cylindrical part of the mouthpiece. The bore is opened further if a system or filter is to be fitted.

During the fitting, the lip of the mouthpiece is re-touched to give it its required form, then the push (also called peg or floc) is turned to fit with precision into the stem of the bowl. This is a highly delicate operation carried out on a lathe with a special cutter, which is in fact an industrial diamond (bonded diamond powder). This is the best tool to ensure perfect fitting.

If the system to be fitted requires to be screwed in, this is done with a tapping tool. The two essential parts of a pipe can now be assembled.

The next operation is called levelling; it consists of aligning the stem and mouthpiece which have slightly different external dimensions. This is done on a fast-turning wheel, fitted with emery cloth.

Gérard Chapel leads us into another workshop. Surprisingly, only women work here. Some ten oper-ators carry out one of the most delicate tasks, pol-ishing, destined to eliminate all rough traces on both the bowls and mouthpieces. There are four phases to this operation, each phase using a finer emery cloth. A lot of attention and precision is required, so as not to alter the shape of the pipe. An error in polishing can create a flat surface which would not be acceptable. This is why women who have sen-sitive fingers are employed; their training takes about a year.

The pipe is now almost finished. We leave the machine shops for much quieter work-rooms. Before the final finishing processes, pipes go through a further selection, based on half a dozen precise standards of quality (they differ from country to country) which consider the texture of the briar, the absence – or otherwise – of minor flaws, their number and location. The selector needs a great deal of experience. In France, this classification goes from the rare straight

The sixteenth operation, rasping, is entirely done by hand on good-quality bowls to eliminate all rough edges and shape the model. The operator uses a specially designed rasp for briar, which he may have made himself (facing page).

The drilling of the draught hole must be exact; a slight deviation could result in the rejection of the bowl (above right).

At Courrieu's, bowl polishing is a delicate operation; no flat facet can be tolerated (below).

grains, which have a regular "flame" without faults, down to the lower "second" and "third" qualities, which have a varying amount of fillings. Between the two extremes, the first quality consists of the category AB, well grained and without flaws, and the AC of average texture and a few imperfections. The A quality is rarely used these days: it includes the "bird's eye" texture which is seldom found in the younger briar roots currently dug up. Then follows the "mixed A" quality which allows for two or three minor fillings, and the "ordinary mixed" with up to five such fillings, perhaps slightly larger. These "mixed" qualities offer excellent value for money to smokers with limited resources.

The ultimate phase of manufacture is the finishing. The best first-quality pipes are generally left in a "natural" state and are only waxed. The others can be stained (tinted or coloured). The range of tints is quite wide, and the darker ones have the advantage, perhaps the inconvenience, of masking imperfections and putty fillings. Whatever the tints, colouring is carried out by hand. First a base,

then the tints are applied with either a brush or a wad. The pipe bowls are then flamed to fix the colour, and then suspended on a rack to be dried by infra-red lamp. The buffing on felt wheels eliminates the sheen which remains on the bowls after flaming, and ensures a uniform colour. Certain bowls can be tinted in a way that shows up the contrasts of the briar.

Stained pipes can be waxed or varnished. While waxing presents few difficulties, varnishing demands, as does polishing, experienced hands. Varnish, applied with a wad, dries very quickly and must be applied in one movement on the bowl, as a pause would show and the pipe would be discarded. It is essential that no varnish goes into the combustion bore, since that would make the pipe unfit for smoking. This operation is all the more delicate as the tops have to be varnished. In other countries, and particularly in Britain, a slightly different method is used, combining varnishing and waxing on a specially prepared "dolly" wheel.

Certain bowls, which have a number of black spots (excess of silicate) are destined for sandblasting. A

A Rhodesian model before draught hole drilling. One can see the rough edges still to be rasped (right).

mixture of sand and glass dust (or metal) is "blasted" on the bowls. It attacks the softer parts of the briar and eliminates the spots, the harder parts appearing in relief. To avoid dust filling the workshop, this is carried out in a glass cage, using fitted rubber gloves. Sandblasting not only has the advantage of "saving" briar bowls. Sandblasted pipes are lighter in weight, they give a "lighter" smoke, and their quality is excellent. Although sandblasting is now becoming less used, some London makers have recently specialized in the process.

Surface carving, at least in Saint-Claude has all but disappeared. This is carried out on bowls with prominent faults with a special fraise or cutter. It eliminates all flaws and small splits and imitates sandblasting. It is a long process which is applied to ordinary and therefore cheaper pipes, defying economic considerations. These days, surface carving is still carried out also on better briar, such as the work of Italian carvers, on freehand models.

Whether natural or varnished, pipes receive a final polish, either on a soft chamois leather or a felt "dolly" wheel using a polishing compound. Most are then tubed, meaning fitted with a system (or filter) and then blown through under compressed air to eliminate all dust and particles left in the bore of the bowls and mouthpieces.

That leaves the stamping. All pipes are marked with the brand of the manufacturer, the name of the series and probably the shape number or quality, and finally the origin of the pipe (Saint Claude or France in this case). Stamping is done on the stems with a heated stamp using a machine activated with the foot. It is at that point that pipes are fitted – when required – with metal bands and that the mouthpieces are also marked.

The pipes are checked for the last time and receive a final buffing on a felt (or cotton) wheel, before being put into individual bags, boxed and shipped.

Thus are born – not only in Saint-Claude, but also in other factories in France (Courrieu at Cogolin), in Great Britain and Ireland (Dunhill, Comoys, Duncan, Peterson), in Germany (Vauen), in the Netherlands (Hilson, Big Ben), in Italy (Savinelli, Lorenzo), in Denmark (Stanwell, Nording, Svendborg) – more than ninety per cent of all pipes made in the world. Produced in series and (partly) by machines, they offer smokers, a wide range of models of good quality at reasonable prices.

Hand-made pipes. As far as the others are concerned, they are created by the genius of individual craftsmen who are often real artists. Their pipes are often unique models, made out of the best briar available, and they form the aristocracy of pipe-making, and merit their high prices. They are sometimes made "to order", according to the specifications of the client. Their manufacture follows the same operations as those above, but differs essentially in the working methods and the tools used: a craftsman-artisan works with his hands.

We should distinguish between the two methods that they employ: there are those who make their pipes by hand but use a chuck to hand-turn them (hand-made shapes), and those who produce entirely by hand, hence the name "freehand". The difference is important, since the second method can take the grain of the briar fully into account. For the "turners", manufacture starts by drawing with a thick pencil the basic shape of the model on the face of the *ébauchon*, according to their imagination or the instructions of the client. The block is then cut roughly on

a ribbon saw following the given design. The operations which follow are similar to series production, but for one exception: it is not a machine which turns the bowl or the stem, but a tool held by the artisan.

On the other hand, for those we sometimes call Master Pipe-Makers (the pipe artists who are often Italian or Danish), work starts with the choice of *ébauchons*. As already noted, they are cut from blocks which are of exceptional quality. The briar suppliers pick the best pieces and know where to send them. But they are quite rare and sometimes the pipe-maker himself will go to the saw-mills to pick his own pieces. His experience and instinct will tell him whether the blocks are promising or not. Briar is an unpredictable material. The cost of any waste will be reflected in the price of each pipe. Apart from the time spent in selecting the right briar, each freehand requires about ten hours work in the workshop.

For these master pipe-makers, there are no regular models, only the *ébauchon* will determine the final shape. They work by hand without turning machines, and finalize the shape in relation to small flaws that have to be eliminated, sometimes with a file. A freehand

pipe is always without filling. For the rest, the process of manufacture is the same: fashioning of the bowl with a saw or rasp, boring of the combustion hole with a gouge or small boring tool, drilling of the stem, pumicing of the bowl and mouthpiece. polishing, etc. A hand-made briar pipe is sometimes a sublime piece, and always a precious object, born out of creativity and the nature of the material. One can appreciate its grain and its colour and never cease to feel its texture and to admire its exceptional finish. It can be the "love of a lifetime".

There is also another category of artists: the carvers (or sculptors). The work of Paul Lanier, Jean Masson and Roger Vincent has maintained the Saint-Claude tradition of carved pipes. The bowls are sometimes produced in small series when they depict portraits of known personalities, or animal heads. The carver first makes a model which is used to cut six bowls with a reproduction machine. But the machine cannot reproduce the piece with precision. It is then that the talent of the carver comes into its own, turning out by hand exceptional unique models. The subjects and shapes are extremely varied and some can be quite large, such as the "winged monster" exhibited at the

Bergerac museum; it has teeth made in ivory and the eyes are rubies. The piece is some forty centimetres long, and Roger Vincent was very proud to show off his model in his workshop. For some years, Paul Lanier has been regularly commissioned by the Confrérie des Maîtres Pipiers, to produce the piece to be presented to France's "Top Pipe Smoker". Paul Lanier, whose enthusiasm, joviality and dexterity guide his steady hands, also produces portrait-pipes to order explaining that he keeps on postponing his retirement. Each pipe requires some fifty hours work, and reflects the know-how of a thousand years of wood-carving in Saint-Claude.

To start his work, the carver relies on photos of his subject and initially produces a plasticine (or clay) working model; then he makes one in wood in order to ascertain the feasibility of the project and determine the size of briar *ébauchon* he will require. The work can now start on the briar carving. It is extremely delicate, as any false move could ruin the piece and waste hours of work. It also demands that the aesthetic should be combined with the functional, since carved pipes should be capable of being smoked. The motif on the bowl, sometimes running onto the stem, must not interfere either with the boring of the combustion hole or with the drilling of the stem.

THE MOUTHPIECES

Some smokers consider that a good briar pipe depends more on the quality of the draught, therefore in part on the mouthpiece, than on the quality of the bowl. It is certain that a bad mouthpiece may compromise the potential taste of a faultless briar.

The search for an ideal material for a mouthpiece has continued for a long time. It requires precisely inverse qualities to those of the bowl: the less porous it is, the less "foreign" substances it will trap and the sweeter will be the smoke. But if the material has to be compact, it must also be light. For more than half a century, Saint-Claude and other manufacturers have been using vulcanized rubber (also called ebonite) in preference to bone, horn, cherry or amber. This was discovered accidentally by Charles Goodyear in 1839 when he let an eraser melt on a heating stove. Vulcanite is easy to work, light and non-porous. It does not alter the

taste of the smoke and, in addition, it is economical, so that at present the majority of pipes are fitted with vulcanite mouthpieces, generally called "vulcanites" for short. They have nonetheless some faults: they can break and age badly. In use and under contact with light, vulcanites will discolour, become greenish and give out a taste of sulphur which is present in the manufacturing formula. These faults are not found in ideal materials, for example in the more expensive synthetic resins such as acrylic, and in sheet or rod vulcanite, usually worked by hand, which is of a superior quality to moulded vulcanites.

Vulcanite mouthpieces therefore offer a good compromise between price and quality, necessary for the economic viability of series production of pipes. A firm in Saint-Claude, L'Ebonite, specializes in the manufacture of these mouthpieces, producing several hundred thousand a year. As everyone knows, vulcanization is achieved by mixing sulphur with rubber. Manufacture consists of mixing ground sulphur with liquefied rubber, to which is added a small amount of plastic material; the mixture is heated and melted in a hopper, then allowed to flow into multi-cavity moulds. These moulds have a longitudinal skewer which creates the bore of the mouthpieces. The mouthpieces are taken out of the moulds while still warm to facilitate the extraction of the skewer. They are then "stoved" under steam. Heated at 130 degrees Celsius, the steam causes the sulphur to reach 190 degrees thus causing a chemical reaction which produces vulcanized rubber.

All mouthpieces are moulded straight. Those required to be used on bent pipes are reheated and curved by hand on a form. Whether straight or bent, mouthpieces go through a first polishing process before delivery. The pipe-maker will then carry out all the necessary processes for the finished pipes.

One company in Saint-Claude, Waille, makers of the Ewa brand of pipes, have specialized for some years in the production of other, less common, mouthpieces. Heir to a pipe-making family, from father to son since 1860, Michel Waille has revived the manufacture of horn mouthpieces which, before the Second World War and the appearance of synthetic materials, employed almost the total population of a small village near Saint-Claude, Cinquetral. In those days, the majority of pipes

The master carver Paul Lanier in his Saint-Claude workshop. A carved head requires at least a week's work and costs more than ten thousand francs (left).

Carved briar heads are a tradition in Saint-Claude. Houdon's Voltaire was first reproduced by the carver Henri Dalloz around 1862. It has been in great demand ever since (below).

were fitted with horn mouthpieces. Opinions are divided on the material, some saying that its porosity gives a bitter taste. Michel Waille defends horn mouthpieces with passion: they have a fine appearance and they are very comfortable for the teeth. They are however more expensive and the current demand for them is relatively small.

Manufacture starts in effect in Africa and Australia in a natural way. After the animals are slaughtered, the horns are cut off and left to dry in the open air, exposed to the voracity of flies. These like "fresh" horns and lay their eggs in them. The grubs feed on the horns for a month until they, in turn, become flies. The horns are effectively cleaned and all that is needed is to tap them on a hard surface for the "bone" to fall out. It is this which becomes the raw material. It is not only used for the manufacture of mouthpieces, but also for making buttons, handles for shaving brushes and knives, and combs.

Once with the manufacturer, the horns have to be straightened. The operation consists of boiling the horns to soften them, then passing a blow-lamp over them to break the internal nerve, since if the nerve is left intact they would revert to their original shapes. Their curve is then reversed in a small vice called a "mathieu". Next, they are dried for about ten days after which the best can be selected, and it is from these that the mouthpieces will be made. The horns can now be shaped on a turning machine; the draught hole is drilled by hand, and its enlargement is made on a lateral drill.

A German company, Raschig from Ludwigshaffen, supplies "ambrolith" – a synthetic resin – to Jean Nicolas (Lyons), Gilbert Guyot (Paris) and Philippe Bargiel (Crépy-en-Valois), the last three French artisans who can make pipes, from bowl to mouthpiece, entirely by hand. In his remarkable book on the history of pipe-making techniques in France, *Les Pipiers Français* (The French Pipe-Makers), Gilbert Guyot describes the manufacture of these mouthpieces in resin which have the qualities of being non-porous, unalterable and

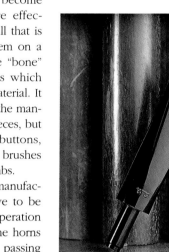

light, and which are incomparable. Depending on the length of mouthpiece required, pieces are sawn from the blocks which come in long strips with a rectangular cross-section. They are then turned by hand and shaped on a wheel fitted with coarse sand-paper. After drilling, the mouthpieces are fitted to the stems of the bowls with a bone or nylon screw, then levelled, pumiced and polished at length.

PIPE MANUFACTURING IN ENGLAND

The process of briar pipe manufacturing in England follows essentially the operations carried out in Saint-Claude. In the nineteenth century, traders (particularly in London) were already interested in handling all sorts of pipes for export to the colonies and the United States. They already had a network of agents, and even local offices as far afield as South Africa, Australia and New Zealand and, of course, a ready market among the troops and civil servants stationed in India and the China coast. Initially, the British traders bought supplies from France, from Saint-Claude in particular. At the same time, they felt that they should help the budding French industry by investing in it. Some of the first to do so were Oppenheimer Pipes and Adolf Frankau. The former, was the British agent for GBD pipes made in Paris by a company founded in 1850. By the end of the century, Oppenheimer had acquired GBD and its manufacturing facilities in Saint-Claude, and this led to the building of a large factory. One purpose of that factory was to supply London with briar bowls for fitting and finishing. Adolf Frankau, the second company, was actually developed by a young man of eighteen, Louis Blumfeld, who was put in charge of the company when the founder died in 1856. He created the brand BBB which was the first pipe name to be registered (No 40) in Britain when the Registration of Trade Marks Act became law in 1876. Adolf Frankau was eventually taken over by Oppenheimer who

A hand-made mouthpiece by the German pipe-maker Rainer Barbi, engraved with his initials. Rainer Barbi's technique for polishing mouthpieces is a trade secret (right).

The Saint-Claude workshops sometimes resemble mysterious laboratories. At Chapuis-Comoy (Chacom pipes), makers since 1825, a worker is bending mouthpieces. They are first heated to 60 degrees Celsius then bent by hand and finally cooled in cold water to retain the curve (right).

used its manufacturing facilities as a basis for future developments.

Another famous maker was Henri Comoy, who arrived in London in 1879 with a bag of tools. His family had been Saint-Claude pipe-makers since 1825. He was one of the prime movers in the introduction of the "London Made" appellation. There were others in the British Isles: Peterson in Dublin (Ireland), Barling, Charatan, Duncan, Hardcastle, Ben Wade, Civic, and, of course, Alfred Dunhill who opened his London shop in 1907, having already introduced a pipe for car-drivers as early as 1904.

These all followed more or less the same course in manufacturing. They originally obtained finished pipes from Saint-Claude (or Paris) but, gradually, under Henri Comoy's lead, felt that they should concentrate on top-quality products, "London Made". The machines were bought in Saint-Claude and some French expert operators even spent time in England to train English operators. Over the years, minor alter-ations were introduced. For instance, London was first to introduce hand-cut vulcanite mouth-pieces from rods or sheet. These were mostly used on top-quality pipes, although some top-quality moulded mouthpieces were filed to obtain distinct shapes, like the Comoy's Phantom. Comoy was probably the first to introduce the widening of the draught hole at the lip of the mouthpiece. There were variations in polishing due to London factories trying out different polishing agents, but the most important difference was in the finishing process: whereas Saint-Claude applied varnish by hand, London manufacturers perfected a way by which they could apply varnish straight on the polishing mop.

A minor revolution in England was the introduction of the metal-stemmed pipe, the Falcon, originally an American idea. This was in about 1953, when the late Dave Morris, then head of the Lewis's of Westminster chain of retail tobacconists obtained the agency for Britain. As there were still restrictions on impor-tations, he made arrangements to have the pipe made in the UK. Falcon has the distinction of being the one and only pipe to be advertised on television. Sceptics said that it would never sell, but Falcon pipes soon obtained between twenty-five and thirty per cent of the market (in volume) in branded pipes.

Most developments had to be abandoned

when the pipe industry started to shrink in the 1970s, although one factory introduced repro-duction machines (based on the type used to turn wooden golf-clubs) for bowl turning. This also cut down training times. Other subsequent small developments have included the use of laser machines to stamp brands on mouth-pieces. At the same time, there were many changes in the grouping of companies.

The best known and most prestigious group is, of course, Dunhill, which now includes Parker (originally set up by Dunhill), Charatan and UK agencies for Butz-Choquin of France and Stanwell of Denmark. Cadogan Investments (formerly Oppenheimer Pipes) makes and markets GBD (London-made), Comoy's, BBB, Dr Plumb's, Kaywoodie, Loewe, Orlik and Medico. Peterson of Dublin has now merged with Duncan Pipes; and Falcon, which had remained independent from the others, has now also merged with Merton of London. The last named used to do a great deal of business in cheap lines, but realized in the 1970s that these were to become a thing of the past. Merton has now become the leading importer of quality pipes, such as Savinelli (Italy) Big Ben (Holland) and Amphora. Barling Pipes are made in the Isle of Man by a factory that also makes meerschaum pipes from African material, under the brand name Manx as well as for other brands. Another firm, Pomeroy & Cooke makes similar meerschaum pipes under the Jambo label, many of which are sold through mail-order. There are a few small com-panies that have managed to weather the storm and are still active, but the important devel-opment in British pipe-making has been the birth of small companies specializing in top-quality merchandise, with a few lines for the middle-price market.

Most of the creators of these companies learned their trade in the best "schools", like Dunhill and Charatan. They all emerged in the 1970s when the mass market was disappearing fast, but then it was evident that quality was the most important aspect. William Ashton-Taylor, for example, had learned pipe-making at Dunhill and had always dreamed of owning his own business. When this became possible, he launched the Ashton brand which is hand-made right through. His range includes fine straight grains and he soon discovered, as others did, that the strength of English pipe-making was in classical shapes. He has also perfected a very

To the question: "Of all the pipes that you have carved, which was your favourite?" Eyup Sabri answers: "The one-offs, those that I have never dupli-cated." Eyup Sabri is undoubtedly one of the best meerschaum carvers. He was born and works at Eskisehir, in Anatolia, where the principal sources of meerschaum are found (facing page).

Philippe Bargiel, in his workshop. Former craftsman at Sommer of Paris, now working at Crépy-en-Valois, he is now the only craftsman using the traditional methods of making meerschaum pipes (right).

light sandblast which has become greatly appreciated in all markets. Initially, demand came from overseas, the USA in particular, but now many specialists in Britain stock his pipes.

The brand name James Upshall was taken from a maternal ancestor of the late Ken Barnes who was with Charatan and decided to create his own pipe-making factory in Wiltshire. The company is now run by Barry Jones, who was Charatan-trained, and worked with Ken Barnes from the start. Basically, he follows the old Charatan principles of hand-turning and is now recognized as one of the leading pipe-makers in England. Like Ashton, his shapes are classical and he uses the best Greek briar that he can obtain. He also turns specials in what can only be called the Charatan tradition. The best pipes, classified under strict specifications are stamped James Upshall, while the lower quality is marked Tilshead (the village where the factory is located). Barry Jones' pipes are entirely free of faults. He employs a number of young and enthusiastic operators.

Dennis Marshall, who had also worked at Charatan and other companies, created the Millville brand. With his son John, he turns unique freehands and also classic shapes. For the English market, he has specialized in ranges of upper middle-quality briars, but at very affordable prices.

Finally, Leslie Wood is not only a former Dunhill craftsman who hand-turns his own brands, Ferndown and Elwood, but is also an expert in fitting silver or gold bands and other adornments on pipes. He not only applies that skill to his own products, but is also in demand from other companies requiring his skills.

MEERSCHAUM PIPES

For the last thirty years, and with a few rare exceptions, meerschaum pipes have only been made in Turkey. Until then, from the start of the eighteenth century, which saw the appearance of meerschaum pipes in Austria, Turkey was supplying the raw material to European pipe-makers. In 1961, Turkey put a stop on all exports of raw meerschaum, so as to create a Turkish monopoly to develop a profitable economic activity which would generate foreign currency. Originally lacking experience, the Turkish pipe industry, still in its infancy, produces products with imperfections often judged unpardonable by connoisseurs of meerschaum. Lately, however, Turkish artisans have been

Tools used by Philippe Bargiel. They consist of chucks, tightening rings, nozzles, polishing wheels, fraises, etc. made of wood. They have not altered since the nineteenth century (left).

sent to western Europe for training and some progress has been made.

Meerschaum is a comparatively rare mineral, being a natural silicate of magnesium. Sources of meerschaum have been found in Tanzania, Somalia, Spain, Greece, the Crimea and Turkey. The main exploitation is currently carried out around the small town of Eskisehir, between Istanbul and Ankara. No one knows the exact quantity mined each year, nor the extent of the meerschaum fields. To reach the layers, miners have to go down to a depth of some 80 metres, although meerschaum was originally found at a depth of 25 metres. At that depth, the meerschaum is superior in quality, but the "lumps" tend to be smaller. Let us reassure the connoisseurs, worried that the pits around Eskisehir may run out; there is a rumour, which has been around for some time, but is persistent (and kept secret for unknown reasons), that a magnificent new field has been discovered in another part of Turkey.

The manufacture starts in Turkey by moistening the lumps of meerschaum, to facilitate carving. They are then cut on a saw. Currently, a block of average size provides enough material for two pipes, leaving some off-cuts. These off-cuts are used for meerschaum linings,

or reduced to powder to make reconstituted meerschaum, which can be poured in a mould with the addition of a binding substance. The powder also serves to mask flaws before the finishing of a pipe.

Meerschaum is a particularly soft material and the carving (or turning) of the block is done by hand, using different cutters and scrapers to arrive at the, still rough, shape of the bowl.

The combustion hole is bored and the stem drilled. These operations are done by a machine, with the worker holding the piece and boring against a fast-turning bit. This method does not guarantee precision work: the bowl is bored as deep as briar, but since the line of the stem is occasionally out-of-true, the result is approximate. The stem is then drilled to fit a plastic ring, into which will be placed the push of the mouthpiece, also made of plastic. Often, the lack of precision of the drilling can create some inconvenience for the smoker: a slight bias may cause difficulties in adjusting the mouthpiece and risks the breakage of the stem when weakened by the saturation of tar.

The bowls go back to the worker for finishing. They are first of all filed to eliminate the worst irregularities and then sand-papered. This polishing can be unsatisfactory, and does

not please the most exacting smokers. At this stage, the small flaws can be rectified by filling with dampened meerschaum powder. The differences of texture on the bowls can be masked by the next process, by which they are dipped in a bath of stearin or melted paraffin wax. Unfortunately, stearin is not the ideal material to produce the patina which gives the outward beauty of a meerschaum pipe, as it deteriorates after a time and the flaws soon reappear.

There is a legend of Count Andrassy's cobbler, who fortunately discovered the "secret", his hand being covered with shoemaker's wax when he made his first pipes; he deduced that the material should be treated with a greasy substance. In that way, the pipes developed a fine patina with usage, which overcame the first unattractive colours of the absorbed tar. After a few trials, he opted for beeswax, which has been used satisfactorily for two hundred years. No one knows why the Turkish pipe-makers preferred stearin, although one can suggest an answer: stearin is opaque and hides flaws, at least on a new pipe, whereas beeswax, which is clear, demands a perfect surface.

Quickly taken out of its bath, then allowed to cool, the pipe is polished for the last time and buffed with lime. It only remains to position the resin mouthpiece which has had its plastic push fitted, and to put it in a case. All Turkish meerschaum pipes are destined for foreign smokers, either exported or sold to tourists.

Alongside the manufacture of pipes in series which fortunately are improving in quality, there are also carved pipes. While they are often rather coarse, a few talented craftsmen, such as Eyup Sabri in Eskisehir, produce some fine pieces. Some are rather large and are meant as show-pieces. It is difficult to know whether to recommend smoking the others which are not properly treated and risk deterioration.

The almost miraculous existence of the French craftsman, Philippe Bargiel, sculptor by trade and former pipe-maker with the firm of Sommer (now gone), makes us appreciate how much the Turkish pipes could be improved. He is probably one of the last to make meerschaum pipes in the traditional way. Not a traditionalist by nature, he has nonetheless a love for meerschaum and he is clever enough to be able to procure raw meerschaum, and also raw amber which he uses for the restoration of antique pipes, his other speciality. Finally, by contrast with other pipe craftsmen who take their secrets to the grave with them, Philippe Bargiel, who is in his fifties, hopes to be able to train one or two apprentices as craftsmen to follow in his footsteps.

For the lover of meerschaum, it is a real pleasure to visit this amiable expert, in his workshop at Crépy-en-Valois, some 60 kilometres north of Paris. Philippe Bargiel is impassioned by his art which he will talk about with ardour, and will not hesitate to drop his tools to answer any questions in detail. What are the differences between a Turkish pipe and a traditional one? "A vast subject!" he exclaims, before going into details illustrated by numerous small drawings. First, the methods of boring and drilling are the other way round: here, it is the pipe that turns and not the tool which is held by the craftsman. He can therefore control his work with precision. Then, the combustion hole is not bored as deep; this is a precaution which will prevent the bottom of the pipe from falling out when saturated by tar. The hole is therefore higher and, in order to reach it, the draught bore finishes in a slight upward curve.

The stem is then tapped to fit the boxwood screw on the mouthpiece. This is the most delicate operation of all. The screw must fit without effort in the axis of the stem and mouthpiece and be in line to avoid ultimate disasters. For this work, the craftsman uses a number of tapping tools in various sizes, the diameter of the screw being precisely calculated in relation to the stem and mouthpiece.

Although bone has often been used in the manufacture of meerschaum pipes, boxwood remains the best material for the screw. Bone is

The queen of pipes: meerschaum. The lightness, porosity and purity of this silicate of magnesium is unequalled. It is a rare and expensive mineral, which is found deep in the soil of Anatolia (left).

Once polished, cut and lovingly fashioned, amber is an ideal material for mouthpieces, being both smooth and resistant. Unfortunately, it has become too expensive and amber mouthpieces have all but disappeared (left).

quite hard but the strength of boxwood has an amount of flexibility which absorbs shocks. If a pipe is dropped, for example, the shock waves bounce on a screw which is too hard, causing the breakage of the stem or, if amber, the mouthpiece. Finally, by contrast with the plastic fittings of the Turkish pipes, a boxwood screw does not alter the taste of the smoke.

The polishing process of the bowl is equally difficult. The artisan works on a "dolly" wheel, some 20 cm in diameter, made of soft cloth, which is quite supple so that the bowl can be held against it with ease and it will not compress the surface of the bowl in contact. Any compression would, with use, produce a light patch. The traditional finishing of a meerschaum bowl demands the use of what is called a "horse tail". It is a type of fern with a fluted stem, which grows on river banks or in marshes. The stem, used damp for polishing, contains microscopic grains of silicate which make it abrasive. To this day, nothing finer or more precise, nor more convenient has been found to polish meerschaum.

The carved bowl is then dipped into a bath of melted whale oil. This treatment of meerschaum, absent in Turkish manufacture, is nonetheless indispensable. Whale oil, or spermaceti, is a grease found in the frontal bulge of the sperm-whale. "Whale-lovers should be reassured", adds Philippe Bargiel, "that the content of one bulge would be enough to treat several million pipes." Whale oil, which has been used in cosmetics and even as a fine lubricant for industrial machines, has the advantage of melting at low temperatures, and particularly of being both clean and non-degradable. But since industry, under pressure of the whale protection cam-

paigns, does not use it any more, it has become a rare product.

Whale oil is ideal for meerschaum, since it is a "living" material which is self-cleaning. Without it, meerschaum is rapidly saturated by tar and becomes unsmokable. Warming up with the pipe, it melts and mixes with the tar which it draws towards the exterior of the bowl's wall. As it cools, the wax on the pipe retains the tar, while the whale oil returns inside the meerschaum. Thus, the tar mixes with the wax and the result is a fine patina. If you scrape the patina, which may be from light yellow to deep red according to the age of the pipe, only to a tenth of a millimetre, you will find the immaculate whiteness of the meerschaum underneath. The meerschaum keeps its absorbant qualities indefinitely; without them it would have no interest.

Finally, the pipe is plunged into a bath of melted beeswax; it is transparent and therefore the meerschaum must be without flaws.

In England, there are two factories making meerschaum pipes, one in the Isle of Man and the other in Northamptonshire. They use African meerschaum, commonly called Tanganika meerschaum. It is less pure that the Turkish variety but also less fragile. It comes in blocks similar to briar *ébauchons* and, after wetting, is turned in the same way. The treatment of the bowls is similar to the traditional method, but in view of the lower level of purity of the material, they are often calcined or tinted. The pipes, which are standard models, are generally fitted with vulcanite mouthpieces and the prices of the finished products can compete favourably with those of briar pipes.

We saw earlier how ambrolith, a synthetic material imitating amber and

In 1968, Robert Doisneau wrote an article on the last manufacturer of clay pipes at Saint-Quentin-la-Poterie in the Var département of France, Job Clerc. He photographed one of the women workers taking a pipe out of a mould. This was a model of Bacchus, a classic in clay pipes (right, above).

From the middle of the nineteenth century to the depression of 1929, the small town of Andenne, in Belgium, was an important centre of the clay pipe industry. In 1943, there was only one artisan left, Emile Lévèque. One can see, in his workshop photographed at the time, an assembled two-part mould held in a "gin-vice" (right, below).

used often by Philippe Bargiel, was made. Real amber, the favourite with smokers up to the Second World War, is now very rare and very expensive. But Philippe manages to obtain some at a more reasonable price. Amber is a fossil resin, created by ancient forests millions of years ago. It was mostly found on the south coasts of the Baltic, in Germany, Poland and Lithuania, but most fields may now be exhausted. It is sometimes found on the beaches of Pomerania and among the shingle on the banks of the River Oder. It comes as a rough stone, in colours varying from off-white to dark red via yellow. It is only when polished that its real purity is evident. For pipe mouthpieces, yellow amber has always been preferred since it hides the draught bore. Some rare pipes have been made in amber from time to time, but they cannot be smoked; heat would most probably make them explode.

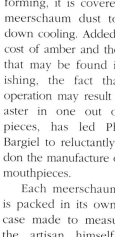

The manufacture of a straight amber mouthpiece does not present any difficulty. The block is cut with a saw and papered with fine emery to spot likely flaws. The piece is then drilled and shaped. It is a little more difficult to make a bent mouthpiece. Unlike ambrolith which softens in boiling water, real amber has to be plunged for a few seconds in oil heated to 120 degrees Celsius. It is taken out and with a special cloth (any other method would leave an imprint) held in the hands, while the shape is formed as rapidly as possible. After forming, it is covered with meerschaum dust to slow down cooling. Added to the cost of amber and the flaws that may be found in polishing, the fact that this operation may result in disaster in one out of two pieces, has led Philippe Bargiel to reluctantly abandon the manufacture of bent mouthpieces.

Each meerschaum pipe is packed in its own fitted case made to measure by the artisan himself. The

At Andenne c. 1930 (facing page). Three to four tonnes of clay being delivered to the factory in a typical local horse-drawn cart (top). The kilns at Lacroix & Cie and the drying shelves (centre). The kilns were heated to a temperature of 1050 to 1100 degrees Celsius.
The pipe-maker has put down the mould on his right. He uses the plug to take the bowl out with extreme care (below).

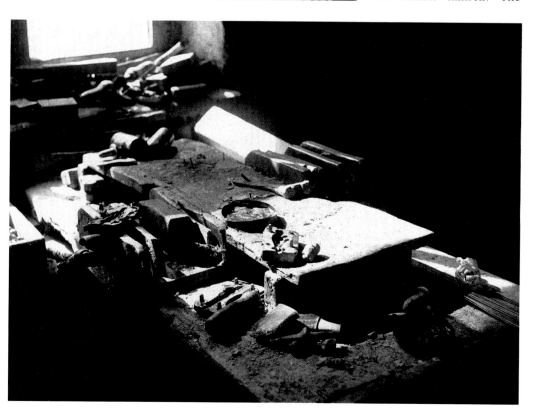

pipe has to fit exactly to avoid friction. A good case must be both light and firmly made. Norwegian pine is the best material for such cases.

THE CLAY PIPE

Clay pipes were in widespread use during the nineteenth century, but are now a part of history since their existence is confined to a decorative role, in museums and private collections.

After extraction, one type of clay was often mixed with another from a different source, then soaked and kneaded in a wooden tub by a specialist worker, with an iron bar. This binds the clay and produces a uniform colour. The pipemaker then took a piece of clay, enough for a pipe and fashioned it into a "roll" (or "dolly") on a table. The rough shape was thick at one end (for the bowl) and thin at the other (for the stem). After a short drying period in the air, an oiled skewer was inserted to form the draught hole.

The roll then went to the moulder who placed it in one part of a two-part mould, then clamped the second part onto the first by means of a vice. The combustion hole was formed by inserting a plunger or chuck, forcing the surplus clay to the top. The pipe was allowed to dry and the surplus clay was scraped off with a sharp knife; a horn or copper scraper could be used. Finally, the pipe was polished by the "finisher" with an agate called a "stone".

Thus fashioned, batches of pipes were placed into shallow trays called "saggers", covered with silicate sand, and placed in kilns for about twenty hours at a temperature of 200 to 300 degrees Celsius. When taken out of the kiln, the pipes cooled and were then dipped in a bath of soap, wax and gum which varnished and whitened them. The "enamel finisher" carried out the final decoration, applying varnish or colour (slip) with a paint brush. The pipes were fired a second time for about twenty minutes. Before shipping, they were wrapped in tissue paper, then packed on layers of straw to avoid breakage, in wooden cases.

The last French manufacturer of clay pipes on an industrial scale was Laville at Montluçon who used, until 1975, moulds salvaged from the Gambier company. Clay pipes are made in Holland for souvenir and touristic purposes.

The pipe-making firm of Leonard, in Belgium, at Andenne, near Namour, has specialized since 1932 in making pipes for shooting galleries, but since the 1960s it has returned to the manufacture of "real" clay pipes. Pascal Leonard, is the grandson of the founder, and today still uses original moulds and also makes more than one hundred models, including pipes in the shape of the heads of the present Belgian royal family and a reproduction of Gambier's Jacob. In France, in the village of Vernègues near Salon-de-Provence, the artist Michael Coquet makes, among other products, a number of ceramic pipes enhanced by hand-painted decoration,

The rolling of the clay was done entirely by hand, a task often given to women and juveniles. In 1943, behind Emile Lévèque, clay rolls are partially dried before being moulded (facing page).

A three-tier kiln at the important Wingender factory at Chokier, Belgium, c. 1900. The bottom tier is reserved for white clays, and the middle and top tiers respectively for the second and first firing of "black" clay pipes. The base of each tier has a round opening and the fire is at ground level. The kiln was heated for four hours with coal and for seven hours with wood (left).

such as blue motifs in the style of Moustiers, animal heads and ancient royal regimental emblems. We should also pay tribute to the work of the French craftsman Gérard Prungnaud, at Saint-Quentin-la-Poterie, in the Gard département, whose work is of a very high quality.

Clay pipes were still made in Manchester (England) by John Pollock & Co until the last of the Pollock family retired a short time ago and the company was taken over by a snuff-making company of Sheffield: the pipes are still in production.

CORNCOB AND PYROLITE PIPES

During their recent history, the Americans have perfected two types of pipes. The first, the corncob, invented in 1869 by a Missouri farmer is ephemeral to the point of being disposable. The second, invented a century later, is in pyrolite, born from new materials indispensable to the aeronautical industry. This is a material so durable that it can be reproached for being soulless! Its manufacture has now ceased. In spite of their undeniable qualities, these pipes have not found a significant market in the Old World.

The corncob pipe has the advantage of a very cheap price, and its lightness and porosity makes it quite pleasant to smoke. But corn (maize) degrades rapidly and has a smoking life of only six to twelve months. The manufacture of the pipe is very simple. When the ripe cobs of corn have been picked, they are left to dry for a number of months (a hard hybrid has been developed specially for pipes). When thoroughly dry, they are cut with a saw to the desired length. The marrow is extracted, the bowls turned and polished. They are sandpapered and then pumiced after having been coated with plaster, and sometimes honey which gives them smoother smoking qualities. Stems and vulcanite or plastic mouthpieces are inserted;

The real birth of a pipe starts with a design on paper. To obtain the best quality product, each element of a future pipe is studied in detail.

100

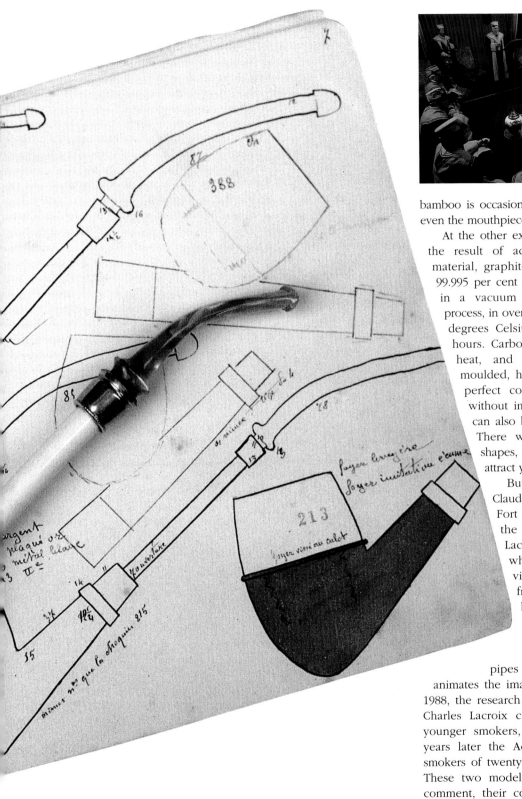

The preoccupation of Saint-Claude manufacturers is to create new pipes to attract smokers. For them the installing of a young smoker into the Confrérie des Maîtres Pipiers is a sign of optimism and hope (left).

bamboo is occasionally used for the stem and even the mouthpiece.

At the other extreme, the pyrolite pipe is the result of advanced technology. The material, graphite-pyrolite is composed of 99.995 per cent carbon, which is produced in a vacuum by a very sophisticated process, in ovens heated at more than 2000 degrees Celsius for a period of eighty hours. Carbon is a good conductor of heat, and the pipes, which were moulded, had the quality of ensuring perfect combustion of the tobacco without impairing the bowl. Pyrolite can also be coloured and decorated. There were a number of classic shapes, finished in bright colours to attract young smokers.

But let us return to Saint-Claude to the main office of Cuty Fort (which regrouped in 1987 the Chacom, Jeantet, Jean Lacroix and Vuillard brands), where Jean-Charles Lacroix, vice-president of the Confrérie of Master Pipemakers, but with particular responsibility for new designs, is planning a new pipe. In fact, the real birth of most pipes starts with a pencil which animates the imagination of the creator. In 1988, the research and design office of Jean-Charles Lacroix created a model aimed at younger smokers, the Mini-Poyat, and two years later the Ace of Pipes, intended for smokers of twenty-five to thirty years of age. These two models created a great deal of comment, their conception being resolutely contemporary. For pipes, this "rebirth" is a promise for the future.

TOBACCOS

However much the smoker values his pipe, it is, after all, only an instrument for providing pleasure to the taste buds from the delicious plant, with its thousand varieties, that is tobacco. There is nothing like a pipe. Unlike a good briar or meerschaum, the paper of a cigarette alters the taste of the tobacco. But even the finest quality pipe, well broken in, smoked according to the rules of the "art", is worth very little without a good tobacco. The ideal tobacco does not exist. Even though the majority of tobaccos sold in the shops are of the highest quality, one smoker may find excellent a blend that another detests. Good tobacco is a matter of taste. The smoker responds to the variety of products that are offered, but the range is so wide that he needs to have a basic idea of the different blends and mixtures in order to make his choice. Unlike cigarette-smokers, but like connoisseurs of good wines, a true pipe-smoker is above all a connoisseur.

THE WORLD OF THE NICOTIANAS

Together with the humble tomato and potato, and the deadly nightshade, the tobacco plant belongs to the Solanaceae family which, according to its etymology, "comforts" its users. The botanists gave it the name of Nicotiana in honour of Jean Nicot who was reputed to have introduced the plant into France. The genus comprises some sixty species and several thousand varieties, but only two species are cultivated for smoking. The first, named *Nicotiana tabacum*, has beautiful red or pink flowers with a long pale corolla, and it is mainly used in the production of tobaccos for cigarettes, cigars or pipes. The second, *Nicotiana rustica*, which has yellow flowers and small round leaves, provides tobacco for certain users in Middle Eastern countries, such as narghile (hookah) smokers.

It is generally recognized that tobacco originated in the Americas and that, growing wild, it was smoked by American Indians for several thousand years. Its current name, adopted in Europe during the second half of the sixteenth century, derives from an Ameridian word and is used today in some sixty languages and dialects. You can take your pick: etymologists say its origin may be *tobago*, from the Antilles

A Virginia tobacco plant. Three to five months after planting, the leaves at the base are ripe, and ready to be harvested. Virginia tobacco is grown in eighty countries and represents sixty per cent of the world's production (facing page).

This watercolour by Louis-Michel Philipeaux dates from 1813. Three years earlier, Napoleon had created the State monopoly for the manufacture of tobacco. France had, at the time, eleven factories which processed about nine thousand tonnes a year (left).

After being dried and fermented by the producer, the dark compressed tobacco leaves arrive at the factory (preceding pages).

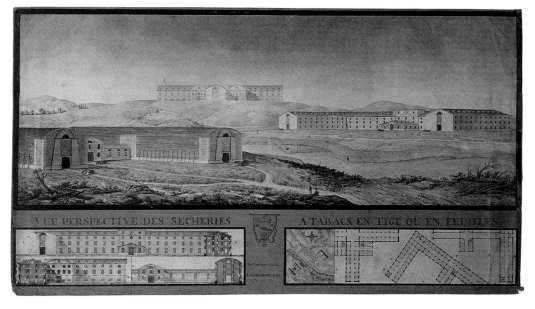

MANUFACTURE DES TABACS

LE TRIAGE

DEBALLAGE ET ARROSAGE

LES SECHOIRS

LES HACHEUSES

LE TORREFACTEUR

DEBIT DE·TABAC

MANUFACTURE·ROYALE

TABAC

VE

VANDER ELST

Scientific or popular, there were numerous images of tobacco in the nineteenth century (facing page). This representation of a tobacco factory (above) in the *Le Monde Illustré*, follows the phases of manufacture and gives precise information on the mechanization of the factories at the time. For the public at large, the images of tobacco are those they see daily, on shop signs (centre, France 1825) or advertisements on matchboxes (below, Belgium 1820).

islands, or *tobaco* which, according to Spanish sailors, was the name given to rolled leaves smoked by the Arawak Indians from Hispaniola (now Haiti and the Dominican Republic). We know how the plant gained popularity in the rest of the world, first of all spread by the early conquerors of the New World in the sixteenth century. Nonetheless, in 1993, a team of French scientists, trying to protect the mummy of the Pharaoh Ramses II from deterioration, discovered traces of tobacco in the embalmed body. Where did that come from? Had it been grown in the Nile valley? Had it been imported from Asia? Could prehistoric migrations explain its presence on the American continent? These questions were taken very seriously and discussed in the popular press. But most Egyptologists and tobacco historians were quick to agree on a commonsense opinion: the fragment most probably came from the tobacco pouch of an archaeologist who had examined the mummy in the nineteenth century. Whatever the answer, these questions do not disturb the sleep of tobacco-growers, who are found in most parts of the world today, except in the Arctic and Antarctic. World production, which keeps on growing, has doubled over the past thirty years and has passed seven million tonnes a year.

Tobacco is a delicate and demanding plant. It will grow and flower only in temperate climates with a warm atmosphere; a temperature between 25 and 30 degrees Celsius seems to suit it best as it does not like a temperature of less than 15 degrees and will die at less than three degrees. It also needs deep and fertile soil which is slightly acid and well watered. These conditions are found in many regions around the globe, in particular in tropical or subtropical areas, where tobacco occupies a total of over five million hectares.

China is the world's largest producer of tobacco with about one-third of the total world production being for its own domestic use, followed by the United States, India and Brazil; of the European countries, Italy and Greece lead, respectively with seventh and tenth place in the world's "league" table. But although all these regions grow the same plant, they do not produce the same smoking-tobacco. There are four main categories of tobaccos, each covering a number of types which are the basis of various blends, to suit the taste of the markets they are aimed at, and also to fit the manufacturing processes. Professionals generally call them by their English names.

Flue-cured is the name for light tobacco of the Virginia type which is dried artificially, and is the base for the majority of cigarettes and for pipe tobacco often blended with Oriental leaf. Virginia represents about two-thirds of the world's production. It is grown

mainly in the USA, in Virginia naturally but also in the Carolinas, and in a number of other countries such as China, Brazil, Argentina, Japan, Poland and Zimbabwe.

The light air-cured is a tobacco dried naturally. This category includes the Burley, which had been developed by 1864, and also the Maryland. Burley was first produced in the USA, but later introduced with success in Italy, Brazil, Thailand and some African countries, such as Malawi. It is a light tobacco which has the advantage of being able to absorb flavouring agents and does not "bite" the tongue. Maryland is often used in blends to soften the strength of other tobaccos.

Dark air-cured tobaccos are used as a base for cigars, dark cigarettes and pipe tobaccos. They are grown in India, Indonesia, the Philippines, Brazil, Cuba and France.

Oriental tobaccos are sun-cured. They are found in a number of blends and mixtures as their lightness and sweetness add aroma to the occasional "bite" of other tobaccos, such as Virginias. They are grown around the Mediterranean and the Black Sea, in Italy, the former Yugoslavia, Albania, Greece, Turkey, the south-east of Russia and also in parts of Syria.

Some other tobaccos, products of particular processes, fall outside these categories. One such is Perique, reputed to be named after the French planter Pierre Chenet. It is grown only in the parish of St James in Louisiana, USA, and has been matured in barrels with plum juice and fruit pulps, according to a secret recipe, since the early nineteenth century. It is a rare tobacco which, in small quantity, adds a fruity and subtle aroma to a blend. Also outside the main categories, Latakia is a dark leaf from Syria, also produced in Cyprus and Lebanon. It is sun-cured and fumigated over open fires using wood from the region of Aleppo. It gives pipe tobacco a distinctive "burnt" and "spicy" aroma. There is also Kentucky, produced in the American state of the same name, and in Tennessee, and (outside the USA) in Canada, Malawi and Italy. It is a dark

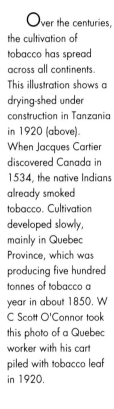

Over the centuries, the cultivation of tobacco has spread across all continents. This illustration shows a drying-shed under construction in Tanzania in 1920 (above). When Jacques Cartier discovered Canada in 1534, the native Indians already smoked tobacco. Cultivation developed slowly, mainly in Quebec Province, which was producing five hundred tonnes of tobacco a year in about 1850. W C Scott O'Connor took this photo of a Quebec worker with his cart piled with tobacco leaf in 1920.

Albanian peasants in 1913. The leaves that have just been harvested will be dried in the sun for Oriental tobacco, prized for its lightness (facing page).

Tobacco was imported into Java by the Dutch in the seventeenth century. Essentially, the island of Java produces dark tobacco for local consumption, and it is sun-dried (right).

tobacco matured and "fired" with hickory, oak or maple wood.

TOBACCO GROWING

There was a time when growing tobacco was like gardening. The first plants grown in Europe were lovingly watched over by horticulturists, impatient to see a new flower bloom on their continent. This probably took place in around 1550 in Belgium, since Dutch merchants had brought back a few seeds from Florida. The Dutch botanist Rembert Dodoens recalls, as early as 1554 in his book *Gruydeboeck*, an extremely rare plant which he had seen growing in a few Belgian gardens. What he called *Hyosciamus luteus* was none other than *Nicotiana rustica*. Two years later, in his garden at Angoulême, or perhaps in the Franciscan monastery, the monk André Thevet, back from Brazil, grew the tobacco plant, because of its fine flower and long corolla. But it took another half century for commercial tobacco plantations to be established in Europe.

There was also a time when tobacco cultivation bordered on an adventure, when planters and settlers cleared large areas of the New World to make fortunes in tobacco. The first was the Englishman John Rolfe who, in 1611, wanted to copy the new English colony founded by Sir Walter Raleigh in Virginia. At the time, the plant later known as *Nicotiana rustica* was called "appooke". John Rolfe improved the techniques by importing the best seeds from Trinidad and Venezuela. Five years later the Rolfe plantations began to thrive. And, eight years later, the export of tobacco from Virginia to England was started. In the meantime, Rolfe had married Pocahontas, the daughter of the American Indian chief who had initiated him in tobacco-growing. From 1620, Virginia required more workers for its plantations, and so slaves were brought from Africa. Also, lacking settlers, one hundred and fifty young English women were brought over, more or less voluntarily, to increase the population. For these slaves and for the English women, another type of adventure began.

No trace of this adventure remains in tobacco-growing today. For a long time now, the cultivation has been entirely mechanized, scientifically controlled and commercially motivated, consisting of a long succession of technical operations. To understand how much know-how goes into a pouch of tobacco, we need to follow the main stages in this complex process.

Tobacco is planted under plastic sheeting in long beds which have been chemically disin-

In the Dordogne, in the Valley of the Vézère, the tobacco plants bloom white in summer, while leaves ripen in the sun. As elsewhere in France, harvesting will take place in August and September (facing page).

In this plantation in North Carolina, the stems have already been cut and the leaves are allowed to droop before being carried to the drying-shed. North Carolina is one of the seven major producing States in the USA. (facing page – top). Seen from the air, the large American plantations show row upon row of perfectly aligned plants, which will gradually disappear during harvesting. Here, tobacco workers from Farmville (Virginia) are picking the leaves (facing page – below).

fected. It is here that the minute seeds have been sown (one gramme in weight contains several thousand seeds). Planting is carried out every year at variable dates depending on the climate; for example, late March to early April in France, October in Cuba and January in Florida. Each square metre of seedbed receives about two thousand seeds which will produce a thousand seedlings, provided that they are constantly watered. After two or three months, the seedlings which have grown to about ten centimetres and have produced four to eight small leaves, are transplanted mechanically to the tobacco fields which have been carefully prepared. The density of planting varies according to the tobaccos; for example, seven to nine thousand plants per hectare for Kentucky fire-cured, and up to two hundred thousand plants for certain Oriental tobacco. According to the variety and the climatic conditions, it takes between three and five months from transplanting to harvesting. During that time, the plants require a great deal of attention and maintenance work: earth dressing, manuring, weeding and

watering together with some pruning, done by hand, such as taking off the lower leaves, or topping and nipping the buds to increase the size of the leaves. In the meantime, the tobacco plant, which is delicate, must be constantly guarded against attack by insects and viruses, and by bacteria such as mildew or "blue mould" which in the 1960s destroyed a great part of the Cuban plantations.

The plants destined for dark tobacco are considered to be ripe when some yellow streaks appear on the top leaves and a green coloration shows on the leaves at the base. There are other signs that indicate the maturity of plants that will produce the lighter (or blond) tobacco, such as the green/yellow colour of the leaves, the leaf-tips curling downward and the veins appearing quite pale. Tobacco leaves for cigars are picked just before full maturity. Leaves for cut tobacco used for cigarettes or pipes need to ripen fully. There are two methods of harvesting, depending on the region, either picking the leaves with the stalks or taking just the leaves. The first method consists of

The island of Reunion has a perfect climate for tobacco growing, and a factory manufactures most French brands from local sources. On the island's plateau, the harvesting is still carried out by hand (above).
In the Dordogne in September: the leaves still on the stems have been cut late in the morning and are left to droop for a few hours. In the evening, they are taken to the drying-shed where they are hung on horizontal wires to dry for a month or two (left).

cutting the stalks with all the leaves. The ends of the stalks are pierced to suspend them from a hook, and then they are taken to the drying sheds. Later the leaves are picked off the stalks before processing. Burley, used in many blends, is harvested in this way. Since the development of the tobacco harvester, drawn by a tractor (there are fully-automatic harvesters), this operation has become mechanized. The second method consists of gathering the leaves, picking them as they mature, starting from the base of the plants. In most countries, this method of harvesting has also become mechanized. The leaves are gathered into bunches and tied with string by special machines. The bunches are hung on rods up to fifty metres long and taken to the drying sheds. This harvesting, carried out in stages, takes three to four weeks. It has the advantage of increasing the yield by ten to twenty per cent over the stalk-cutting method, as the leaves that are left can continue to grow. This means that the whole harvest will be uniformly matured. The disadvantage is that it is very labour-intensive. Nevertheless, it is used to gather Virginia-type tobacco.

DRYING AND FERMENTATION

The first phase of the transformation of the leaf is the drying. There are two methods in use, depending on the region where the tobacco is grown and the variety: natural and artificial drying. (This distinction has already been seen in the drying of briar blocks.) The first is air-curing, when the leaves are simply hung up to dry – some two hundred leaves per cubic metre – in a well-ventilated shed, for one or two months. This method is mostly used for dark tobaccos, in South America, Cuba and France. The artificial method, flue-curing, shortens the drying time considerably, the drying shed being heated by hot-air pipes. This lasts about a

September-October. The autumn colours appear in the fine old drying-sheds at Saint-Sulpice in the Dordogne. Long air-curing is necessary for dark tobacco. The leaves lose their chlorophyll and turn yellow, then oxidation eliminates the sugar. In two months, they will have lost ninety per cent of their initial weight (facing page and right).

The same phase of transformation in the factory at Bouaké (left), created in 1957 by the Ivory Coast Tobacco Company, which changed its name to Société Ivoirienne des Tabacs (SITAB) in 1971. The factory produces all tobacco products, including cigars. The Ivory Coast produced 2,500 tonnes of raw tobacco in 1992.

week, in a temperature of from 35 to 75 degrees Celsius and is strictly controlled. Most Virginia tobaccos are treated in that way. The speed of drying limits the oxidation of the leaves, keeping the sugar-level which otherwise disappears in a long air-curing. Therein lies the difference between light (blond) and dark tobaccos. In one, the sugar releases an acid reaction when the tobacco is smoked, while the other, without sugar, gives an alkaline reaction. Other methods of drying, such as fire-curing are not so common. This, the traditional method of the American Indians, is still practised to produce Kentucky and the famous Latakia. Sun-curing should also be mentioned but this is only used for Oriental tobacco. Whatever the method, tobacco loses from eighty to ninety per cent of its weight while drying. This phase is a simple desiccation. In fact, the drying modifies considerably the chemical composition of the plant over the next three successive phases. While the leaves turn yellow, venti-lation must be reduced to a minimum; the leaf still "lives" and yellows while breaking down its chlorophyll and transforming its proteins and starch. The second phase is the proper desiccation of the leaf, a period of oxidation. As noted, that varies according to the method of drying. In limiting oxidation, flue-curing maintains the yellow colour. Finally, the third phase dehydrates the central rib of the tobacco leaf.

After drying, the leaves are stored. Both dark and Oriental tobaccos continue to ferment while blond (or bright) tobaccos simply age. It is only at that stage that the leaves start to give out their characteristic aromas. These operations are meant to ameliorate the consistency of the leaf and its flavour. The fermentation of dark tobaccos completes the oxidation, eliminating all traces of sugar and chlorophyll. At the same time, chemical reactions help to make the ammonia and nicotine more volatile, a vital factor in producing aroma and taste. It is during this time that the colour of the tobacco

Fermentation of dark tobacco at Bouaké. The heaped leaves heat up spontaneously to 50 to 60 degrees Celsius after a month, during which time the temperature is carefully controlled (right, above).

A trolley full of bunches of leaves at Bouaké, tied together, they will be piled as they are for fermentation (facing page).

Dried leaves are taken to be weighed. The fermentation is in lots of two to three hundred kilos per cubic metre (left).

118

Workers at Bouaké prepare a mass fermentation. The bunches are piled in large cases which can contain several tonnes of tobacco (right).

becomes more uniform, which improves its combustibility, so that it burns much more evenly.

There are three methods of fermenting dark tobaccos: "bulk fermentation" which consists of loading the leaves in large movable containers containing from six to two hundred tonnes each. This accumulation provokes instantaneous heat from the first day, reaching 40 to 50 degrees Celsius after a month. To obtain uniform fermentation, the leaves are turned over two or three times during the process. Another method, used particularly in France, allows a reduction of the level of nicotine in dark tobacco which can be as much as fifty per cent; this is fermentation in "cases". The leaves are placed in cases that take about a hundred kilos each. They are stored for six to eight months at normal temperature, then in a store heated to 55 degrees Celsius for eight days, to be returned to the original room for a number of months. The temperature does not rise so high in these cases as it does in bulk fermentation although the nicotine breaks down more. A third method of fermentation, which is quicker, is used to treat leaves which

are more matured, such as those from the base of the plant. The leaves are stored for about ten days in cases in a "hot chamber", where the temperature rises to 60 degrees Celsius and where the level of humidity is eighty-five per cent.

Oriental tobaccos, which are dried in the sun, ferment more naturally and moderately. The leaves are simply bagged in bales of fifty kilos, and stored next to each other in a one- or two-tier shed. The mild Mediterranean air deals with the rest. This slow fermentation only raises the temperature by 3 degrees Celsius. A "hot chamber" is also used for Oriental tobaccos by producers who want to achieve fermentation out of season. This process has the advantage that it hastens fermentation, but it requires constant attention to avoid the tobacco darkening too much.

The blond (or bright) tobaccos such as Virginia which are dried naturally, and others, such as the Burley and Maryland also dried naturally, are not fermented (they would lose their yellow colour) but only "aged" during a period varying according to the country of production. However, this process

The tools and equipment needed to prepare large quantities for fermentation are disappearing (left). Now, the "free" leaves are more frequently piled automatically in the large cases by a blowing apparatus.

demands that the leaves should have a second drying period at high temperature, to reduce the level of humidity to a minimum. They are then cooled and treated with steam to soften them so as to render them less brittle. They are finally pressed together before being stored. The next stage consists of separating the central rib of the leaf mechanically so as to eliminate any fragments in the final product. A proportion of the ribs are chopped and will be included in the final blend; their function is to control the smoke and to reduce the levels of nicotine and the related tars.

FROM THE GROWER TO THE MANUFACTURER

From the hands of the producer, the raw tobacco leaf passes to the manufacturer. The shipment takes time, since most tobaccos are exported to be manufactured far from the producing country. Europe and the United States are both the prime exporters and the prime importers, on the one hand for the Virginia-type tobacco and on the other, for the dark and Oriental tobacco. Public health legis-

lation which led to stagnation in the one and a decrease in consumption in the other, has for some years caused a decline in imports. Tobacco is also an important source of foreign currency for developing countries. Brazil and Zimbabwe account for almost half the world exports of flue-cured tobacco. In Malawi, which produces Burley, tobacco constitutes about half of the country's exports. For Greece, the export of Oriental tobacco is the second most important source of foreign currency.

In many countries, producers sell their tobacco to wholesalers, or work as co-operatives. The practice is slightly different in the United States, where they assemble in large covered markets where each can sell his production. Whatever the method, the manufacturer does not buy the whole of a harvest, or a given quantity of a certain variety. He does not look to buy a whole plant, but a quality determined by the level of the leaves on the plant. Each leaf develops different qualities according to where it was situated on the tobacco plant at the time of harvest. Each level is also subdivided by other factors, such as the development of the leaves, their colour, their texture,

After fermentation and humidification, the tobacco is shredded. Shredding transforms the leaves into "cut" tobacco (left).

Kentucky, c. 1930. The expert buyers, the "blenders", select the grades for their companies, in the large buying-sheds where growers sold their harvests (facing page).

their combustibility and their aromatic potential. In purchasing a given grade from a given level on the plant in a given country, the manufacturer knows exactly what he is buying.

As an example, the Danish Orlik Tobacco Company, which manufactures the Orlik, W Ø Larsen and Sweet Dublin brands and has eighty per cent of the Danish market, uses every year in its production some one hundred and twenty different grades. The buyer is generally also the expert in charge of mixing the tobaccos, in other words, the blender. And it is the art of the blender which is all important.

THE ART OF BLENDING

Apart from a few rare exceptions, raw tobacco is not found for sale in the industry. Only blends of natural or aromatic tobaccos are offered for sale. The majority of pipe tobaccos contain between ten and thirty tobaccos, or more precisely ten to thirty different grades. Amongst them the "basic" tobaccos give the product its essential charac-

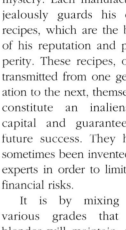

teristics and dominant feature, while the "filling" tobaccos do not alter the nature of the whole. As these blends have the virtue of being able to "tickle" the palate and the sense of smell of smokers, it is important, year after year in spite of differences in the harvests, that the same quality be maintained. Thus the smoker will always find, under the same brand name, the same taste and consistency. As each element of the composition is susceptible to variation from one year to the next, this perfect "identity" can only be obtained by using a wide number of tobaccos. Here we enter into the world of mystery. Each manufacturer jealously guards his own recipes, which are the basis of his reputation and prosperity. These recipes, often transmitted from one generation to the next, themselves constitute an inalienable capital and guarantee of future success. They have sometimes been invented by experts in order to limit the financial risks.

It is by mixing the various grades that the blender will maintain, year

A buyer in Malawi. Malawi is the second largest tobacco-producing country in Africa after Zimbabwe, and supplies mainly Burley which is exported all over the world (above, left).
Today, in the United States, 750,000 tonnes of tobacco are produced by 600,000 growers, who sell to the highest bidder. Left: an auction sale at Lumberton, in North Carolina.

in, year out, the principal characteristics of the finished product. He may also create a new mixture. In effect, the art of the blender is to marry various grades to obtain in the end one single taste, with an essential character that identifies the product. Thus, in an ideal blend, even an experienced smoker cannot distinguish between the grades used. Having achieved the type of blend required, for instance a Virginia, the blender must decide the precise nature of the product, either light or strong, since the range presents several possibilities. The decision having been made, the blender can select the required grades.

At the point of purchase, only a few highly qualified blenders sample the pure grades, as it is difficult to predict their transformation once mixed with the others. The effects can be surprising: at a recent tasting of pure grades organized by the Paris Pipe Club, one of the smokers, overpowered by the strength of the tobacco, simply passed out! Most are content to study and touch the leaves to be assured of the essential qualities that will be found on arrival at the factory: colour, texture and density.

After opening the bales or the bunches of ten or so leaves of a given grade, the manufacturer will carry out a number of processes before the tobacco is ready to be smoked. The plants have been stripped of the centre rib by the producer or, in the United States, by specialized workers called "packers". The first task of the manufacturer is to prepare the blends and mixtures.

All the blends, whether new or not, are first of all produced in small quantities, to be tested by panels of smokers who will give their appraisal according to a rigorous standard. They comment on the appearance of the product, its colour, aroma, consistency; and, when smoked, its taste and aroma. Up to the 1960s, white clay pipes were used for that tasting, as they are more neutral and permit a better judgement. With the cut of tobaccos becoming wider and coarser, the clay pipes have been replaced by briar pipes with large bowls. Each taster gives an overall opinion. In the case of new products, a complicated system of marking the results decides the manufacturer whether or not to test the product on informed smokers from tobacco retailers to members of pipe clubs. These smokers, who are rewarded by some tobacco or pipes, are asked to note the aroma, the taste, the combustibility, the cut, the colour and to give a general opinion. It is only after this last test that a new product is put on the market, as it stands or with modifications.

MANUFACTURE

Before being mixed and then shredded, the pieces of leaf, or "strips", are placed together on a conveyor belt to go into a tunnel where they are humidified. This important operation can affect the shredding: leaves that are too dry can become "dust"; those that are too damp can become pulp. Once humidified, they are placed in a blending silo. Then, in the case of aromatic tobaccos, they are "sauced", or flavoured. This is to give them a complementary taste by introducing additives which will help to preserve the level of humidity. These additives, their composition and mixing are part of the secrets of manufacture. They are numerous, diverse and, in some countries, regulated to avoid adding, to the injurious effects of nicotine and tar, any chemicals that may be suspect. Among these additives, one finds sugar, liquorice, maple syrup, glycerine, molasses, fruit extracts, cocoa and rum. Sauced tobaccos are tested in the same way as natural blends.

The next operation, the shredding, is carried out in powerful machines capable of dealing with several tonnes of tobacco per hour. It gives the product its final appearance: the fine cuts of tobacco which are found in cigarettes as well as in pipe tobacco, the tobacco that in France is called *scaferlati,* and in English simply "cut tobacco". There is an idea in France that *scaferlati* means pipe tobacco, but it actually refers to all cut tobaccos. Shredding is not applied to cigar tobacco, since the leaves are simply rolled after removing the stalks. In pipe tobacco, there are varieties from fine to coarse which determine the essential characteristics of the mixtures. It is considered an indication of quality. The wider the cut, the slower is the rate of burning, with the result that the palate is more sensitive to the make-up of the blend. On the other hand, the finer the cut, the faster is the rate of burning and the release of nicotine. Most smokers prefer cuts which are at least 0.7mm, which exclude pipes that are too small. Fine cuts are normally from 0.4 to 0.6mm, medium cuts around 1mm and broad cuts from 1.5 to 2.5mm. Rarer coarse cuts can be as much as 3.5mm.

Zimbabwe is one of the world's ten largest producers of tobacco. Its flue-cured Virginia is exported worldwide, and provides an important contribution to the country's balance of payments. Facing page: samples of dried tobacco from the Zambezi valley.

Once shredded, the cut tobacco which is still damp is then dried. It is a question of returning to a level of humidity which allows the tobacco to be kept in good condition, about fifteen per cent humidity. English tobaccos have a higher level of humidity than Continental ones. This raises an argument: English tobaccos burn more slowly, but some Continental manufacturers say that less humidity gives more tobacco! Blond (or bright) tobaccos are dried in rotating steam-heated driers. Dark tobaccos are "toasted" on metal trays heated to 200 or 300 degrees Celsius. This toasting brings out the strength of the taste and aroma, characteristic of French tobaccos. The cut tobacco is then cooled. But the manufacture of aromatic tobaccos is not yet complete. Before packing, they receive a last additive, "top flavouring", to enrich the aroma, unlike saucing which modifies the taste. The composition and dosage of top flavouring are well-kept trade secrets. A number of products can be used, such as spirits (whisky, rum, etc.), extracts and essences of fruit and menthol. As with all the subtle dosages of mixtures, the aromatization of tobacco requires the experience and the "nose" of the professionals.

Gérard Pellissier works at the research centre of Seita, the French tobacco monopoly company, near Orleans; he is one of the two "aromatic experts" in charge of flavouring pipe and cigarette tobaccos. Graduate of the Aromatic School at Versailles, which trains perfumers as well as technicians for the food industry, he is one of the two men in France in charge of "tickling the nostrils" of smokers. He has access to around a thousand various essences, such as natural essential oils, often made at Grasse in southern France (on a synthetic molecular base) which have the advantage, unlike others which may vary from season to season, of being stable. But a thousand perfumes do not necessarily give a thousand basic aromas. For example, for the aroma of clove, used for its spicy quality, Gérard Pellissier uses three or

four slightly different essences. In the world of tobaccos, flavouring is the art of infinite variations. Enough said. "In questions of aromas," confides Gérard Pellissier, "the competition between manufacturers is intense, and silence is the rule."

The curiosity and the sense of adventure of smokers has no limits. Some manufacturers offer, apart from normal cut tobaccos, particular products which have different cuts and appearance. First, the "pressed tobaccos": instead of being shredded after blending, humidified and sauced, the leaves which have been preheated are put under a pressure of

FABRICATION DU TABAC. · LE HACHAGE.

about one tonne per square centimetre to produce a compact "cake". The cake is then cut in thin slices called "flakes", which the smoker will find in his pack; he has then to rub the flake in his hand to fill his pipe. This is called "flake cut". This task is already carried out for the smoker in "ready rubbed" tobaccos, the flakes having been loosened in a rotating drum. Cavendish and Black Cavendish tobaccos – a process of double fermentation and not a type – are normally sold ready rubbed. Pressed tobacco can also be sold "granulated" which, as the name implies, consists of small grains or cubes. "Twist" tobacco, which was popular until the nineteenth century, has almost disappeared, although still manufactured by two companies in England. The leaves are spun into a long "rope" two to three centimetres in diameter, which retailers can cut to the amount required by their customers. This preparation is similar to "curly cut", which is still obtainable. Strips of dark and light tobacco are rolled into thin rods and cut into slices, which can be put straight into a pipe. Another particular cut, appreciated for its combustibility, is "crimp cut"; this consists of short-fibre tobacco which has been lightly pressed, then cut in short strands and later "toasted".

After a rest of about twenty-four hours, all pipe tobaccos are automatically weighed and packed, to be conditioned in packaging which

W. Ø Larsen
Nº 10

Dunhill
Blenders own

W. Ø Larsen
*Fraser Flake cut
Burley*

Red Virginia

Latakia

Dunhill
*Ribbon cut
turkish*

W. Ø Larsen
*Selected blend
Nº 32*

W. Ø Larsen
*Selected blend
Nº 50*

Bell's three nuns
Nº Nicer

W. Ø Larsen
Selected blend Nº 4
Loose leaf

Black Cavendish

W. Ø Larsen
Bright Virginia

Dunhill
Rubbed Flake

Cavendish

Dunhill
Nº 10

Dunhill
Alfred's own

Dunhill
Nº 34596

Dunhill
June 86

depends on the quality or the presentation required: simple wrapping, plastic pouches or metal tins.

THE SUBTLETIES OF TASTES

With dark or light cut or pressed tobaccos, natural or aromatic, varying widths of "cuts", the consumer has a wide choice. Nonetheless, it is another classification, more subtle and vague which does not correspond to a precise standard, which normally decides the smoker's choice. Four countries are the major producers of pipe tobaccos: the United States, Great Britain, Holland and Denmark which have each imposed on the world of smokers what we call the "taste" of their products. The inverted commas are necessary as the concept is extremely vague. It only reflects a general trend, occasionally contradictory, which does not necessarily correspond to the geographical origins. Thus, one can produce a "Dutch taste" tobacco, even called "Dutch tobacco" in France, with Brazilian leaves. Some generalizations can nonetheless be made without fear of making a mistake or misleading the reader.

Tobaccos said to be "American" are more often than not blends of light (blond – bright) aromatics, based on Virginia and Burley, spiced with a touch of Perique or Latakia. The whole gives a smoke famed for its sweetness and lightness. But the essential of their aroma comes more from the strength of the saucing and flavouring than from their natural qualities. They have an excellent level of humidity and a dominating taste of sugar, obtained at the time of saucing by the introduction of products such as sugar, maple syrup and a wide variety of fruit extracts. They often have the aroma of gingerbread or, as some English smokers put it: burnt custard! It should be noted that American legislation favours the strength of this flavouring as it allows the sale of tobaccos containing up to fifteen per cent additives, while the British legislation allows only two per cent. There are over two hundred mixtures of this type in the USA. Among the better known, the classic and highly sugared Prince Albert has not been sold in

France for some years, but is found elsewhere round the world, along with Edgeworth and Half and Half. Some of these tobaccos are exported or manufactured in Europe under licence.

By contrast, the tobaccos said to be "English" are not always aromatic. The basics are still the same, Virginia, Burley, Perique and Latakia. They distinguish themselves by two particular preparations, highly appreciated by connoisseurs. To start with the mixtures are blends of Virginia, Oriental and Latakia, the last two giving them their taste and robustness. They are also characterized by their colour: an English mixture presents between the yellow Virginia and the dark Latakia, subtle and refined aesthetic contrasts. The second great speciality of Britain are the Flake Cuts; as already mentioned, these are pressed and sliced tobaccos, normally made from blends of basic American Virginia. Their taste can be as strong as the mixtures, but their range also presents some lighter elements. British manufacturers offer over one hundred and fifty brands, many being exported around the world. Amongst them is the famous Dunhill Mixture – Britain's most prestigious brand – given the fair name of Early Morning Pipe, encouraging the smoker to light up after his early morning tea, also reminding us that the British are, above all, tea drinkers! This does not stop Dunhill from innovating new tobaccos. Two new blends were introduced in 1992: Black Aromatic, a mild Virginia matured for a long time to give it a dark colour, to which is added a red Virginia and a touch of Burley; and Mild Blend consisting of different Virginias softened by Cavendish. All these products, as is the case with most English tobaccos, are packed in metal tins for export, although on the home market, the majority is now sold in plastic pouches. But while Dunhill's prestige goes around the world, the market in the UK is dominated by the brands Condor (Gallaher) and St Bruno (Imperial Tobacco) which between them have half the market.

The so-called "Dutch" tobaccos come in two different kinds. The oldest comprises traditional products of Holland, based on dark tobacco from the former Dutch colony of Indonesia

One of the many basic tobaccos offered by W Ø Larsen of Copenhagen to help the smoker prepare his own mixture, Fraser is a flake-cut Burley. It needs to be rubbed before mixing with other cut tobaccos. Burley easily absorbs flavouring and is essential in aromatic tobaccos on sale to the public (facing page).

This still-life by an unknown artist, depicts, apart from cigars, products which were popular at the turn of the century and may be disappearing: twist-tobacco and packs of Caporal scaferlati (left).

(Java and Sumatra). Certain strong American Virginia tobaccos are added, and occasionally Maryland. These blends which are not aromatic develop a strong taste in the mouth, and may be disappearing – much to the advantage of a more recent Dutch speciality: the aromatic blends which use Virginia and Burley. Since they were introduced in the 1950s these have become popular around the world, appreciated by younger smokers for their lightness. They are soft and have a strong fruit aroma. They are also often presented as Cavendish ready rubbed, ensuring a good level of humidity and therefore slow burning, or in crimp cut for smokers wanting faster burning. The most famous are Amsterdamer, the Amphora range with several Cavendish blends and whisky aroma, and Clan which now offers a light variant for smokers who want to follow the current tendency for lighter tobaccos. Dutch tobaccos are extensively exported and also manufactured under licence in a number of countries.

The "Danish" tobaccos are also aromatic blends similar, for their light smoke, to Dutch products. Denmark, however, the country which has the greatest number of pipe-smokers in relation to the size of its population (almost as many as England with a tenth of the population), has a number of experts who have developed some specialities of pressed tobaccos in which they are undisputed masters: flake cut, curly cut and Cavendish. Danish blends are based on Virginia, Burley, Perique and Latakia. Harald Halberg produces some twenty products, amongst them Mac Baren's famous mixtures, Golden Blend and Plum Cake. The main Danish manufacturer, Orlik Tobacco, manufactures several brands and markets one of the most popular tobaccos on the market, Orlik Golden Sliced, a light flake based on Virginia with a touch of Burley. The company also supplies two Virginia loose leaf cut tobaccos.

To these four main types of

blends, which are also seen as classic "tastes" by most smokers, we should add the French dark tobaccos, which have a virile robustness and are distributed in many countries. Seita (the French tobacco company) markets half a dozen dark blends, which are variants of the traditional *Caporal* taste. The most popular is the *Caporal ordinaire*, commonly called *petit gris* (small grey) which is a blend of French and Oriental tobaccos. It is quite economical and is sold in cube-shaped paper packs. However, the sales of strong dark tobaccos are declining in France by ten per cent every year in favour of light aromatic blends. Clearly, this decline reflects the economic situation and the demography of rural regions, where they were traditionally consumed.

PERSONALIZED MIXTURES

Since these principal basic types cover a vast range – many hundreds of different tobaccos – the majority of smokers are perfectly satisfied. There are nonetheless two world-famous tobacco merchants, also pipe-makers, who can help smokers in search of originality and perfection, to create mixtures "to measure". They are Dunhill in London and W Ø Larsen in Copenhagen, each of whom have slightly different methods.

At Dunhill, at the tobacco counter of the Duke Street shop, there are twenty-four drawers full of natural or aromatic grades of tobacco, which await the customers in search of new flavours or balance to satisfy their taste buds. There are in fact two types of customer who visit the emporium. First, those who know exactly what they want and who have already had their ideal mixture registered and numbered in Alfred Dunhill's *My Mixture Book*, which he started in 1907 when he opened his shop. The company has a great sense of discretion and does not reveal the names of famous customers whose favourite mixtures are on the register, particularly if they are still alive.

"The National Smoke" was the slogan of the popular American "crimp" cut Prince Albert ("PA" to its devotees) in its Christmas promotions. At the start of the century, R J Reynolds Tobacco marketed glass tobacco jars, filled with PA, in one pound or half pound sizes (above). Most smokers of P A bought the "toppy red bag" which cost five cents in 1913 (below).

A display on the theme of travel, by Amsterdam's tobacco specialist Hajenius, consisting of classic mixtures in tins (facing page).

One of the aromatic mixtures from W Ø Larsen, manufactured by the Danish company Orlik, the No. 10 Sweet Brown (right). It is made up of several pressed Virginias of different colours, contrasted with a touch of Black Cavendish. Its precise recipe (particularly the flavouring agents) is a well-kept secret. Below: This old tobacconist sign (France, late eighteenth century) depicts a habit which has almost disappeared: taking snuff. The snuff-taker tramples a medusa, symbol of tyranny.

Among those who are not, we find King Edward VII, the Duke of Windsor and Rudyard Kipling. The sales assistants take great pleasure in advising other customers who are still looking for the ideal mixture. A long dialogue establishes crucial points, such as the proportion of such and such a grade, the nature of the cut and the aromatic qualities. Once the mixture is prepared, the customer can taste it. But an experienced smoker will know that a few puffs are not enough to have a definite notion of the tobacco; for unknown reasons, the flavour of tobacco can vary from one place to the next, or from one day to the next. The customer having accepted the mixture, it is given a personal number and entered on the register, which to this day has about 38,000 numbers. It is then kept in a round metal box of fifty or one hundred grammes. Dunhill also offers its customers the *Mixture of the Month*, which is always new, in the hope of giving smokers some variation on the normal routine.

At No 9 Amagertorv, in the pedestrian precinct of old Copenhagen, W Ø Larsen's customers probably find the widest selection of tobacco in the world, some four hundred different

products of all brands. But the company markets also some forty Larsen tobaccos which include basic, natural and aromatic blends and mixtures, in a variety of cuts. Home products are packed in tins of fifty and one hundred grammes. There lies the difference between Larsen and Dunhill: W Ø Larsen's customers do not leave with a prepared mixture but, advised by the sales staff, they leave with ready-made products which they can mix at leisure at home. The advantage of this method is that customers can alter the aroma of their tobacco at will, going from a mild mixture in the morning to a stronger one later in the day.

It is paradoxically in the United States, where there is often a critical view taken of smoking, that lovers of tobacco are easily served. Traditional sales of loose tobacco are thriving, and every large town has at least one tobacco trader who can supply the tobaccos required for personal mixing. The sympathetic president of the Pipe Club of France, Roger Almerge, always asks his friends going to the USA to bring him back some American Virginia or Burley for their aromatic qualities and humidity content, since French legislation forbids the sale of

"The *gris* (grey) that you take in your fingers and roll", goes a song about the economically-priced French Caporal tobacco. It appeared in the middle of the ninteenth century, and quickly became popularly synonymous with the word tobacco. This dark non-aromatic fine-cut tobacco is still one of the bestsellers in France, although its consumption is diminishing by ten per cent a year. Its coarse character cannot but be improved by a Stanwell pipe (facing page).

loose tobacco. Similarly, in Great Britain, the sale of loose tobacco (also traditional) has been revived over the past two decades by the enterprise of specialist tobacconists who can offer their customers much more choice than the ordinary tobacco outlets.

One needs experience to perfect one's own mixture without being disappointed. Even experience is sometimes not enough to obtain the "perfect mixture". One of the most experienced smokers and expert collectors of this century, the naturalist Eppe Ramazzotti of Milan, author of two books on the subject, admitted at the end of his life: "I have mixed tobaccos for fifty years but have not yet found the ideal one." He was not alone!

Although there are no basic rules in the matter, smokers who prepare their own mixtures follow some simple principles. To reinforce a blend judged too bland only needs the addition of a small dose of dark natural tobacco. The converse is also possible by adding some lighter blond tobacco to a strong Oriental mixture. It becomes more complicated when one wants to alter the aroma or taste of a mixture; the use of Latakia or Perique can be crucial, since even a small dose can change the "quality" of a mixture. Finally, the homogenization of the product is essential: the cuts and the humidity content must be similar, this means that pressed tobaccos need a little more rubbing and drying in order to be mixed with cut tobaccos.

In addition to these simple principles, the composition of a personalized mixture requires one gramme of imagination, three grammes of know-how and experience and at least ten grammes of that basic "product" – patience. Good luck!

A THOUSAND AND ONE PLEASURES

It is impossible to evoke all the pleasures that tobacco gives to pipe-smokers. Each smoker not only has a distinct personality, but also his own preferences, fixed ideas and vocabulary. Between the gluttons who want to taste all tobaccos and flit from one to the other, the

After entering the tobacco business in 1906, Alfred Dunhill became a passionate pipe-smoker. He is seen here preparing a mixture (left and bottom of facing page).

136

Thirty-eight thousand customers' recipes are entered entered in the venerable register, *My Mixture Book* (left), started in 1907 and still in use. Among the customers: King George VI and the Spanish King Alphonso XIII.

gourmets who savour one product or another according to the time of day or the time of the year and who happily compare their tobacco to a vintage Bordeaux, the exhibitionists who want to astonish those around them, the countrymen who stick to their "regular" regardless of innovations, there is one common bond – the pipe and not the tobacco.

Nonetheless, they agree on a simple truth – that tobacco is the "soul" of the pipe.

To start with, there is the aroma which escapes when a pouch is opened. It is an authentic natural product appreciated by the smokers of natural cut tobacco, a simple "smell of tobacco" which some wrongly believe to be the smell of the newly harvested plant. Dark tobacco evokes other senses, as in the words of Louis Pauwels: "It smells of new-mown hay, fresh clay, wool, damp leather, a forest fire, a coach-load of men." If some lovers of natural tobaccos have a sense of the authentic, others have a sense of the dream, the imaginary voyage; a summer's day and an Oriental spice market which comes out of a tin of English mixture, dominated by the Latakia, the tobacco dried

over wood. However, most smokers today, particularly in Scandinavia, the Netherlands, Germany and the United States prefer to discover the familiar perfumes of chocolate, hazelnuts, apples or cherries, rum or whisky, even if the tobacco does not give the actual flavours suggested by the aroma. The olfactory pleasure of flavoured tobaccos is a sort of trap into which the smoker falls with pleasure, like a child astonished by a disguise.

Then there is the "material" itself. First, the appearance of the tobacco, its cut, its colours which may vary from ivory to black via gold (only non-smokers think that there is only one colour) and particularly the contrasts in certain mixtures, especially the English mixtures. These are difficult to explain, but can be compared with contemplating a fine briar. The smoker is confused by the secret alchemy of the beauty of nature and the work of man, a certain harmony and some civilization. Then, all smokers like to feel the texture of the mass of tobacco in the pouch. It may be not only a sensual feeling, but also the anticipation of the pleasures that are to follow. The pleasures given by the material, seen and touched, are intimately united: the smoker likes them to respond to and augment each other.

Then comes the pleasure of smoking. We should say the pleasures since, as with a good dinner, the flavours change as time goes on. Just after lighting, the smoke is light and is felt by the nose. Then, as it gets thicker, it goes to the palate. The sort of meal it evokes goes back to the days before sweet desserts, when the final choice was between fruit and cheese. Whatever the case, the smoker is satisfied at the end of his smoke. He will have sampled some of the thousand pleasures that are found in today's tobaccos, whether they are more or less natural, more or less strong, more or less sweet, or fruit-flavoured.

As with all pleasures in life, there are no rules in matters of tobacco. All tastes are respected and no one would think of imposing a hierarchy. A certain unanimity is, however, found among some dedicated smokers who advise against aromatic tobaccos. Curiously, while words are lacking to describe their pleasures, there are many terms to qualify the "defects" of sauced tobaccos. When smoked, they bite the tongue, their sharpness is felt in the throat and after a smoke they tend to leave the tongue thick and rough. It is true that some additives are sometimes thick, and perhaps a little too mysterious. It is nonetheless true that the ideal is to like tobacco for what it is, a natural product; that way it will never disappoint you.

MANUFACTURE IN BRITAIN

Great Britain is the only major country in Europe that does not have a tobacco-growing industry. France and Italy in particular can call upon their own producers to grow some of the tobacco required, but the UK has to import everything.

Historically, initial supplies came from the then colony of Virginia, supplemented in due course, in this century, by tobacco from the African colonies. Rhodesia, now Zimbabwe, became one of the most important "Empire" suppliers. All tobaccos had therefore to come by sea and a number of seaports soon became important entry points for tobacco. They included London, Bristol, Liverpool and Whitehaven, and later Belfast in Northern Ireland. Still today, the majority of UK tobacco factories are found near or within easy reach of these ports. To start at the most northerly point, Whitehaven on the Cumberland coast was the entry port which supplied Kendal where traditional tobacco is still produced, and later Glasgow in Scotland.

Liverpool competed with Bristol for the trade with America, and pipe-tobacco is still manufactured there by Imperial Tobacco. Bristol, now the headquarters of Imperial Tobacco, has a cigarette and cigar factory. In nearby Cardiff, in Wales, Gallaher has its cigar factory.

London, being the capital, could boast a number of pipe-tobacco manufacturers and blenders, but this is no longer the case. Nonetheless, its importance to the tobacco trade is remembered with "Tobacco Wharf" in the redeveloped area of London's dockland. Pipe-tobacco is still made in Northern Ireland, near Belfast, where both Gallaher and Rothmans have factories.

At the present time, Gallaher, Imperial Tobacco and Rothmans are the major pipe-tobacco manufacturers in Britain with the majority

share of the home market. Smaller manufacturers and blenders have now disappeared, or have their tobaccos made on the continent of Europe. The only independent manufacturers are the two companies in Kendal, which produce the traditional types such as "Twist" and "Plug" and a variety of loose tobaccos.

The important feature of British tobaccos is that they are very restricted in the types of additives that can be used for flavouring, although chocolate, vanilla and certain other extracts are permitted. This means that, over the years, the flavour of tobaccos has been produced by the natural aroma of the plant, and by the long experience of the manufacturers in blending. Indeed, at one time, it was not possible to import certain Continental and American pipe-tobaccos, as they contained additives which were not approved in the UK. These rules have been somewhat relaxed, and there has been a growing demand for imported aromatic tobaccos. The most successful has been the Dutch brand Clan, which is distributed by Gallaher, and which gave British smokers – particularly the younger ones – a taste of aromatic tobaccos. This has led the domestic manufacturers to produce aromatic blends to compete with the increasing popularity of Continental aromatics.

Thus Dunhill introduced Dunhill Aromatic for the mass market, which was something of a gamble since all other Dunhill tobaccos are in the premium sector. At the same time, a Dunhill Ready Rubbed was launched; if anything, it is just as aromatic as the variant bearing the name. The brand Craven, which had been popular years ago as a mixture was revived in three blends: a mild flake, a mild ready rubbed and an aromatic. Sensibly, the cut was medium-to-broad and in the aromatic variant which had the appearance of a mixture, the colour of the tobacco goes from yellow to dark with some strands in a subtle mid-brown.

With Clan as its leading aromatic, albeit imported brand, Gallaher did not need to introduce one of their own. But the company, like others, appreciated the increasing demand for lighter tobacco, which it added to its Condor brand, one of the leaders but considered strong by some smokers. Imperial Tobacco reduced the number of its brands in 1988, but has also appreciated the demand for aromatics. This led, in the 1990s, to the introduction of Dutch Blend to fill that gap.

Loose tobacco has been traditional in the UK for generations but the introduction of packed tobaccos had gradually reduced the demand. As the number of brands also diminished, this created a revival, since retailers found that they could sell loose tobacco at a better price and make better profits. This revival of interest is also present in the United States, but the sale of loose tobacco is forbidden in some other countries, such as France. In Britain, specialist retailers were threatened by the wider distribution of the better-known tobaccos in a variety of outlets. Their answer was to provide smokers with a wider choice that was not obtainable elsewhere, thus enhancing their status as tobacco specialists. Imperial Tobacco had never ceased to supply loose tobaccos. Other manufacturers such as the Kendal-based traditional makers were quick in responding to the renewed trend. But, at the same time, importers started to obtain loose tobaccos, many of them aromatic. This revival of a trend has helped the specialist trade a great deal and some tobacconists can now boast that over eighty per cent of their sales of pipe-tobaccos are in loose form.

TOBACCO AND HEALTH

It would be a pity for so much care,

"Caporal tobacco is now an integral part of what the poets call the 'sweet perfumes of the morning'." Caption to the *Morning Pipe*, drawn by Honoré Daumier (above).

Tobacco and pipes, social phenomena which sometimes attract hostility, have often stimulated cartoonists. In this strip published in the *Revue Illustrée* in 1890, Godefroy amuses his audience with the cunning of the smoker, a working man, who clears the bench for his own use in *A Good Pipe* (below).

refinement, experience and pleasure to disappear, before going up in smoke, in the face of the anti-smoking campaigns in many countries. These are getting more and more virulent, creating guilt among smokers, and reaching worrying extremes. In some twenty years, the smoking habit has passed from the status of an accepted practice to one of an addiction, a culpable vice and even a crime. Smoking in public places is now often forbidden, and sometimes punished by prison sentences, as in the Philippines where, recently, a hundred persons were incarcerated for the "offence".

Pipe-tobacco does not merit this indignity. It cannot be denied that tobacco – just like alcohol, tea, coffee, good food and finally nearly all ingested products – can be a deadly poison if used in excess; but the way it is used in pipes prevents too much toxic danger.

Nicotine is a strong alkaloid, extremely toxic, deadly in its pure state. It acts on the heart and the nervous system. A cigarette or a pipe only contains a very low dose, the surplus of which is dissipated in the smoke exhaled from the mouth. With this very low dose, nicotine acts on the majority of smokers only as a slight sedative and has tranquillizing effects which are useful for stressed smokers. The danger for smokers is therefore not nicotine as such, but the addiction that it can provoke.

It has been recently shown that pipe-tobacco smoke, which is more alkaline than that of cigarettes, assists the absorption of nicotine by the buccal mucus. Most pipe-smokers do not inhale smoke, but exhale immediately from the mouth. According to the report *Smoking and Health Now,* published in 1976 by the US Department of Health, only thirty-five per cent of pipe-smokers inhale smoke, as against ninety per cent of cigarette-smokers. Thus, wise pipe-smokers avoid all substances that might endanger the respiratory system. At the same time, they avoid the inhaling of large doses of carbon oxide, taking into account that pipe-tobacco smoke contains on average only about half the amount found in cigarettes. Similarly, the danger of tar is eliminated. It is not only because pipe-smokers do not inhale, but because they smoke in short puffs, that the levels of tar and phenols are greatly diminished.

All this explains why the risk of lung cancer is no higher with pipe-smokers who do not inhale than with non-smokers. Another study by the same American agency shows nonetheless that pipe-smokers, on the whole, run a slightly higher risk than non-smokers. To ensure that pipe-smoking is inoffensive, some precautions are recommended.

First of all, pipe-smoking should be avoided when there is any slight wound or sore within the mouth, in order to avoid infection. The other recommendations concern the "juice" of the pipe, rich in tar, which is created by condensation in the draught hole of the mouthpiece. Therefore, both the mouthpiece and the bore of the stem should be cleaned frequently. Furthermore, certain factors reduce condensation due to overheating of the bowl and a bad draught; a good density of briar guarantees a reasonable temperature and a thick cut is preferable as it slows down the rate of burning. A system or filter sometimes impairs the draught and should be taken out as it can provoke deeper breathing. For the same reasons, a pipe must be filled properly.

Provided with what he considers to be the "best" tobacco, forewarned of the dangers, and observing these simple recommendations, the smoker can now relax and savour moments of pure pleasure.

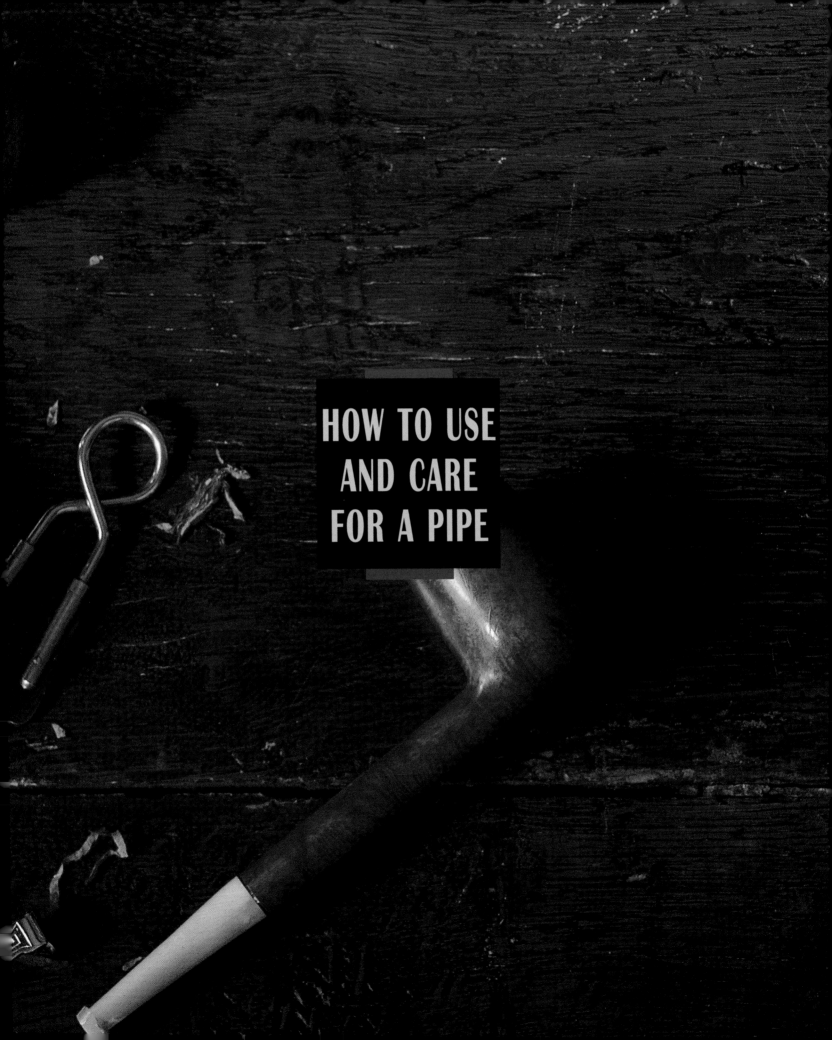

HOW TO USE AND CARE FOR A PIPE

If, as Alfred Dunhill quite rightly affirms in his book, *The Gentle Art of Smoking*, there is nothing esoteric or mysterious in the art of pipe-smoking, there are nonetheless certain rules to follow and certain hazards to overcome in order to enjoy it fully. But all experienced smokers know that it is not enough just to follow the rules to be guaranteed a good smoke. Happy are the cigar connoisseurs who are certain that they will not be disappointed when lighting a Cohiba! All pipe-smokers have experienced the day when, having filled and lit a pipe according to the rules, it proves to be almost unsmokable . . . only to revert to being a "best companion" after a few weeks' rest. Nothing can explain this mystery which happens to two natural products "wedded" to each other: on the one hand, briar and more rarely meerschaum, and on the other, tobacco. It is a "marriage" for better or for worse.

HOW TO CHOOSE A PIPE

The old Irishman was right, when he asserted that the purchase of a pipe was just as risky as the acquisition of a new tweed jacket. Everything starts on the day when you decide to step into a pipe shop. Whether you are an experienced smoker or a novice, you need to follow certain rules which, although not a guarantee against all risks, will nonetheless limit them.

The first rule is to enter the right shop. To buy a pipe, particularly your first one, you should go to a specialist. Of course, you may in theory find a good pipe in a normal tobacconist. But it would be a miracle if the trader, generally in a hurry, who sells packs of cigarettes and other products at a quick rate, were able to advise on this delicate purchase. As far as I was concerned, I was lucky enough to enter by accident, when I was fifteen years of age, the Garnier shop in Paris, to buy my first pipe. Everything went well with the advice of an

amiable and competent assistant and I chose a carved bull's-head, which at the time was the lucky charm of my favourite fictional character, the detective Nestor Burma, whose adventures by Leo Malet I read avidly. Thirty years later, this pipe, obtained for a modest sum is still delicious to smoke. I shiver at the thought that I might have bought a mediocre pipe from a corner shop and might have given up smoking a pipe after a few unfortunate trials, in favour of cigarettes. It is a fact that only a specialist dealer – who presumably services and repairs pipes – has a wide enough selection and sufficient experience to guide a novice. He also knows that the purchase of a pipe by a dedicated smoker, and more so by a beginner, requires a peaceful environment, a friendly atmosphere, a sympathetic listener and, particularly, time.

If you are just starting and have no preconceived idea of the pipe you want, it is best to be guided by the amount of money that you want to invest. In this domain, there is one rule that has few exceptions: the dearer the pipe the better quality it is likely to be. Three essential factors determine the price of a pipe: its size, as a larger pipe will be dearer than a small one; its texture and grain, in other words the regularity (more or less) of the "flame" or bird's-eye and, finally, the quality of manufacture. As far as meerschaum pipes are concerned, they are generally expensive, being made of a relatively rare material, and also fragile. But if you can afford it, for your first experience, do not hesitate to buy a Dunhill briar. And do not listen to the pessimists who pretend that it is like "giving jam to a pig"! The better your pipe, the more pleasant will be your first steps in .pipe-smoking, and you will be encouraged to discover the wonders of the world that you have uncovered. Nonetheless, it would be a pity to ruin a pipe so well conceived by using it badly. Thus, you need to give it as much care in smoking as the craftsman did in making it. Rest assured, if your means are limited, a real profes-

Pipe tools are an integral part of the ritual of pipe-smoking. They are not all indispensable; their value is not necessarily related to their usefulness – it is purely part of the pleasure of smoking (preceding pages).

Age does not matter as far as smoking is concerned. It is perhaps best not to start too early. This little Breton on the postcard (left), sucking his father's pipe, is happy to do so, provided that it has never been smoked. One of the most celebrated addresses in the world for pipe-smokers: Sommer's Au carrière d'écume (The Meerschaum Quarry). Unfortunately, this shop closed in 1989. Its fittings were made of solid mahogany and dated from 1855 (facing page)

sional specialist will always be able to suggest a range of more economical pipes, perhaps less perfect, but sufficient to assure an excellent beginning. For the rest, it is a question of taste . . . and luck. When the salesman has spread a range of different shapes in front of you, let your taste be your guide.

Your eyes are the first thing. Do not buy a pipe shape that does not satisfy you on the pretext that it has other qualities. A smoker easily tires of a pipe he did not particularly like in the first instance. In the case of a briar pipe, if the general appearance, shape and colour pleases you, look at it more closely. Try to see the presence, which is only too frequent, of tiny holes or filled cracks in the wood. If they are not too deep, they will not impair the smoking qualities. But know that, sooner or later, they will show up, as fillings do not react in the same way when the pipe is smoked. On the other hand, if they are too deep, you run the risk that the pipe will "explode" one day! If the interior of the bowl shows signs of fillings, avoid the pipe; they may release unpleasant flavours while you "break" the pipe in, and that will not encourage you to persevere.

After this examination, and if you are pleased with the pipe, do not hesitate to try the lip between the teeth. Many specialists will provide plastic covers and you can judge how the pipe looks in a mirror. (The shop will generally have one.) The pipe must please you, of course, but it must also "fit" your face. While there is a certain amount of leeway, a very small pipe in the middle of a large face is as incongruous as a very large pipe hiding half a small head.

If you are still hesitating between several models, choose a classic shape that will not disappoint you; select a medium shape which has "plenty of wood", in other words, one that has fairly thick walls and will not heat up too quickly. Avoid pipes that are too large and take longer to smoke and often discourage beginners, and pipes that are too small and leave you "hungry". Opt for a fairly long mouthpiece which will cool the smoke before it reaches the mouth. When choosing between two pipes that are similar in size, select the lighter one which will feel better in the teeth and which has probably dried longer and lost its resin. To start with, go for natural wood or sandblast (those subjected to a jet of sand or grit under pressure, which makes them lighter), rather than those that are varnished and can flake if smoked too quickly or compromise the

To choose a pipe, you need time. You need to sit down and think in a calm atmosphere. This is always possible in the Astley shop in Jermyn Street, London. For forty years, Mr Walters was an attentive and expert adviser to the firm's customers (right).

"It suits him so well" To choose a pipe, you need to respect and even improve your face. This was well understood by the American painter, Norman Rockwell. In this self-portrait he removed his glasses, but not his pipe (*The Triple Self-Portrait*, facing page).

taste if the varnish has run into the bowl; and those colours that hide imperfections badly. Avoid, like the plague, the leather-covered pipes which were popular with misguided smokers in the 1950s, and can hide horrible flaws. If you are a novice, also avoid surface-carved pipes – more rare these days – which look like sandblasted pipes; they are "carved" with a fraise or cutters, and also hide imperfections. Finally, as a beginner, do not chose oval bowls; certainly less bulky in the pocket, they are often difficult to smoke, as the tobacco burns irregularly.

The range of pipes is so wide that any smoker can find the one that suits the personality and the occasion. The most liberal Republican member of the US Congress during the 1960s was the elegant Millicent Fenwick, who knew how to choose a suitable pipe to fit her fine profile (right, above) . . .

For the final decision, call on your sense of touch. Your hand is a decisive factor in selecting a pipe. You will cherish a pipe that feels good in the hand. It is a difficult notion to explain, but it comes down to the pleasure of feeling an object in the palm of the hand, handling it, and caressing it. All experienced smokers know that a pipe spends as much time in the hand, being looked at, as between the teeth, and that the pleasure of feeling the warmth of the object is often worth as much as its taste.

Do not forget, when you choose a pipe, to examine the mouthpiece. Today the majority of briar pipe mouthpieces are made of vulcanized rubber (vulcanite). And the majority of meerschaums have mouthpieces of synthetic resins resembling amber. Their general appearance is conditioned by the model of the pipe, but the shape of the "bite" (the area just behind the lip) and the bore can vary according to the taste or requirement of the smoker. These details are more important than they appear at first sight, since they determine the way smoke will reach the mouth, and the way the pipe will be held in the teeth. The only rule is to select a bite that will feel comfortable in the teeth. One can choose accordingly between a nar-

row lip (therefore a narrow bite) which fits nicely between the teeth, and a wide lip/bite (called a fishtail) which spreads the weight of the pipe, but can be unsteady. You must, of course, try them out, even if later you change the mouthpiece. As for the draught bore, avoid one that is too narrow and restricts the passage of the smoke. Some mouthpieces which are recommended, such as those from Peterson Pipes, have a bore that directs the smoke upwards towards the palate. Finally, nervous smokers with a tendency to bite or chew, should choose a thicker and rounder bite rather than a flat one.

One last detail will help you in your selection: the presence or absence of anti-nicotine systems (gadgets), sometimes screwed on the push (peg or floc). You can either throw them away or use them and clean them. The only advice that one can give is to avoid them in order to maintain the full flavour of the tobacco and the full pleasure of the pipe, as they tend to create more condensation inside the mouthpiece and the stem and alter the taste of the smoke, giving it a back-taste of old nicotine. To avoid the effect of tobacco without losing its qualities, it is best not to inhale (most pipe-smokers do not), to smoke slowly and to clean the pipe as often as possible. Systems can nonetheless be useful when the pipe is new as they tend to soften the initial bite of the tobacco. But do not hesitate to get rid of them once the pipe is comfortably broken in.

What pipe have you chosen? It will most certainly be a briar which today accounts for virtually the whole market. They present a very wide variety, but most come under categories which permit identification according to their shape, size and the way they are made. There are two models which constitute the basic classifi-

. . . while this less elegant bulldog understands the need for a large pipe (left).

His Royal Highness Prince Bernhard of the Netherlands enjoying one of his bents. On the 31 March 1973, at a Chapter Meeting held exceptionally at the Soestdyk Palace, the Confrérie des Maîtres Pipiers of Saint-Claude received him as a Member of their brotherhood (right).

Large or small pipe? That depends on the shape of the face and also the quality of tobacco one wants to smoke. Beginners are best advised to avoid large pipes . . . (below, cartoon c. 1871)

cation for the non-initiated: the straights and the bents; in this the English language is used by most smokers, worldwide. In each of these families, the differences are great depending on size, the degree of the curve, the shape of the mouthpiece and the bowl (including the stem). The imagination of pipe-makers seems to have no limits. But about fifteen standard shapes have established themselves over the years to become the great classics, of which every smoker has at least one example in his personal collection. So as to discourage in advance any irrational classifications, most classic shapes are found in either straights or bents.

The simplest and most popular straight is the Billiard. No one is certain of the reason for the name, except that it is something to do with "as straight as a billiard cue". It is therefore a straight pipe with pure lines, the bowl being at right angles with the stem. The angle between the bowl and its stem is crucial, as an acute angle may add bitterness to the smoke. There are derivations of the Billiard: the Poker, also the Stand-up Poker, has a flat base permitting it to stand upright; the Apple, like the fruit, has a rounded shape (it also exists as a bent); the Bulldog, massive and squat as its name indicates, has a wide bowl towards the top; the fine and light Canadian has a long oval stem and a short mouthpiece, and is appreciated by aesthetes, even though its characteristics make it fragile and sometimes

"He went into his office. There was still a smell of tobacco, in spite of the window being open onto the Quai des Orfèvres. He put the files on a corner of his desk, tapped the bowl of his still warm pipe on the window-sill, came back to his chair and automatically looked for another pipe which should have been on his right. It was not there. There were three pipes, including one meerschaum, near the ashtray. But the good one that he was looking for, the one he often returned to, that he always carried with him – a large briar with a slight curve that his wife had given him ten years before for an anniversary, the one he called his good old pipe – was not there." The opening lines of *Maigret's Pipe* by Georges Simenon (right).

Piet Mondrian's pipe and glasses (below). The pure lines of the pipe reflect the work of the Dutch abstract painter, photographed in 1926 (facing page).

difficult to repair after an accident; the Pot is designed for the strength of its bowl, with plenty of wood, and gains in aroma what it loses in weight; the Dublin is slightly laid-back (as were some old clay pipes), the bowl widening towards the top; the Liverpool is a Billiard with a long stem, short mouthpiece; the Lovat has a similar bowl but a short saddle mouthpiece; the Prince has a rounded bowl, flattened at the bottom, which contains less tobacco and is therefore appreciated by smokers who are quickly satisfied. Note finally that pipe-makers offer a number of straight models with panels: Panel Billiard, Panel Apple, etc.

Among the bents the Bent Billiard is as popular as the straight, with its well-known "S" shape. Its centre of gravity, which is lower than on a straight, makes it lighter in the teeth. With a slightly rounder bowl and fitted with an olive-

band (or mount) it becomes an Army Bent. Mounted (or banded) pipes, found in all models, are not only sought for their strength. A band reinforces the stem at its most vulnerable point where the mouthpiece is fitted, but is also appreciated for its appearance. The Bent

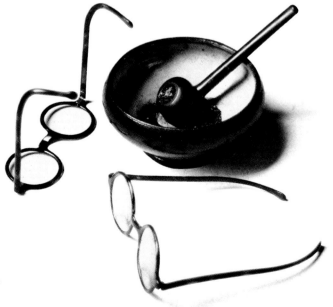

Rhodesian, robust and squat, has less curve on the stem and mouthpiece which are thicker than on the Bent Albert, which some consider for its finesse and the incline of its bowl as the most elegant of the range of bents. A similar bowl fitted with a much longer mouthpiece is found in the famous Churchwarden (named after the Churchwardens of yesteryear, who smoked them in council or even, it is said, during the sermon), which was particularly appreciated in England and Germany.

Alongside the classic models in briar, there is one category of exceptional pieces where master pipe-makers can express their creativity, the freehands, unique pipes made entirely by hand and often to order. A freehand is never duplicated, and some creations are extremely original. Although firms like Charatan in London, were already making freehands in the 1930s, the concept was re-created in the late 1950s and spread to many shops in the 1960s. Originally, the masters of freehands were the Danish makers but, for some years, German, English and particularly Italian creators have gained a reputation for this kind of work.

In the whole history of pipes, it is interesting to note how national habits and traditions have influenced the sizes of pipes in different countries. In Britain, clay pipes were originally quite small, and although they grew as tobacco became cheaper, they never grew to the same sizes as those made on the continent of Europe. Therefore, when briar became the dominant material, the British demand for smaller pipes persisted. In the regular series, there were four basic sizes, namely lightweight, small, medium and large. This was reflected in due course in the categorising of sizes in groups by Dunhill.

The lightweights were a creation of the 1920s and 1930s which meant simply what they were called: light pipes with a small capacity which gave a shorter smoke, seen by the smokers who used them as being more economic, and recommended to beginners. They also suited the finer cut tobaccos that were much in use then. In general, the trend in Britain was for small- or medium-size pipes which were also suitable for finer cut tobaccos and were cheap to buy. As we have seen, *ébauchon* blocks are sold by weight, so that the smaller the *ébauchons*, the larger the quantity the bales contain. The shapes were generally Billiards, Apples, Princes and bents and also a shape which has now virtually disappeared, the Bullcap, which the French call *Tomate* (tomato). The French name is an excellent description. Not only was it a very popular shape in Britain, but it also became the best selling shape in Australia. The UK manufacturers exported large quantities of these pipes up to the late 1960s. They were made plain or with lines around the wide upper part of the bowl, and also with varying numbers of panels – four, six or eight.

The large pipes were made basically for export, particularly to the United States and were called American shapes. As world travel expanded after the Second World War, American and other visitors to England asked for large shapes and many British smokers started to appreciate them more since they found that they need not fill them right up with tobacco! Currently, large pipes are far more common in British pipe shops than they were thirty years ago. One other reason for this situation is that after the war, the duty on pipe tobacco was such that the cost of an ounce of tobacco in Britain was about double that of twenty cigarettes. Now twenty cigarettes are dearer than an ounce of tobacco, but this does not seem to have persuaded smokers to go back to the pipe.

One exception to the pre-war trend for smaller pipes came from Ireland, where the Irish Bulldog was popular. It had to be cheap, and therefore it was made from a low quality of briar, but it also needed to be large enough for an "Irish thumb" to be placed in the bowl – the Irish were reputed to have big thumbs! At the same time, the Irish smokers were able to purchase fairly cheap tobaccos.

As we have seen, the Americans preferred large pipes, which were almost a tradition with them, and smokers in France on the whole preferred models which were medium to large. For them, the popular *gris* tobacco was always cheaper than the equivalent pipe tobaccos smoked in Britain. Similarly, German smokers liked larger shapes, a trend that could be traced to the time when they smoked large ceramic pipes. During the Second World War, the pipes made in Germany were quite small due to the shortage of tobacco, but as soon as the trade restrictions eased in the late 1940s and the early 1950s, larger pipes were again in demand.

With all these trends, the nature of the preferred tobaccos was, and still is, important. Taking America as an example, smokers there are more likely to use broad and coarse-cut tobacco than are those in England.

To complete this review of pipes available in pipe-shops, let us leave briar. Today, other pipes make up only five per cent of the total number of pipes sold worldwide. Among those, the most prestigious is the meerschaum pipe. The material is actually a mineral, a silicate of magnesium, light and white in its natural state, which can float on water; the first users called it meerschaum or "sea foam". Apart from its lightness, meerschaum possesses all the necessary qualities for transformation into a pipe: its porosity guarantees a light smoke, and its softness is ideal for turning or carving. Its disadvantages on the other hand are its high price (as a comparatively rare material) and fragility.

Nowadays, meerschaum comes mostly from Turkey, more precisely from Anatolia. Its scarcity, and also economic considerations, led the Turkish government to ban exports in its raw state, and to assume the monopoly of the manufacture of pipes. All meerschaum pipes found currently in the world's shops, with rare exceptions, are imported from Turkey. They come in all sizes and shapes, and are also carved. Unfortunately, Turkish pipe-makers have neglected to apply some of the traditional methods of manufacture, methods which had been perfected over the years by Hungarian, Austrian, French and other craftsmen, which enhanced all the qualities of meerschaum. Thus, some of their pipes can produce unfortunate surprises: a meerschaum that saturates with tar, the bottom of a pipe that drops off, a stem that breaks. To avoid this last accident, if you have been tempted by a Turkish meerschaum, make sure that the mouthpiece is well aligned with the stem, by separating them a little to check this aspect.

All smokers must see meerschaum for what it is: a luxury refined product which does not tolerate imitations, with incomparable qualities which must be respected. Otherwise, it is best to abstain. Fortunately, it is still possible to obtain a meerschaum pipe made in the traditional way. The former pipe-maker from the Sommer company in Paris – now alas closed – has set up his own workshop not far from Paris. Philippe Bargiel must be the only one left in the world who respects the tradition. Most pipe specialists know him, some stock his products, or you may go directly to him. His main problem is to obtain raw meerschaum, but he manages to do so. The traditional amber mouthpiece is fortunately not indispensable, since real amber, very difficult to find these days, is very expensive. Ambrolith, a synthetic resin which is amber-coloured will be (almost) as good. It must be said that the pipes that Philippe Bargiel creates with love are expensive, but not excessively so. They are worth trying once in a lifetime.

One should also be careful with "meerschaum-lined" pipes, which are now fairly common. They are generally briar pipes, the bowls of which have been opened up to receive a meerschaum cup. In itself the principle is good: the meerschaum protects the briar and lightens the pipe. But there are two types of cups for these pipes: one made of off-cuts from meerschaum blocks, and the other, in far greater number, made up from meerschaum

One could never imagine Albert Einstein without his teasing eyes, his ruffled hair and his pipe. The author of the Theory of Relativity was famous for saying: "Before answering a question, I always light my pipe." (right).

Harry Dickson is to fantasy what Sherlock Holmes is to detective tales. It is after lighting his pipe with care that the hero Jean Ray relates his ghost stories to his friends. He is here depicted by Nicollet, smoking a Calabash and illustrating the first chapter of *Treachery in Agarttha: The Myth Exposed* (facing page, above).
A grand meerschaum classic, made until the 1950s: Calabash bowl and amber mouthpiece. This model is no longer obtainable except in museums and antique shops. To make it today would be extremely expensive (facing page, below).

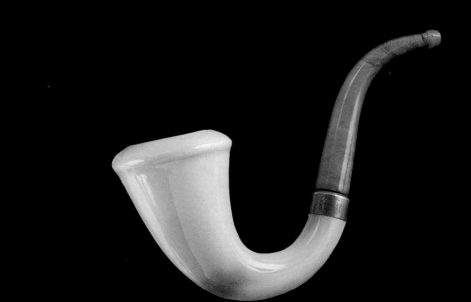

powder bound together and moulded. The first are the best since real meerschaum is used, although they are not worth a great deal if not treated properly with whale oil. As for the others, the less said the better, since their lives are short!

Among meerschaum pipes, one should include the Calabash, made from an African gourd, called a calabash, into which a meerschaum cup is placed. It is a fine and rare type, as shown being smoked by Sherlock Holmes in films. But all fans of the Baker Street detective know very well that there is not one mention of the Calabash in the works of Conan Doyle.

Finally, beginners will note with curiosity in certain shop windows clay models or corncob pipes. The first, which are still made in Holland, Belgium and France, have the advantage of preserving the taste of the tobacco, but they are brittle. One can still find some porcelain pipes, particularly in Germany. Smokers find them fragile and heavy, and they give a rather raw smoke. Corncobs, sometimes called Missouri meerschaums, are common in the United States and are extremely cheap, but they only last a few months. The porosity of the corncobs ensures a sweet and light smoke, well appreciated in the United States. Do not look any longer for asbestos pipes nor for pipes in violetebony wood. The first, generally Dublin shapes, used to be made in England, but are now forbidden since the carcinogenic effects of asbestos were discovered; the others, made in Saint-Claude until the 1960s, from a very rare wood, became too expensive.

A last word: to those who are tempted to make a gift of a pipe to a smoker, we advise a great deal of circumspection. As we have seen, the chance that a smoker will like a new pipe depends on a number of fine distinctions, often not appreciated by others. Thus, if you do not know the smoker intimately, as well as his tastes and his habits in the matter, it is best to offer him a tobacco pouch, a lighter or, better still . . . a fine book on pipes.

Matches or lighter? King Frederick of Denmark chose the latter when photographed by Patrick Lichfield (below).

BREAKING IN AND CARBONIZATION

You have just acquired a new pipe, or perhaps the first one. You are embarking on one of the essential and most delicate aspects of the art of smoking. Whether you have chosen a regular model or a unique work of art, the quality of your pleasure will depend on getting the best aroma from your tobacco. This pleasure will be spoilt if you omit the first important thing: the "breaking in" or carbon lining of the pipe.

All briar pipes need to be carbon lined before regular use. There is no point in subjecting the wood to the attack of heat, tar and nicotine before it is prepared. The pipe could become unsmokable. To prevent that, it needs to have a progressive layer of carbon applied to the walls. This layer will protect the bowl. Contrary to what the uninitiated may think, the carbon layer is not burnt briar – something to avoid – but a combination of tobacco residues. The layer has to be of uniform thickness but there is unfortunately no strict rule to guarantee the success of the operation. One thing is certain, breaking in needs constant attention to avoid burning. A burnt new pipe would be irretrievable.

We believe that, to obtain a good carbon layer, certain practices must be avoided, although some people recommend them. You will be greatly disappointed if you fill the bowl with spirit, honey, jam or oil in the hope of obtaining a better flavour. Common sense will tell you that briar, an ideal material for pipes, does not need further treatment to fulfil its role. No need either for the supreme heresy of mistaking briar for a crêpe-suzette, and "flaming" the inside of the bowl with spirit. No pipe worthy of that name can withstand such treatment. As for "automatic carbonizing", praised by the author of *The Ultimate Pipe Book*, this is far removed from the spirit of the dedicated smoker who will avoid it. Rich burghers in olden times used to employ a professional carbonizer to avoid undertaking this task themselves; perhaps it was a better solution.

So, how do you proceed to obtain the best result? It needs patience, moderation and vigilance. You must first avoid burning the briar. Start by filling the bowl to about a quarter of its capacity (the art of filling is discussed later), light it and smoke slowly; do not worry if it

"The duration of a smoke," wrote Jean Giono, "depends on the rhythm of breathing, the cleanliness of the pipe, and of the tobacco. The

rhythm is quickly found when the mouthpiece has had a cleaner passed through it and you have a decent tobacco . . . with tobacco, above all, the slowness and experimentation are distinctive side-dishes." Above: Jean Giono, photographed by his friend and biographer Pierre Citron. "He who lives without tobacco is not fit to live," exclaimed Bertrand Russell, philosopher and mathematician. This great pacifist still smoked at eighty-six years of age (facing page).

goes out – initially, you should avoid too much heat. It will be evident if the pipe is too hot, as it will sweat and feel humid. In this case, let the pipe go out and relight it when cool. After four or five pipefuls, you can progressively increase the amount of tobacco, first to a third, then after a few more smokes, to a half, and so on . . . You may need to smoke up to twenty times before you can fill the bowl to the top. During the operation, at each step, you will need to ensure that the carbonizing is regular, relighting as and when necessary. Do not assume that a pipe has to be smoked

Therefore, the carbonizing of a first pipe may be risky for a beginner. This risk can be avoided if a new pipe is initially only smoked once or twice a day, and no short-cut for carbonizing is used. This has the double advantage of letting both the pipe and the tongue rest between smokes.

Meerschaum pipes present a danger, as they normally taste good from the first smoke. Nonetheless, they will only be perfect when well carbonized. The method is different from that used for a briar. Meerschaum will not degrade nor compromise the taste of the

The warmth and patina of old briars beloved by smokers . . . (right).

in one session, without relighting. Experienced smokers relight all the time. Another important rule is to let the pipe cool down before refilling it, to avoid burning the briar.

The pipe will be broken in and carbonized when the layer is uniform. This uniformity is best obtained by gradually filling the pipe. The point is that the top of the bowl which first receives the flame of a match or lighter will carbonize more quickly than the bottom. You can now smoke your pipe as you wish. This preliminary process is somewhat of a chore. But pipes from which the smoker can obtain immediate pleasure are rare. You often get a taste of bitterness and some pipes may take longer to break in than others.

tobacco if the pipe is filled right up from the start. But, contrary to briar, meerschaum changes colour during use, from milky white to yellow and then brown before attaining, for the best pipes, the deep red colour that smokers are proud of. As the lower part of the bowl darkens more quickly, meerschaum specialists recommend filling only half the bowl at the start, in order to obtain a relatively gradual coloration. Pipes treated with whale oil demand some extra precautions. For the first thirty smokes, preferably one a day, the smoker should avoid touching the bowl. The easiest way of handling the pipe is to hold it with a piece of cloth, or simply to hold it by the stem. The reason for this precaution is that the mixing of whale oil and beeswax may, initially, cause fingermarks to be left on the bowl. It is also advisable to smoke slowly and not relight if the pipe goes out. Otherwise, the whale oil is likely to melt unduly and run to the bottom of the bowl and into the stem. To avoid any chance of this, it is best to place the pipe vertically after smoking, the un-emptied bowl being lower than the stem so that the whale oil will run back.

In the case of a carved meerschaum, however, some expert smokers control the colour transformation by varying the amount of tobacco each time they smoke. In that way, they obtain subtle colour variations between the different parts of the pipe.

Clay pipes also smoke well from the start. In the light of their fragility and limited life, this is essential. Sometimes carbonizing may be difficult, as heat tends to close the pores of the clay. If this happens they can no longer absorb tar. A strong intensity of combustion can calcinate the bowl and make the pipe unsmokable: a black spot appears on the outside and nothing will stop it getting larger while altering the taste of the tobacco. To avoid this problem, one should smoke slowly, at least for about the first twenty smokes, and avoid tobaccos that are too dry. The same precaution must be taken with porcelain pipes, which carbonize in layers and risk breaking under intense heat.

The English writer and journalist Walter Harris smoked his first pipe at university. His reputation as a pipe expert is undoubted, particularly at Astley's where he is a faithful customer. He is seen here lighting an Astley, according to the rules (right).

THE FILLING

It goes without saying that before you can break in (carbonize) a pipe, you must fill it. The filling, on which will depend the taste and comfort of a pipe, needs a certain amount of expertise in fingering (in the literal sense) which is acquired by experience, but will soon become automatic. The operation consists simply of filling the bowl with tobacco so that it will smoke evenly – which supposes that it is sufficiently "packed" – without the smoker having to resort to deep puffing. It is a question of the correct measure: not too much, not too little.

The best way is to fill the bowl slowly with small pinches of tobacco, regularly pressed down with the finger which demands the instinct of the smoker regarding the "springiness" of the tobacco; I use the index finger. But prior to filling the smoker must ensure that the draught is free by blowing through the mouthpiece. The first pinch which goes to the bottom of the bowl must not be pressed. But each subsequent layer is pressed down gradually. For the beginner who has not yet mastered the technique, there is a simple test: before lighting, put the pipe in the mouth and draw on it; the air must pass through but offer a slight resistance. If unsatisfactory, empty the pipe and start again. If it takes too much effort to get the air through, it means that the tobacco is too compressed and this will prevent it

The tobacco is tamped down after lighting the first time (top). The second lighting will light the pipe properly (centre). Then the pipe is smoked slowly to avoid burning the briar (bottom). The pipe-maker Savinelli used to advise: "Hold your pipe firmly from time to time, and count up to ten. If you can do that without burning your hand, continue to smoke. If you can't, let it cool or even go out."

burning properly. If too easy, just put in a little more tobacco. If the amount of tobacco is insufficient, it will burn quickly and the heat will "bite" the palate. Some experienced smokers check the amount of tobacco as they fill the pipe. Finally, it is worth checking that the top surface of the tobacco is fairly even before lighting.

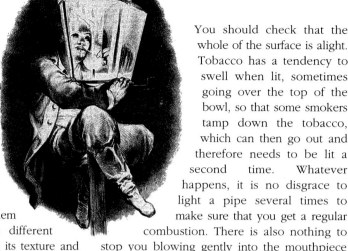

There may be a slight problem as each tobacco demands a different density of filling, depending on its texture and level of humidity. This can easily be overcome and the novice is advised initially to use a fairly fine-cut tobacco, a little on the dry side, rather than a humid coarse-cut which would pack too tightly. But the beginner can be reassured: there is no need to achieve speed records. Take your time and shortly you will find that you fill your pipe correctly without thinking about it. But also, to avoid losing time, there are a few practices to be avoided, although some people recommend them. One is to put a hard piece of tobacco "stem" (tree-trunk, as some say in England) at the bottom of the bowl to ensure a better draught. The uninitiated will soon find that the piece of stem will clog the pipe . . . it is then best to empty it.

LIGHTING

It is no good, as will be appreciated, to fill a pipe well but light it badly. As in other circumstances in life, fire must be handled with care. Even if a bad combustion of the tobacco is not too serious, the smoker will never forgive himself for burning the wood of the bowl through sheer inattention. This is a risk with smokers who tend to incline the pipe when they light up. The best and simplest way is to hold the pipe vertically, pass the flame all over the top of the tobacco, and draw in with short puffs.

You should check that the whole of the surface is alight. Tobacco has a tendency to swell when lit, sometimes going over the top of the bowl, so that some smokers tamp down the tobacco, which can then go out and therefore needs to be lit a second time. Whatever happens, it is no disgrace to light a pipe several times to make sure that you get a regular combustion. There is also nothing to stop you blowing gently into the mouthpiece once the pipe is lit, to fan the glow and ensure a good spread of the embers.

Whether you light your pipe using a match, a lighter or a taper is immaterial. Normal size matches have the inconvenience of burning quickly, causing burnt fingers, and therefore necessitating the use of several. There are special matches, such as Swan Vestas in England, which are a little longer, and are sold by tobacconists. A lighter would seem to be the ideal instrument, particularly a gas lighter which, unlike a petrol lighter, has no smell. There are special lighters made for pipes which have the flame at an angle, and therefore aim directly towards the bowl. All this does not stop serious dedicated pipe-smokers from using, shamelessly (as I do), a good old petrol Zippo lighter, which is ideal in the open air. Even if, at first, the sharp smell of the petrol worries you, it does not, as some people think, alter the taste of the tobacco.

SMOKING YOUR PIPE

To start with, there are no rules for smoking a pipe well. If the ideal is to smoke peacefully, with short puffs, the essential is to obtain the maximum enjoyment, which some smokers achieve with long deep puffs. Here, freedom is the rule. It is only limited on the one hand by not causing excessive heat through rapid smoking, and on the other by repeated

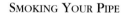

The "dada" painter Marcel Duchamp loved to tease with his weird haircuts, but he wisely kept to the best classic pipes, such as this large Apple (facing page, photographed by Man Ray in 1921).

On June 27, 1965, at London Airport, a photographer catches Bing Crosby lighting his pipe near fuel tankers. The next day, a journalist commented that it was an example of "what should not be done". All the same, with a correctly filled pipe and lighting within the rules, the risks of accident are nil (above).
The American physicist Robert Oppenheimer, "father" of the atom bomb, knew how to light the least offensive of "furnaces" . . . (below).

relighting required by slow smoking. The world record for slow smoking with a normal pipe and without relighting, is over three hours. No one will be surprised that this record is held by a Swiss. Maybe he has his own method, well known among competing smokers, enabling him to smoke slowly without the pipe going out. This is done by pressing the ash lightly with a pipe tamper. You can use a special cover to retard combustion. These covers are specially made for the purpose, although not admitted in competition. Instead of using a cover, the ideal method is probably to hold the palm of the hand a few centimetres from the bowl.

The same lack of rules applies when the pipe is about to go out. Some smokers light it again, others do not. Some light up again before the pipe cools down while others stop when there is still a little tobacco in the bowl. If you smoke in the open air and it starts to rain, you can always smoke the pipe upside down; the tobacco will not fall out if the pipe has been filled properly in the first place. Whatever the circumstances, it is necessary to press down the ash with a pipe tamper or similar tool. On the other hand, it is not advisable to relight a meerschaum before it has been adequately broken in.

After smoking, all good pipe-smokers are united by three important rules. The first is to let the pipe cool before emptying it, so that it absorbs all the humidity and stays dry. The second concerns the way the pipe should be emptied. It should only be necessary to tap the bowl lightly to make the ash fall out of the pipe. You should avoid the seemingly simple practice of carelessly tapping the bowl into an ashtray, or tapping it against the heel of the shoe. You may damage the top of the bowl or, if the pipe is held lightly, snap the mouthpiece

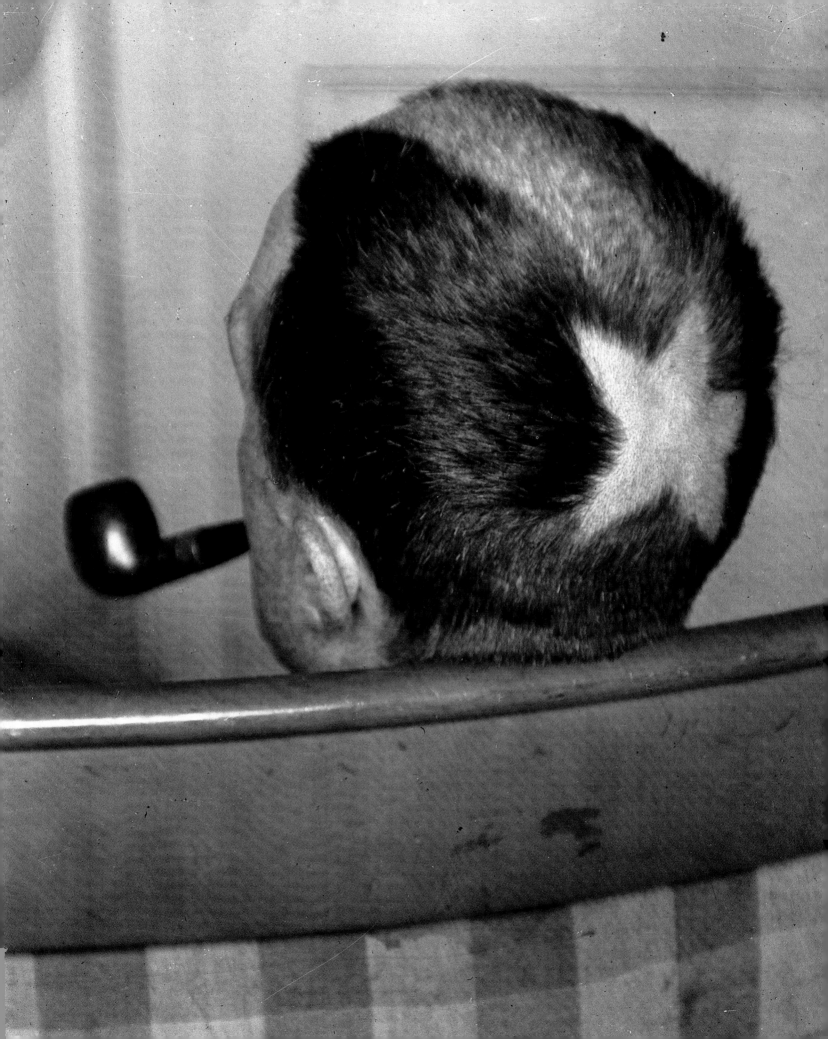

without emptying the pipe. If the ashes do not fall easily, it is best to use a proper tool for the purpose. The third and last rule is that the pipe should have cooled down completely before you refill it.

Last, but not least, avoid leaving ashes at the scene of a crime you have committed! As noted by Conan Doyle in the *The Sign of Four*, "It is a point which is continuously turning up in criminal trials, and which is sometimes of supreme importance as a clue. If you can say definitely, for example, that some murder had been done by a man who was smoking an Indian lunkah, it obviously narrows your field of search. To a trained eye, there is as much difference between the black ash of a

The briar bowl, which heats up less than clay, permits the smoker to hold his pipe in comfort, as shown by Jean-Paul Sartre (facing page, photograph by Henri Cartier-Bresson in 1946).
Pierre Loeb, friend of the surrealists, used a similar hold (left, photographed by his sister Denise Colomb).

165

Trichinopoly and the white fluff of a bird's-eye as there is between a cabbage and a potato."

CARE OF A PIPE

Provided that they are well looked after, briar and meerschaum pipes can last a lifetime and improve with age. Dedicated smokers will not begrudge time, patience and know-how spent in carrying out the small ritual of cleaning their favourite pipes. It is an indispensable operation, as a dirty pipe is a calamity for the smoker and for those around him. When it becomes clogged by tar and other substances released by the combustion of tobacco, a pipe starts to secrete, through condensation, an acid juice which makes it unsmokable. It also emits a bad smell which will offend those in the vicinty. Only Stalin, who never cleaned his Dunhills, would (with impunity) submerge those around him in clouds of evil-smelling smoke.

To clean your pipes, there is one first unbreakable rule: never try to clean a pipe thoroughly while it is still warm. Since the wood of the stem and the mouthpiece will have swollen as a result of the heat, it is difficult to separate

them without the risk of splitting the pipe. On the other hand, without removing the mouthpiece of a warm pipe, you can put a pipe-cleaner through the pipe, and this will absorb the surplus humidity and nicotine. Some smokers leave the pipe-cleaner in position until their next smoke. But this basic precaution, to be repeated after every two or three pipefuls, is not sufficient to guarantee a well-cleaned bore. It is essential to remove the mouthpiece to achieve an adequate clean.

There is one obvious rule (which should, nevertheless, be stated): never clean a pipe in water. To clean the inside of the bowl, one of the most efficient ways is to use a piece of paper, twisted into a cone which you can turn inside the pipe,without forcing it. You can also use emery paper, as long as it has a fine grain. For the stem and the mouthpiece, once again use a pipe-cleaner. If this is not enough to remove all substances which might have hardened, there are pipe-cleaners with hard bristles. An efficient way is to use a solvent, normally spirit-based, that is available from tobacconists. All you need do is to dip a pipe-cleaner in the solvent before passing it through the pipe. Some "gourmet" smokers – including the author of these lines – like to dip the pipe-cleaner in a drinkable spirit, such as cognac or whisky. Some Germans have a liking for lavender-scented eau de Cologne!

Many smokers find their own favourite way of cleaning a pipe. There are still smokers in England who would like to use birds' feathers which were highly suitable for cleaning clay pipes and quite efficient for briar. Unfortunately, they are no longer found in shops. Another tip comes from a British pipe expert who suggests that one of the best tools for cleaning the bore of a stem is a long electrical screwdriver. The edge of the screwdriver should be between three and four millimetres, which is the same as the majority of draught bores. It will not only scrape the excess tar but also reach right through pipes with long stems – without risk of damage – which the average pipe-tool cannot always do. It is also useful for

Clark Gable used his pipe as a seductive weapon. Imagine him without it (right). "The man who talked to geese" favoured large bents – the Austrian zoologist and psychologist Konrad Lorenz. Note that the smoke does not worry the bird (below).

A good pipe on a cold day, to warm the soul and the hand. Facing page: Peter Fleming, photographed by the traveller and writer Ella Maillart in China in 1935. From this journey on foot across central Asia, Ella Maillart brought back *Forbidden Oasis* and Peter Fleming his book *News From Tartary*.

cleaning out the accumulation of tar that sometimes occurs in the recess that takes the floc (push or peg) of the mouthpiece. He also advocates the use of a piece of kitchen paper, rolled to a taper, to ease penetration into the stem bore; this will mop up all excess humidity in that part of the pipe. In addition, it is worth obtaining thin pipe-cleaners (as sold for metal-stemmed pipes) for the initial cleaning of bent mouthpieces, as their very nature occasionally causes a slight obstruction which makes it difficult to push a normal-size cleaner through; the end of the metal core of a modern pipe-cleaner can catch the inside of the bend in the mouthpiece. Finally, our expert considers that leaving a pipe-cleaner in a pipe overnight (or while resting the pipe) is unnecessary, since the air should be allowed free access, but he will not dispute that some smokers swear by that method!

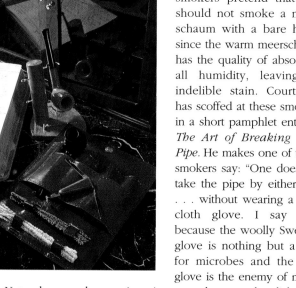

Some tools for the well-prepared smoker: pipe-cleaners, knife with tamper, pipe-case, pipe-holder and pipe-rack under glass (right).

As for the frequency of cleaning, it depends on the shape and other features of the pipe (Peterson pipes, for example, have a small condensation well which needs frequent cleaning) and the nature of the smoker. Wet smokers, who produce a lot of saliva, need to clean their pipes more often than dry smokers. Note also that a badly-filled pipe will produce more humidity. Whether you are a wet or a dry smoker, cleaning must be done in private, as the operation releases harsh smells from the residues.

Once the inside of a pipe has been cleaned, you should take care of its exterior. Smokers are judged by their peers, connoisseurs of fine pipes, who will note what they have between their teeth. To make a briar pipe shine, nothing is better than wax. American experts recommend "Canuba" wax, an exotic product with great properties. Many smokers use normal natural wax, used to polish wood and easily found in d.i.y. and paint shops. It immediately revives the dullest of pipes. Specialist tobacconists stock pipe polishing products, such as the highly recommended Dunhill Pipe Bowl Polish.

The cleaning of vulcanite mouthpieces is a little more delicate. All smokers will find that, at some point, the colour of the vulcanite alters to an unpleasant yellowish green. This occurs more quickly if the mouthpieces have not been looked after. There are two products which have been specially made to revive discoloured mouthpieces. For myself, I prefer to give them an application of olive oil with a cloth, and I leave the vulcanite to absorb the oil for twenty-four hours. After that time, the mouthpiece may not have returned to its original colour, but it will almost have done so.

The care of meerschaum pipes is relatively simpler. Some fussy smokers pretend that you should not smoke a meerschaum with a bare hand, since the warm meerschaum has the quality of absorbing all humidity, leaving an indelible stain. Courteline has scoffed at these smokers in a short pamphlet entitled, *The Art of Breaking In a Pipe*. He makes one of these smokers say: "One does not take the pipe by either end . . . without wearing a fine-cloth glove. I say fine, because the woolly Swedish glove is nothing but a trap for microbes and the kid-glove is the enemy of meerschaum, since it covers the natural polish with an artificial coating, vaguely oily and indelible. Believe me, it's true." If that sort of fetish suits you, and you do not mind losing one of the pleasures of a pipe – its touch – then go ahead. A simpler precaution is to avoid smoking a meerschaum with a damp hand and to hold it by the mouthpiece. If the bowl gets dirty, it is sufficient to clean it with a paintbrush or a piece of cotton-wool dampened with soapy water, then rinse it with clear water, avoiding the inside of the bowl and drying it with care. Finally, if the colouring of a meerschaum treated with whale-oil is irregular giving it a poor appearance, hand it to a master pipe-maker who will give it another whale-oil treatment. This cannot, however, be done a second time.

Cleaning is not the only aspect of the care of a pipe. As the pipe is smoked, a layer of carbon

The ashtray is the pipe's ally, giving it time to cool. But the smoker should avoid knocking the rim of the bowl when emptying the ash (facing page).

accumulates inside the bowl. One fine day, the smoker will find that he cannot put in enough tobacco, and that the tobacco has lost its flavour. A tobacco which had previously been full of aroma becomes insipid. The signal is unequivocal: it is time to de-carbonize ("de-carb") the bowl. The operation must be undertaken with care. The smoker should take out sufficient carbon to revive the pipe, but not too much, lest the briar be damaged. Most smokers leave a layer of one to two millimetres thickness, while others, better advised, check the thickness regularly. A de-carbed bowl must

after a de-carb a pipe is never quite the same. Perhaps they are right. This regular – sometimes daily – operation is best recommended to fastidious and patient smokers. The tools needed are the same, namely pipe tools, reamers or knives. On the other hand, meerschaum pipes need regular reaming. For one thing the accumulation of carbon impairs the absorbant quality of meerschaum and, as the carbon swells under heat (unlike meerschaum), there is the risk of splitting the bowl. The de-carb of meerschaum requires a fine sharp blade, applying light pressure so as not to compress

The lighter with a horizontal flame was specially designed for pipe-smokers (right).

present the same surface as a new one, having the same shape, albeit slightly reduced. Most tobacconists stock a cylindrical tool with short teeth, called a pipe scraper. The efficiency of a toothed tool to achieve a regular de-carb is doubtful, but a pipe-reamer is a better proposition. The ideal is a small blade, sharp enough to scrape the carbon with ease. I use the triangular blade of my Laguiole knife, which I find ideal. But take care not to let the blade of the knife slip, in case it cuts into the briar.

Another technique, commonly used, is to scrape the carbon regularly before it gets to the point when the pipe needs a de-carb. Those who favour this method maintain that it guarantees that the pipe will keep its freshness;

the material which would again compromise the absorbant quality of the meerschaum. To avoid cutting into the meerschaum, a round-ended knife, like a butter knife, is recommended.

For those who may not have the time, who feel lazy or are clumsy, a specialist pipe-shop or a repair craftsman will undertake the job.

ACCESSORIES

Pipe-cleaners, knives, scrapers or reamers to de-carbonize are all part of the necessary accessories of the smoker. Without them, he could not indulge in his pleasure.

In the first place, there is a small metal instrument, quite cheap, called a pipe-tool, which is multi-functional. Without it, the smoker feels lost. It is normally made up of three parts which swivel around a central ring. One resembles a small spoon, sometimes with one serrated edge, which can be used to empty a pipe and even scrape it if the smoker fears the results of using a knife. A second is a simple metal spike which is useful to clear an obstruction. The last has a circular flat end and is simply a pipe-tamper. There are many versions of the instrument, from the simplest to the most sophisticated. The smoker would be advised to choose the simplest, therefore the cheapest, as this small tool runs the risk of getting lost!

While the simplest tool is advisable, such as the screwdriver suggested earlier for cleaning, there are some simple cheap tools that are made of soft steel and may bend during use. On the other hand, a good quality (even silver-plated) tool can be a welcome gift to a smoker. The same applies to pipe tampers. It is a pity that tampers which include miniature statuettes are so difficult to find today. They are useful to keep in the pocket, and since they often depicted historical or other personalities, they are the basis of some interesting collections. Falcon Pipes, in England, still supply a tamper that fits a finger, thus eliminating the risk of burning fingers!

The so-called "hedgehog" scraper can be dangerous, since it may tear the interior of a briar bowl. By contrast there is, in Britain, the Buttner reamer which has movable blades that can adapt to most sizes of pipes. A very efficient scraper came some years ago from Switzerland; it consists of four different-sized scrapers with four slotted blades. There is a single handle that will take the scrapers, but it is an instrument for use at home, although the box in which it is contained can be carried in the pocket or, better still, in a briefcase. A special tool which had a variable blade came from Japan in the 1970s and created quite a stir; it was in effect like a pocket nozzle chuck and was extremely well made. The only problem was that is was fairly expensive in relation to other products, and in England and continental Europe the sales were minimal. It can still be found in the United States and there may also be some stocks in Europe.

Another indispensable accessory, particularly for those who do not like their pockets to bulge with a metal tin or too large a packet, is the tobacco pouch. Since the disappearance of the oiled-silk pouch and the "bull-purse" from Spain, the smoker has to be content with a simple leather pouch, available in various sizes, which often has an interior lining made from a rubber-based material. All materials are suitable, provided that they are waterproof and do not risk altering the aroma of the tobacco. Many smokers add a humidifying agent. In this domain, imagination knows no bounds. The classical example is a piece of potato or carrot, since these vegetables do not impair the taste of tobacco. Others prefer to add orange or lemon peel, which is meant to freshen the tobacco. But the best of all is to obtain a small piece of meerschaum from a pipe-maker, wet it and place it in the pouch. This method is quite efficient and avoids the nasty surprise of finding that the potato has gone rotten . . . which would also affect the aroma.

The best material for the lining of pouches has always been the subject of argument. Originally, latex rubber was considered the best, but plastic materials were then introduced. Latex rubber had the disadvantage of perishing relatively quickly, although manufacturers could replace it. Unfortunately, costs rose and there came a time when it was no dearer to buy a new pouch than to have an old one repaired. In the long run, technology won the day, and more resistant rubber is now available. Plastic linings are found on cheaper pouches and can be as satisfactory as rubber, but smokers expect a rubber-based lining on the better-quality pouches.

However, to keep tobacco at home or in the office, a tobacco jar is the best. It is indispensable to smokers who indulge in making up their own mixtures from tobaccos bought in the shops. The range of jars is quite wide. Modern tobacco jars may contain a built-in humidifier. Older jars – often in stoneware, porcelain, clay or sometimes metal – are just as efficient, provided that the smoker controls the humidity and that they have proper sealed lids. Apart from the same humidifying agents as are used in pouches, the best being meerschaum, one can

Briar and silver. This silver-mounted bulldog "Cad" is resting on the silver lid of a tobacco-jar, which itself is made of ceramic. These silver and gold jars and cigarette boxes, adorned with tortoise-shell and precious stones, are the work of Birmingham goldsmiths and silversmiths, dating from the turn of the century (above).

use damp blotting paper placed inside the lid of the jar, or a piece of wet sponge inside a small perforated metal box. Old jars are sometimes cheaper than modern ones, and smokers are often attracted by their decorative quality which, according to antiquarians, represents a good investment.

STORING OR RACKING PIPES

The storing – or racking – of pipes is a sensitive subject, as there are two distinct schools of thought: those partisan of the bowl at the top and those of the bowl at the bottom. The arguments raised concern the best way to rid a pipe of humidity just after smoking. The Anglo-Saxon side, with Alfred Dunhill in the lead, advises that the bowl should be at the bottom, as the humidity concentrated in the bowl is absorbed by the carbon and dries naturally in the air. On the other side, the partisans of the bowl to the top ask if it is really necessary to flood the bowl with disagreeable "juice", since the mouthpiece can easily be cleaned. Both theories have their value and their respective supporters can be reconciled by the ingenious compromise of inserting a pipe-cleaner which will absorb residual humidity whatever the position of the pipe. In any case, a pipe which has just been smoked will not benefit from being confined in a closed container, such as a box or a pipe-bag, for a few hours. This is particularly true of meerschaum pipes; put away while still warm in a case meant for protection while travelling, they will soon acquire a disagreeable bitter taste. Even when cold, a meerschaum should not be confined to its case. But the smoker should definitely avoid exposing a meerschaum treated with whale-oil to heat, such as sunlight or a spotlight. The oil could melt on the exposed area and would run elsewhere, thus upsetting the even coloration.

Taking into account the individual's preferences, any method is fine for storing pipes. Of course, there are special pipe-racks conceived for the purpose, but they are not always practical, as the sizes of pipes do not always conform with the prepared spaces. As the object of the exercise is to protect the pipes from undue shocks, dust and other domestic "attacks", the best thing is to put them away once cold – except meerschaums – in a box, a drawer or a glass cabinet. Certain firms, such as Savinelli, produce small glass or closed cabinets, specially made for pipes, inside which they can be racked.

The types of pipe-rack available in Britain begins with the single pipe stand, which may be in wood or metal. Years ago Italian single stands in ceramic were very popular. There are other stands for two or three pipes, in which pipes can be rested, and actual racks (that hold pipes with the bowls at the bottom) for anything from three to eight pipes. Racks taking more than that number are normally up-market products. Their designs are quite modern and teak is often used, although models in other hard woods – such as oak – are found. One long-standing model is the "five-bar-gate" – which looks like a gate and has been manufactured and sold in Britain since the beginning of the century; there is evidence that it was already popular in the last quarter of the nineteenth century.

Pipe ashtrays are also available to smokers. They normally have a cork "knocker" in the middle which enables the tobacco to be knocked out of the pipe-bowl without endangering the pipe. Provided the action is carried out while holding the bowl firmly, there is no risk to the fitting.

To choose one's pipe, to know how to smoke it and to look after it well, will make it a life-long companion. This is the measure of the real passion that characterizes the relationship between a smoker and the object of his pleasure; a special relationship in which freedom, sensibility and fantasy come into force, as the smoker may own several pipes – sometimes dozens or hundreds – from which he will pick his favourite according to circumstances. This contrasts sharply with the automatic and slavish habit of cigarette-smoking. And if the cigar is closer to the pipe, it is because it also arouses in the smoker the passion of the gourmet. But it is only the pipe which creates a special sort of magic.

Storing pipes has never been the least important task of the smoker: shocks, dust and heat can be fatal. This English smokers' casket, dating from 1820, was used for travelling. It contains three meerschaum pipes, which should not be confined for too long. The casket is made of amaranth and adorned with brass fittings and also contains a ceramic pipe as well as various accessories (below).

Sir Walter Raleigh's pipe-case dates from 1617, a year before his death. The case protected two clay pipes, two removable mouthpieces and a pipe-tamper shaped like a finger (above). There is nothing like a clay pipe to enable the smoker to appreciate the flavour of tobacco. The picture (facing page) shows a collection on pipe-racks.

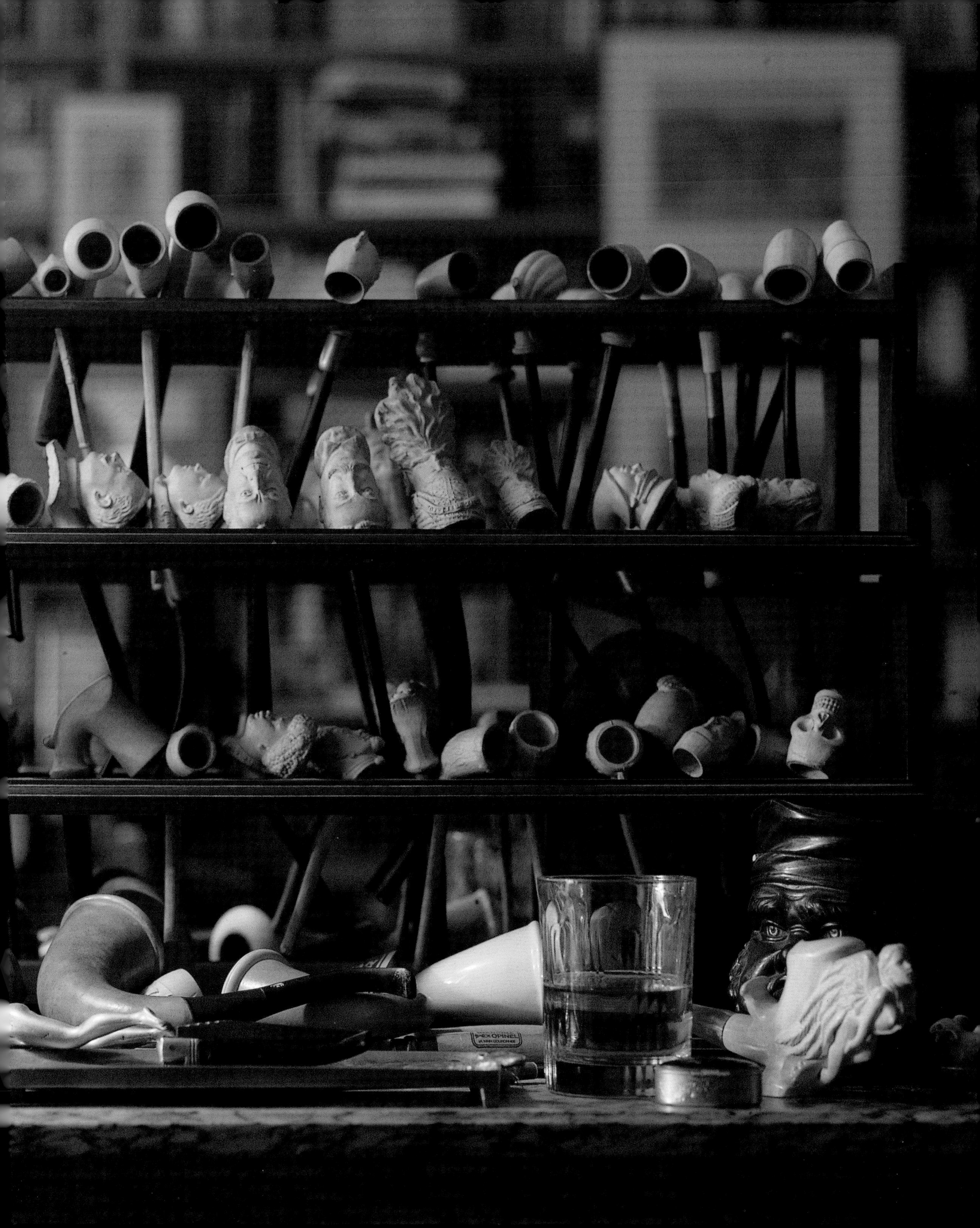
OPINEL

PASSION AND CREATION

Apart from the simple smokers, the most enthusiastic of whom meet in pipe-clubs, or associations, there are two types of people who live their lives "under the sign of the pipe": the collectors and the pipe-makers. For them the passion for pipes is not just a question of smoking; some do not even smoke. They consider a pipe as an object of platonic love rather than a source of pleasure. Even if their sometimes feverish activities make them spend their spare time and even their working hours on their passion, discovering antique and secondhand shops, and other sources, and doing up a unique piece, the ultimate aim is "contemplation". They are ready to do anything for the beauty, scarcity and perfection of a piece. Thus, above their differences, collectors and creators have the same aim, to meet absolute criteria and conduct a never-ending search.

THE COLLECTOR'S PASSION

There is a distinction between those who collect for sheer pleasure, in other words those who buy and own an important number of contemporary pieces to smoke, and those who have a passion for antique and exotic pipes. The first are ardent smokers, but the others not necessarily so; for them, what counts is the beauty, the rarity or the historical value of the object. Those among the latter group who smoke the pipes in their collection are rare. Not only do they want to avoid damaging them, but also they respect the history of the pipes which occasionally have emotional backgrounds for those who own them.

We had to meet an important collector of clay pipes in order to find an exception to that principle. When Alain Demoly received us in his Paris apartment (a true museum to the glory of Gambier, Fiolet and Dumeril-Leurs), he was smoking with a great deal of pleasure a Gambier Jacob, the best-selling pipe of the nineteenth century in France and elsewhere. "Clay pipes are the best," he explained, "as the flavour of tobacco develops fully." But Alain Demoly smokes only the Jacob, a pipe which

can still be found in quantity, new and at reasonable prices, in antique and secondhand shops. He would never think of smoking one of his finest and rarest pipes, which other collectors may still be looking for, but which he has found. Among the best, certain pieces in varied colours reveal remarkably fine work: for example, the faun holding Pan pipes, a superb creation of the Fiolet company which is the top masterpiece of the Alain Demoly collection. There are also some of the best of the Gambier production, numbered 400 to 500, probably created by an anonymous craftsman, such as the head of the Marquis de La Rochejaquelein, the leader of the Vendée uprising, a Charlotte Corday, a Punch and a Chinese mandarin. Among the rarest is Gambier's model 800, a fine head of Christ, which had to be withdrawn from sale soon after its launch, following protests from the Church. Interestingly, and this is a common trait among collectors, it is not necessarily the best or rarest pipes which Alain Demoly prefers. He looks very fondly at a Gambier representing a little boy on a chamber-pot, or the one depicting a woman emptying hers out of the window, or also the one commemorating the arrival of the first railway train at Rennes. Examining these fine pieces, it is easy to understand the attraction of the popular imagery of the French clay pipes of the nineteenth century. In those days, pipes were cheap and readily available in all towns and villages. Today, these pipes tell us more about the daily life of ordinary men and women than our history books do. They take you back in time.

Alain Demoly started his collection by accident some thirty years ago. While he does not remember which was his first purchase, he has not forgotten the circumstances: he had bought it as a gift for his uncle, François Demoly, who was one of the greatest and most expert pipe-collectors in France. But Alain liked the pipe . . . and he kept it for himself. A little later, he bought another. His uncle encouraged him and as young Alain was starting out in life, his uncle advised him to stick to clay pipes, the

Clays, meerschaums and briars, from the antiquarian Denise Corbier in Paris, where collectors from all over the world gather (preceding pages). A beautiful white-clay head of Diana of Poitiers, which more than equals the fine meerschaums. This was a showpiece, to be exhibited in a shop window. It is the work of Gambier, the most famous clay pipe-maker of the nineteenth century (facing page).

A fine piece from the nineteenth century: a coloured satyr by Fiolet. Rare and sought after, it belongs to Alain Demoly (left).

cheapest. From that wise advice was born a life-long passion.

Uncle François, an industrialist whose means allowed him to limit his acquisitions to exceptional pieces, started collecting soon after the Second World War, and he continued to enlarge his collection until his death in 1991. It is an extraordinary collection which includes pipes of all ages and materials. The collection was unfortunately decimated by a theft some fifteen years ago. The stolen pieces included one of the finest in history, carved in ivory by a Dieppe craftsman in the seventeenth or eighteenth century. The pipe represented the bust of a woman, and can still be seen illustrated in André Paul Bastien's book *La Pipe* – unfortunately now out of print. The richness and finesse of the execution of this small sculpture has rarely been equalled. The charming face of the young woman is crowned by a wreath representing a vine, with grapes and leaves below which some delicate curls are visible. She has a ruff around her neck and a bodice of fine lace. Below the bust, the base of the pipe is formed by the feathered neck and head of a bird of prey. There is a hinged cover on top of the bowl shaped like a crown, also in ivory, which makes one think that the pipe represents a queen. Behind the head, a sheaf of leaves and fruit hangs from the stem which would have taken a mouthpiece.

The ivory pipes made in Dieppe were so fine that one wonders whether their owners, who must have been wealthy smokers, dared smoke them! If you ask Jean-Charles Rhein, tobacco merchant in the Swiss city of Geneva, also a great collector, which are his favourites, he answers: "The ivory pipes from Dieppe, and my greatest regret as a collector is that I sold the one I had." And Jean-Charles Rhein relates the sad episode of this magnificent piece, representing the bust of a young woman with a pearl necklace and a lace collar, with the base, strangely enough, in the shape of the head of a fish. He had acquired it for about a thousand francs from a secondhand dealer. A few weeks later, he had a visit from a friend, the Spanish

collector Javier Flores who was so taken by the pipe that he offered him eight thousand francs for it. At the time, Jean-Charles Rhein wanted to buy five fine meerschaum pipes from an antique-dealer, but he could not afford it. With eight thousand francs, the purchase became possible and so a deal was concluded. Jean-Charles Rhein learnt later how rare these pipes were. If you have one for sale, do not hesitate to contact him! It would join one of the best collections in the world, some three hundred pieces, some of which are on show in the window of *Tabac Rhein,* rue du Mont-Blanc, in Geneva.

Why does one become a pipe-collector? It is not necessarily because one smokes a pipe. It was Jean-Charles Rhein's profession which led him to collect tobacco-related objects and he also has a number of snuff-boxes, rasps, cases and other articles. As for Carlos Armero, an international lawyer from Madrid who owns about two thousand pipes from all parts of the world, the reason for his being a collector, as he says himself, is "in the blood". Perhaps, "in the genes" would be nearer the mark: his father collected beer-mugs, his mother old scissors, one brother collects door-stops and another post-cards. So how did Carlos' interest in pipes start? "I smoked a pipe in England," he answers, "where I was a student, to give myself a more English air. But, in fact, it started in Macucu!" Macucu? It is a small village near Libreville, in Gabon. The future lawyer, then aged twenty-three, was there on a visit. In the market, Carlos found an old man selling a variety of ethnic brick-à-brac and, among the goods, he spotted a fine old African pipe. Carlos did not have much spare cash and the dignified old gentleman had no real idea of the value of the object. A deal was struck by the exchange of a fountain pen for the pipe. The lawyer from Madrid does not remember now whether the pipe was in wood or metal, as it has since been lost. But, from that day, none of his trips, private or professional, finishes without the acquisition of some pipes. he admits that he is a "travel collector", and that each of his pipes,

It took thirty years of dedicated searching for Alain Demoly to gather one of the best collections of clay pipes in the world. Facing page, from left to right and from top to bottom, are some of his favourites: *Young Dautan,* a self-portrait of one of Gambier's best sculptors; *Fighting Zouave* (Dutel-Gisclon); *Tom Thumb* (Gambier); *Little Pisser* (sic) (Gambier): *Joko* (Gambier) and *Punch* (Gambier). Above left: *The public scribe* (Gambier).

Amongst other treasures, the French collector Eugene Jance owns these pipes in rare wood lined with metal, probably carved by convicts or sailors in the early nineteenth century (left).

Two fine pieces from the Eugene Jance collection: copies of Turkish chibouks made in France. Made in clay, they are decorated with embossed silver gilt and their long stems are covered with velvet. Dated 1820, they reflect the oriental influence of the time (below).

with the detours he had to make and the people he has met to acquire them, evokes the marvellous countries that he has visited and provides a particular souvenir of his travels.

The public is not able to see Carlos Armero's collection which is lovingly kept in the special cabinets which are so prominent in his Madrid apartment. On the other hand, it is well presented in his fine book, *Antique Pipes,* which is available in English. He dedicated his book to Dominique Delalande, Parisian antiquary and collector with the short phrase *A mi dueno* (to my Master). Dominique Delalande is one of the world experts on ancient pipes. Originally from Brittany, a lover of the sea and of boats, he is passionate about tobacco-related objects. This passion dates back to the time some thirty years ago, when he was struck by the sight of the naked form of a pretty woman adorning a

meerschaum cigar-holder. Today, Dominique Delalande undoubtedly owns some of the finest antique pipes in the world. Some of these meerschaums are more than up to the standard of those in the Austrian Tobacco Museum in Vienna, which is the world's leading museum in this field. One example is a bowl which represents the scene of the battle of Arbela, when Darius was defeated by Alexander the Great, probably a diplomatic gift given by Austria to the Russian Tsar Alexander I, who defeated Napoleon. Dominique Delalande's ambition is to gather together all these marvellous pieces in a museum. Among them, his favourite is a simple meerschaum, a "window piece" which was for a long time seen in the Astley shop in London. It is a simple piece as the bowl is just a portrait, an idealized portrayal of Roustan, the mameluke bodyguard of Napoleon; but it is sublime, because the Viennese artist who carved it, in about 1875, knew how to give the fierce face an almost lifelike expression.

In Lausanne, there is another passionate col-

Unusual collectors' pieces, these "Tophane" pipes turned red while being baked. They were made, in the nineteenth century, in the district of Constantinople which bears the same name. "The bowls, made from a fine soft clay, are decorated by the potters with various motifs, using special rollers. They are also marked with a small stamp. They do not carbonize like French pipes and are very cheap. They are used in huge quantities," wrote Theophile Gautier in 1852 (facing page).

This fine meerschaum pipe was acquired by Alfred Dunhill in about 1920. It represents the battle of Sadowa (1866) when the Prussians beat the Austrians; the scene shown is the capture of the Austrian cavalry standard by a Prussian officer with three dragoons. Made at the end of the nineteenth century, this was a showpiece which has, of course, never been smoked (right).

This is the favourite pipe of the Paris antique collector Dominique Delalande: it portrays Roustan, the mameluke bodyguard of Napoleon, magnificently carved in Vienna around 1873 (facing page). One can imagine the pleasure it gave Baron Erwin Vielder von Gorz to smoke this charming flowergirl. He was the happy owner of this meerschaum and amber pipe made in Vienna in 1860. It is now in the Pipe Museum of Gavirate in Italy (below).

lector who is on the point of gathering a collection worthy of a museum. Jacques Schmied is an antique dealer who specializes in ancient arms and sculpture, but loves the pipes that he does not sell; he has opened his museum in the old vaulted cellar of his shop. The event took place on March 21, 1979, on his sixty-fifth birthday. But he had been brooding on the idea for a long time. It was born the day that Jacques Schmied had two American customers whom he had left alone in his office for a short while. They were on their knees, admiring a very fine meerschaum on the bottom shelf of a cabinet overloaded with pipes. This single cabinet was not capacious enough to take the cardboard boxes in which were housed hundreds of pipes, nor was it worthy of the contents. Today, Jacques Schmied owns about two thousand pieces. He does not select them for their beauty, only for their rarity and historical value. Some of them are rare indeed, such as this large pipe from Lorraine, dating from the last century, carved from the root of a rose tree; the artisan knew how to go round the knots, bulges and other natural features while managing with extreme dexterity to avoid the parts allocated to the bowl and the stem. Also spectacular and rare are those pipes made of glass in the eighteenth and nineteenth century, at Murano near Venice, by master glass-blowers, who occa-

sionally "blew" pipes. They could not be smoked and were meant for decoration. One, which is about forty centimetres long, is artistically shaped like a bird, with blue wings. If you ask Jacques Schmied which pipes he prefers, he does not name these, nor the magnificent nineteenth century pipes made from shells. He answers simply: "Those that my wife gave me." Even when they are top experts in the field, collectors are often great sentimentalists.

Was this the case with Baroness Alice de Rothschild? Apparently not. One must not judge by appearances when considering this wealthy lady. A member of the Austrian branch of the family, who was born in Frankfurt in 1847, she was brought up in Vienna and then settled in England. Little is known about her, except that she never wanted to exhibit her collection; she was a difficult character, known for displays of opulence and an extreme passion for the trees and flowers of her garden. The rest is a mystery.

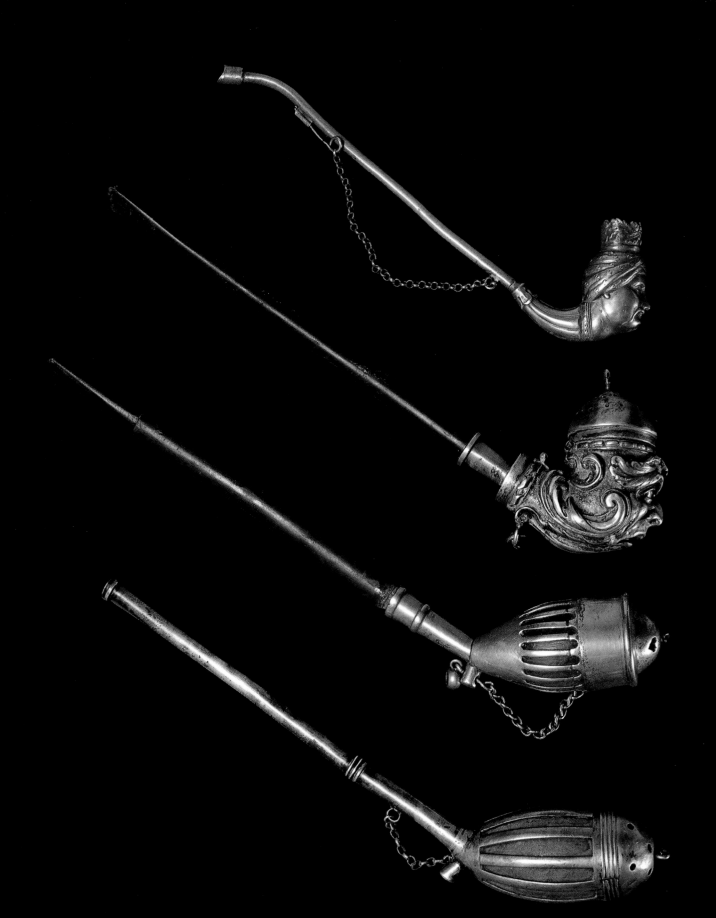

What concerns us is her fabulous collection of pipes. Why did Alice de Rothschild collect pipes, and how did she manage to gather all these treasures? Francine Guibert, curator of the municipal library of Grasse, where the collection is now on show, regrets that she has not the faintest idea! Neither do those who have written books about the Baroness, but have never mentioned this strange collection.

The Baroness gathered in Villa Victoria, above Grasse, four hundred and fifty masterpieces. Many people have spoken or written about her property and her garden with its thousands of flowers. The Baroness used to spend six months there every year, from October until March, and had transformed it into a very large display case for her horticultural hobby, which assumed enormous proportions. In his book, *The Gardens of Fortune*, Marcel Gaucher, son of the Baroness' head gardener, describes the formidable character of the employer whom he calls the "dictatorial gardener". Queen Victoria visited her occasionally. On one such visit, the Queen of Great Britain and Empress of India accidentally walked on a flowerbed. The Baroness went red in the face and shouted: "Get out!" to the sovereign who was hardly used to such a form of address. One single weed, one unfortunate fallen leaf on a path, was enough to rouse her temper. One bemused visitor said: "Along the paths, at intervals, you meet a gardener waiting for a few leaves to fall, so that he can pick them up."

We would have liked to know as much about the Baroness' passion for pipes. Nevertheless, we still have the pleasure of admiring her magnificent collection at the municipal library of Grasse, which was entrusted with it in 1927, by Edmond de Rothschild, Alice's nephew. The Baroness who, in spite of the conventions of her status and of her time had never married, had then been dead for only five years. The pipes shown at Grasse come from all eras and countries: exceptional pottery pieces from Staffordshire, some superb examples from Ulm, some porcelain pipes from Saxony and, naturally, a great number of meerschaums. These perhaps offer a clue: Alice was brought up in Vienna, the "capital" of meerschaums where

some of the finest works of meerschaum art were produced.

We could also evoke the passion of numerous other collectors, such as the American Benjamin Rapaport, whose dedication prompted him to produce his book *A Complete Guide to Collecting Antique Pipes*, an authoritative work. Tony Irving is another collector, from England, whose museum on the south coast attracted thousands of visitors every year. Alas, this museum is now closed and Tony's collection, reputed to be some sixty thousand pieces (pipes and related items) has now been dispersed. The Dunhill family was conscious from the start of the importance of gathering a collection which can be seen in London; Dunhill also has some of the most important archives on the subject. There are others in England who keep a low profile and whose

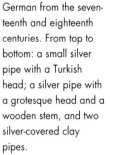

One of the best private pipe collections belongs to Jacques Schmied and is housed in his Lausanne museum. Facing page, these four pipes are thought to be German from the seventeenth and eighteenth centuries. From top to bottom: a small silver pipe with a Turkish head; a silver pipe with a grotesque head and a wooden stem, and two silver-covered clay pipes.

How to be imaginative with a mouthpiece. This one is transformed into a bird's beak . . . This woodcock in meerschaum and amber was made in France in the nineteenth century. It belongs to Jacques Schmied (above).

Two luxury cases for the complete smoker. Each contains meerschaum bowls for a pipe, a cigar and a cigarette. The two subjects, the skull and the eagle's claw holding an egg are classic designs (below, Jacques Schmied collection).

185

An absolutely perfect straight-grain, hand-made by the Danish maker W Ø Larsen. It is the magnificent grain of the Corsican briar which dictated the shape of the bowl. The mouthpiece, also carefully hand-made, contributes to the harmony of the whole pipe (facing page, above).

The tobacco merchant W Ø Larsen, founder of the family business in 1864 (facing page, below).

collections are known to only a few. However, J Trevor Barton, for example, has been featured in magazine articles – ethnic pipes are one of his specialities. Without all these passionate lovers of pipes, the historical traces spread round the world since the sixteenth century would have disappeared. What of the future? Which, among the pipes made today, will be in the forefront of the collections of the next century? It will certainly be those created by the genius of contemporary pipe-makers.

While there are great, important and known collectors of pipes, there are also many who are unsung and unknown. There is for example the head of a long-established British pipe company who is known to have an important collection of antique pipes, but who does not broadcast the fact; his anonymity should be respected. There are also those, like the policeman friend of the editor of the British trade journal *Tobacco,* who used to visit all antique and brick-à-brac shops to find specimens to his liking; he always consulted the editor on his finds. In Britain, there are also the members of the "bottle collectors" clubs, who rummage through garbage dumps in search of old bottles: over the years, they have literally unearthed thousands of old clay pipes and, in the process, have become collectors and enthusiasts. They have also become extremely knowledgeable.

Members of pipe-clubs, which were mostly created in the 1960s and 1970s, discovered through their affiliation, a passion for pipes, old and new. They started collecting new pipes, which they smoked, and also antique specimens, when they could afford it. Some also found that they could trade some pieces or have them sold by auction in order to raise capital to buy others. Their interests are varied, like the man who claimed that he probably had the largest collection of Lovat shapes in England! At the same time, some smokers who have bought or received many pipes over the years, discover one day that they in fact have a col-

lection! It is only when such smokers die that these collections come to light. Some interesting collections have emerged that way, sometimes with antique clays and meerschaums that have been in a family for several generations.

A passion for old briars has grown in the United States, where clubs have been created for the sole purpose of collecting, exchanging and trading what they consider to be "antique" briars, known as "estate pipes". These collectors mostly seek known brands, such as Dunhill, Charatan, Peterson, Barling, Comoys and others, and very often they favour large shapes. While some collectors barter, sell or exchange, they also like to be able to smoke the pipes – a habit that surprises and amuses British and Continental pipe-smokers. Pipe-fairs are organized and they attract collectors from all corners of the United States whenever such gatherings take place. Some pieces are sold for hundreds and occasionally thousands of dollars. This also explains the popularity of the products of the Italian craftsmen, such as Castello, Savinelli and others. They enabled American collectors to get new and unique models which in their eyes would increase in value provided that they were kept in good condition, even if smoked. But there are also collectors whose purse is limited and who specialize, like the collector from New York who has a huge collection of lesser-known brands; his aim is to obtain specimens of all – or at least most – brands ever produced.

The collection of pipes also encourages the collection of related articles. Some choose to collect pipe-tampers, for example, as there were a great number made in the last century and also early in this century. Brass was a popular material, depicting historical or fictional personages, animal heads or birds. Some were also made in silver or gold. Similarly, there are collectors of tobacco-jars – who are not necessarily smokers. They may be collectors of known makes of pottery, but also of brass or pewter items. Finally, collectors also seek the literary side of pipes, mostly in books, but also

The first W Ø Larsen pipes were made by Ole W Ø Larsen, the fourth generation of the family firm; he is seen here examining a crusted-top pipe (left).

catalogues, leaflets and anything written about tobacco or pipes.

THE CREATOR'S PASSION

Today, the majority of pipe-makers work with briar, the material which dominates the contemporary pipe industry. For pipe-artists, the main quality of briar is its intrinsic beauty. It possesses a fine texture, a grain from "flame" to bird's-eye which gives smokers, apart from the warmth of a natural living material, the harmony of its regular design. The art of the master pipe-maker is to enhance its natural appearance, without com-promising the qualities required for a good pipe: lightness, regular combustion, easy draught. Such is the vocation, since the end of the nineteenth century, of a number of prestigious European makers. Between tradition and modernity, the art of pipe-making is transmitted from generation to generation in order to create pipes for the most fastidious smokers. These important houses, known the world over, are above all others

British, Italian, Danish, German and French. We should add a few individual pipe-makers who, because they work alone, by their very nature have a limited production, and rarely attain universal fame.

Denmark. We start with the kingdom of Denmark, to honour this country which revolutionized the art of briar pipe-making, and which has almost as many smokers as France or England, although it has a population of just under six million inhabitants. There the reigning pipe family is W Ø Larsen. Their palace is a fine retail shop, which also contains a museum of antique pipes. It is in the heart of old Copenhagen and has been in existence since 1864. It was started as a small tobacco shop. As it grew, the firm imported larger and larger quantities of cigars, cigarettes and pipe-tobacco, and opened a wholesale department. After the First World War, W Ø Larsen started to manu-facture his own cigars and pipe-tobaccos. Manufacturing activities ceased some twenty years ago, but currently the company offers some four hundred different tobaccos, forty of which are

To mark its Jubilee in 1992, the manufacturer Stanwell produced a six-pipe presentation case, each pipe representing a decade. The pipe of the 1990s was created by Tom Etlang, Master Pipe-maker who collaborated with Stanwell and invented a colouring process to enhance the contrasts of the grain (right).

under the Larsen label, as well as a selection that customers can mix themselves. At the same time, Larsen sold imported pipes until the 1950s. It was then that Ole W Ø Larsen, representing the fourth generation of the family in the business, thought that pipe design needed improving, as he considered that the pipes available at the time were monotonous and dull. He therefore decided to create his own models, to be made entirely by hand. Starting on a small scale, this manufacture of extremely well-made and imaginative models soon earned a well-deserved reputation all over Europe. An interesting detail: the firm's pipes, sufficiently original to be recognized, had no distinctive stamping on the stem or the mouthpiece. In the catalogues of the 1950s all the features are still present which gave the pipes their universal reputation of being among the best briars. W Ø Larsen normally prefers old Corsican briar – now rare – to create the perfect harmony between design and texture. Thus were born, from the start, pipe designs which were as varied as they were original. They were sometimes bizarre, with oval bowl, on a

slant, and well-opened tops, or with pointed bottoms, as well as a great number that are sometimes called "flowers", that is, with the outer rough crust of the briar root left untouched and unpolished. But, in each case, the daring design enhances the shape of the pipe, its grain and the line of the "flame". Forty years on, the concept of Ole W Ø Larsen is being perpetuated by his son Niels, whose favourite pastime is to create fine pipe-tampers in horn. Even if the "flowers" and the pointed bowls have almost disappeared, the originality of design is being maintained in a growing range of models. This range consists as much of regular hand-made models as of shapes of exceptional straight or bird's-eye grains which are grouped under the Perles label and are among the world's most expensive pipes. These models are sometimes fitted with reconstituted amber mouthpieces, made from real amber powder and synthetic resin according to a secret formula. This formula is jealously kept by Mrs Olrik (not to be confused with Orlik, a leading Danish tobacco manufacturer), widow of a famous Danish pipe-maker,

Since Anne Julie Rasmussen and Ruth Eckert retired, Else Larsen (who works at Larsen's but is not related) must be the only woman in the world today who can design and produce pipes (left).

journalist and author of several works on pipes. Among the current masterpieces of the company, we should mention the Rustica series – pipes which have half the bowl (upper or lower) etched and coloured, while the rest has a natural finish. Finally, some Larsen pipes feature magnificent bands made of horn, ebony or palm-tree wood.

The contemporary art of briar pipes, so well illustrated by W Ø Larsen, owes

everything to the genius of a precursor, Sixten Ivarsson. The "inventor of Danish designs" was, in fact, a Swede who had settled in Copenhagen in 1930. The first manifestation of his vocation came in 1946, when the now-famous pipemaker made a pipe for his own use. Five years later, after having carried out pipe repairs for a Copenhagen trader, he opened a small workshop which was to lead to the revolution in briar pipe design. At the time pipe production followed basic rules and only carved pipes and special fittings provided innovations. Ivarsson broke the trend. For each of his entirely hand-made pipes he invented a new concept. More often than not, the briar root inspired his creations. But respect for the material is not enough to explain his genius. Above all, a perfect mastery of harmony and balance made each of his creations a masterpiece of purity and elegance, as well as of inventiveness. Ivarsson's own secret "chemistry" and originality created pieces which will never age.

He quickly gained his reputation, which attracted a great number of smokers to Copenhagen. Shortly after setting up the Stanwell company – whose brand name he finally adopted – Poul Nielsen persuaded Ivarsson to work for him. Extraordinary freehands were born out of this collaboration. These were reintroduced later in Stanwell series, marked with the

famous crowned "S" and sold all over the world. The actual prestige of Stanwell, the leading Danish pipe-manufacturer who has just celebrated his half-century, owes a great deal to Ivarsson. Stanwell's Anniversary presentation case contains six pipes, two of which are signed by Ivarsson.

In Germany, the country which is Stanwell's leading export market, the best selling model is No 11, a copy of a freehand created by Ivarsson. Its feature is a short but large bowl, the top of which has been slightly rounded.

Now over eighty years of age, Sixten Ivarsson still works all alone in his Copenhagen workshop. He has ceased his collaboration with Stanwell and works only on his own account. The majority of his production, not more than two hundred pipes a year each marked "An Ivarsson Product", is exported to Japan and the United States. All that is left for European smokers is to dream or meditate on the words of the genial contemporary pipe-maker, who was asked if he knew the "trick" for smoking well: "Let us say that one must breathe in the same rhythm as the pipe. That's all", he answered simply, in his legendary gruff tone.

We cannot leave Denmark without citing some of those who emulated Ivarsson; they include his son Lars Ivarsson and three others who worked for Stanwell: Anne Julie Rasmussen, one of the rare women who have created pipes, together with another Danish lady who carries out her art with W Ø Larsen and also Ruth Eckert from Vauen. In addition, there are Tom Etlang and Jess Chonowitsh, the masterpipe maker Toa (now working on his own after leaving the admirable house of Svenborg where he had been co-founder), Paul Ilstedt and Ingo Garbe (a German who settled on the small Danish island of Laeso). They all contribute,

In 1941, Alfred Henry Dunhill kept the business going even after the London shop had been damaged by German bombing (right). He was the eldest son of the original Alfred Dunhill and he was an expert on tobacco and pipes, as well as the author of several books and articles; he expanded the company to what it is today.

in the eyes of connoisseurs of the art, to Denmark being the best kingdom.

United Kingdom and Ireland. In relation to pipes, London seems a very long way away from Copenhagen, as British pipe-makers have mostly kept to the proven classicism of traditional shapes, greatly appreciated by English

and timepieces. In 1904, he created his first pipe. A car-owning customer had complained that he could not smoke his pipe in his open car, and Dunhill made him a pipe with a windshield on the bowl. Thus, the first Dunhill was born, and with it Dunhill's passion for pipe-tobacco. In 1907, he opened his first shop in fashionable St James's Street to cater for

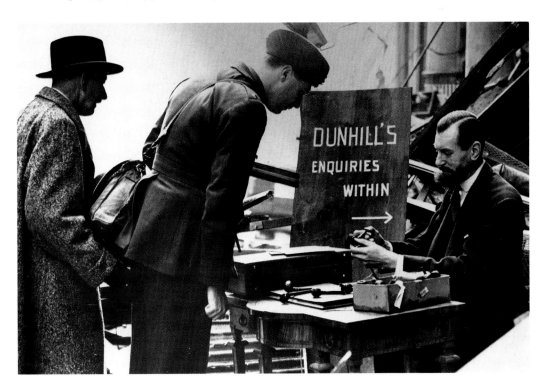

smokers. For them, and for many smokers around the world, a Dunhill pipe is a must. The famous "white spot", inserted into the vulcanite by Alfred Dunhill, to indicate the way to replace the mouthpiece, is the sign of all fine Dunhills and a guarantee of absolute quality. Contrary to many other brands of similar quality, Dunhill has an excellent image worldwide backed by a solid chain of distribution. The company inherited this ideal combination of perfect quality and acute commercial sense from its founder, a genius who could handle anything. Just over a hundred years ago, in 1893, Alfred Dunhill set up his business which dealt with accessories for the carriage trade. With the advent of the automobile, the nature of the business changed quickly. The essential of Alfred Dunhill's genius was his ability to adapt promptly to the new requirements of his customers. First he created a range of products for automobiles, such as overcoats, gloves, goggles

smokers. It was in the sale of cigars, pipes and personalized tobacco mixtures – each recipe being entered in a special register, still used in the Duke Street shop in London – that the company acquired its fame and prestige. Dunhill was not fully satisfied with the pipes he handled and decided to engage two pipe-makers. He set them up in a workshop at 6 Mason's Yard, and gave them a simple aim: produce perfect pipes, whatever the cost. By 1910, the select members of the clubs in St James's and officers of the armed forces could treat themselves to the best pipes in the world, signed Dunhill, at double the price of other pipes. At the same time, Dunhill started to collect all types of articles related to smoking. There is now a permanent exhibition of these articles which represent one of the best collections in the world. The current president of the company, Richard Dunhill, grandson of the founder and a passionate pipe-smoker, con-

An eccentric British pipe: a Dunhill fitted with a golden umbrella to protect the top of the bowl (below).

tinues to add to this collection, some of which is stored in his home outside London. While the current range which comprises twenty-four models in eight finishes is of the highest quality and justifies its prices, it is perhaps regrettable that the creators – the British pipe-makers who work for the brand at Walthamstow, in East London – only produce classic models. The Dunhill production does include a meerschaum, a Calabash and a Churchwarden but even these are classic shapes. At Dunhill's, the real creativity is found in the making of rare freehands, named Collectors and also in limited editions of luxury models, at very high prices. In these special editions, the work of the gold- or silver-smith is added to create, for example, a pipe with an extravagant lid in gold surmounted by an umbrella to protect the top! A pipe of that type, a Billiard fitted with a platinum band inset with diamonds, called rightly the Diamond Pipe, is still for sale – at 96,000 francs – in the Dunhill shop in Paris. We must not forget Alfred Dunhill's own motto: "It must be useful, it must be practical and it must be the best of its type", which remains the standard for the manufacture of Dunhill pipes.

Astley's is a family firm which was founded in 1862 in Jermyn Street, London, and first specialized in meerschaum pipes. It would seem very small compared with Dunhill if its pipes were not so fine. The first thing that strikes you as you enter the art-deco shop, run by Paul Bentley, is simply the number of briars. These fine briars are specially selected, mostly in Calabria for Astleys. Paul Bentley explains what he wants: "The lightest in colour and weight, and the oldest possible. The roots must be at least a hundred years old. They are stored for a year to obtain perfect drying." About three thousand Astley pipes are produced each year. Apart from regular models, the firm's speciality remains hand-made and freehands, the fine making of which justifies their prices. The Astley art is to expose the texture of the wood, its flame-grain or bird's-eye, slightly tinted so as

to create the contrast to respond to the shape of the bowl. But, for Paul Bentley, himself a devoted smoker, the beauty of the briar is not his only concern: "For me," he says, "a pipe must have at least two major qualities. First, it must provide a light smoke, which depends on the quality and age of the root. Then, it must be a magnificent object, which depends on the harmony of the bowl and the mouthpiece which must never be seen as a series-produced piece just fitted to a bowl. Bowl and mouthpiece must jointly contribute, in the same proportions, to the quality and the beauty of the product." Astley has some admirable shapes, such as the Pointed Cutty which reminds one of the old clay pipes with laid-back bowls, pointed heels and slender mouthpieces; and the Barrel Crossgrain which has, as the name implies, a barrel-shaped bowl; and, in particular, the sublime Pointed Dublin, with a bowl like a sharpened blade, although the flame-grain suggests its invisible roundness. Whatever the model or price, all Astley's pipes are marked with a simple white "A" on the mouthpiece.

Let us leave London for Dublin. A welcome invention was the origin of the universal renown of the Irish company, Kapp & Peterson, founded in Dublin in 1875, when the pipe-maker Charles Peterson joined the Kapp brothers, merchants and pipe-makers in the city. This invention dates from 1890, due to the fact that Charles Peterson himself disliked the "juice" which was emitted by wet smoking and which impaired the combustion of tobacco. Today, his System pipe is all the more relevant since humid thick- (and coarse-) cut tobaccos are more widespread. It is simply a reservoir which is bored at the bottom of the stem, near the bowl, and which has a fairly wide opening. This reservoir traps condensation and the particular bore of the stem helps the draught. With the comfort of smokers in mind, Charles Peterson also conceived the ingenious Peterson lip which directs the smoke away from the tongue. The fine classic Bent Army shape fitted with a silver (olive) mount is an

The love that Paul Bentley has for fully-matured Greek and Calabrian briar, carefully selected and dried, is the best guarantee to customers who enter the Astley shop in London (left).

To mark the centenary of the famous "system", Peterson introduced the Sherlock Holmes series, which includes the mythical Calabash of the famous detective, the Original and the Baskerville (facing page).

An inventor of genius: Charles Peterson. His "system" which incorporated a condensation "trap", launched in 1890, is still a feature of current Peterson pipes (above).

The first stage in the transformation of a briar plateau, by Rainer Barbi. The pipe-maker, who works near Hamburg, is one of the briar experts of today (right).

ideal pipe for the informed smoker. Great care is taken in the finish of the pipes, made in a range of three sizes, some are sandblast and some meerschaum. For over a century, the Peterson System has won many converts, amongst whom are well-known pipe-smoking personalities. In 1980, the Dublin company found an old photograph of Mark Twain smoking a pipe that looked like a Peterson, quite large but unusual, the bowl having a long almost flat base. A close look through a magnifying-glass showed that the mount bore the Peterson hallmark. A telephone call to the curator of the Mark Twain Museum in Hannibal, Missouri, confirmed that such a pipe existed, and dated from 1896. To honour the great American writer and to add to the firm's prestige, Peterson decided to revive the model which had not been made since 1900. A number of photos taken at the museum were enough to facilitate the reproduction of the pipe. The Mark Twain Deluxe was introduced in 1985. To mark the centenary of the famous System, and also to introduce new shapes, Peterson created in 1990 the fine Sherlock Holmes series. Next to the models named Watson, Baskerville and Baker Street, one notes the fine lines of the Original, with a bowl which opens slightly at the top and is in contrast to the usual rather heavy Petersons.

Other prestigious makers grace the British Isles. One is Charatan, founded in 1863. They produced classic free-hand pipes and also selected suitable briar blocks to turn Straight-Grains. Charatan is now part of the Dunhill group. Another is Loewe which dates back to 1856 when Emile Loewe opened his shop in London. They still produce extremely well-made pipes, occasionally adorned with silver mounts. Then there is the new generation of pipe-makers, all with impeccable backgrounds: James Upshall, Ashton, Millville and Ferndown, who have contributed a great deal to the quality tradition of British pipe-makers.

Germany. After Denmark, Germany has the highest proportion of pipe-smokers. Today, the

Two Rainer Barbi freehands much admired for their creative designs. Bowls, mouth-pieces and fittings are made completely by hand by the "Master" (left).

most important German manufacturer is Vauen, founded in 1900 after the merger of two older companies. Its fifty-five workers produce about a hundred thousand pipes a year. Seventy-five per cent of them are ordinary pipes which do not bear the white spot on the mouthpiece placed on the "upper range". (Dunhill tried in vain to have the spot withdrawn, but Vauen proved that it was already using this mark on its best pipes in 1911 and that Adolf Eckert, son of one of the founders, had conceived the idea.) Vauen has also specialized in the paper filter which it manufactured in huge quantities, and which has been adopted by Butz-Choquin, Savinelli and others. Since 1961, the company has been run by Adolf's son, Ernst Eckert. His wife, Ruth, was for a long time in charge of product design – a rare situation in the pipe trade. Nothing in her training – she is a trained engineer – destined her for that task, but the daily contact with pipes roused her passion. Ruth Eckert retired in 1990. Today, a team of outside designers create the new products. Although not very original, certain white spot pipes made by hand indicate an aesthetic ambition. The Duke series, for example, includes some very fine sandblasts which are fitted with a double band in polished briar and in gold, and a gold ring round the top of the bowl which is itself polished. There is also a contrasting range in the Konsul collection, the firm's best-selling line, with a black finish, two rings and the top border of the bowl in red. Certain pipes in the Solitaire series, the most prestigious and inventive of the range, turned out of the best plateau briar, are tinted in red or green while still preserving the beauty of the grain. In 1982, the fourth generation of the Eckerts joined the company, in the person of Alexander Eckert whose main interest is management.

In contrast to a firm like Vauen, the workshop of pipe-maker Karl Heinz Joura, in Bremen, is a temple dedicated to the great art. At fifty years of age, Karl Heinz Joura has followed the most original path one could imagine for a pipe-maker. He was the son of a textile-

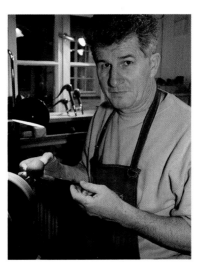

worker and was brought up in the former East German port of Rostock. He was a very keen sportsman, particularly in high diving, and he was enlisted at the age of eighteen by the national sports federation into its amateur team. For a worker's son, this was bliss, as the federation knew how to look after its athletes, in the interests of national prestige. In the same year, he came third in the national championship, just when the Berlin Wall divided Europe into two. Two months later, in Rostock, the young champion abandoned his privileges, stowed away on a cargo boat bound for Kiel and found his freedom. He spent three years in the Cologne Sports College, obtained his physical instructor's diploma and was given a post at the Bremen High School. It was there that a friend introduced him to the pleasures of pipe-smoking. For ten years, he bought pipes like everyone else. A sudden inspiration in 1975 prompted him to make his own and also a few for a number of his friends. They encouraged him and, two years later, he showed his work to a few retailers in the town. They, too, offered him great encouragement and he started selling his pipes in 1979. He then decided to reduce his teaching activities, which he abandoned completely soon after.

All Joura's human qualities, manifested by his experiences, his tenacity, originality, passion and taste for freedom, are found in his work as a pipe-maker. Each freehand is absolutely unique, fashioned out of fine Corsican briar which he goes to select at source. If you ask him what preoccupies him first in a shape, he answers: "Sensuality. I love a pipe to feel fine in the hand." That is why his shapes are often oval, which fit well in the palm of the hand. But Joura also plans more original shapes, with twisted panels inspired by the grain and fine pieces shaped like slender horns. His "ordinary" pipes are each stamped "Joura Freehand" on the stem, and his exceptional pieces carry a nineteen-carat gold spot on the mouthpiece. Joura makes about two hundred pipes a year, selling them in Germany, Switzerland and Italy.

Germany has other high-class master pipe-

Karl Heinz Joura makes two hundred freehands a year in his Bremen workshop. A former physical education teacher, he is considered to be the most gifted contemporary German pipemaker (left).

makers, such as Hasso Baudies in Bremen, Robert Mewis in Oldenburg and Rainer Barbi in Lauenburg. Hasso Baudies' pipes are easily recognized by a small diamond which replaces the "o" of his name.

Italy. The Italians love to have beautiful objects in daily use, and seek to make their lifestyle accessories attractive. This explains why Italy is today the leading producer of fine pipes. The internationally respected firm of Savinelli leads the Italian pipe-makers. The firm was founded by Achille Savinelli in 1876. He opened a small business in Milan selling smokers' articles, including pipes. The shop, on the via Orefici, is still there. With the arrival of the second Achille, after the Second World War – grandson of the founder and born in 1919 – the company started making pipes. A passionate smoker, the young Achille made his first pipe at the age of sixteen. Since his death in 1987, the house of Savinelli, with head offices in Milan and a factory in Barasso on the shores of the lake of Varese, is run by his son Giancarlo and his daughter Marisetta, who perpetuate the work started by Achille. Savinelli's top-of-the-range reaches the zenith of skill, creativity and elegance. Alongside the famous Punto Oro, of which shape 128 – a fine classic Billiard – is one of the best-selling pipes around the world, Savinelli produces exceptional models. The Giubileo d'Oro collection consists of classic models in a variety of finishes without flaws. The Autograph collection has each piece stamped with the signature of Achille Savinelli, and consists of fabulous freehands, some of which the firm call "fan": the bowl is a block of briar with only the base or sides etched or polished; the mouthpiece appears to be thrust into this bowl without a stem, and the contrasting sides open out into the fan. Finally, Savinelli offers some extraordinary and unique briars, often called Corallo because their strange texture suggests coral. They are hand-carved by a secret process, and they are very light,

The great master of Italian pipes, Carlo Scotti, was taken as the example to follow by aspiring young Italian pipe-makers. He always sought the fourth dimension of a pipe, the "heart". He was a past-master in his craft and, until his death in 1988, he personally checked each pipe which came out of his workshop (right).

offering a porosity comparable to meerschaum. As is the case with meerschaums, they also develop a brown patina as they age.

Alongside the real industrialists: Savinelli and also Enea Buzzi and his Brebbia pipes, Lorenzo Tagliabue and his Lorenzo pipes, there are in Italy a number of artist pipe-makers, those who have never produced anything other than unique pipes. In that respect, Carlo Scotti (who died in 1988 and was the founder of the firm Castello) was the first. He could be called the Italian Ivarsson, such was the beauty and rarity of his production which was sought by a privileged few. And yet, up to the Second World War, he was just a retailer dreaming of making his own pipes. He took the first step in a new direction in 1947 when he settled near Como, in Cantù – a small town renowned for its wood-working craftsmen. At first, he copied English classic models, but he soon put his own personality into his pipes and his style became recognized by all. He specialized in rustic finishes of fine designs and took great care in the shaping of the perspex mouthpieces (of his invention) to give his products a supremely elegant line. They are light, sandblasted or etched with sometimes very original designs. One example is the extraordinary model of the 1950s, called "friendship pipes", reminiscent of an Indian Peace Pipe, with a long curved mouthpiece and a slanted bowl. Scotti made fifty pieces which he offered to special customers. Other distinguishing features of this renowned, not to say legendary, make included the small brilliant or ivory strip set into the mouthpiece, the sumptuous grain of the briar which he selected from a secret source in Liguria, and the discreet daring which made each model a modern example of a classic tradition. Scotti's legend, particularly in the United States, was born from the human qualities of a man who refused to make pipes that he could not supervise himself. Orders accumulated, but he never wanted to employ more than five craftsmen. "In this life," he said, "it is

With a kind of magical touch, the free-hands of the firm Castello, made by Carlo Scotti, are both modern and classic. One notes that some are etched and sandblasted, this was Scotti's speciality (facing page, top)
The top-of-the-range of Savinelli, the main Italian manufacturer, are no less handsome than the creations of the individual Italian artisans. This selection includes the famous Octavia, a model with eight panels (seen here in the version with contrasting colours). To match the eight panels to the diamond-shaped stem is quite an achievement (facing page, below).

196

difficult to achieve the best. That is why you have to learn to be patient." He is also credited with a saying worthy of a great artist: "A pipe has three dimensions, plus a fourth – the heart." It is a quotation that Franco Coppo does not deny; he was Scotti's assistant in 1969 and has taken up the reins of the house of Castello.

In Italy, as in Denmark, there has been for some years now a real renaissance in pipes. There are young craftsmen who are passionate about the rare and the beautiful, such as Terenzio Cecchini (his firm, Mastro de Paja, was founded in 1972) and Salvatore Amorelli (whose firm was founded in 1979). The originality of their conceptions and the perfection of their finishes in all detail, mean that each of their pipes is a masterpiece of craftsmanship, not to say contemporary art.

France. This panorama – however incomplete – of the world's finest pipes ends in France, where the first mention must be of Saint-Claude where briar pipes were born. Originality of design is not the main characteristic of French pipe-makers who, proud of a long tradition, say that a pipe must be a good pipe above all else. Their prime concern remains, therefore, the quality of the briar and the standard of manufacture, destined to provide pleasure and comfort to smokers. There are, nonetheless, some fine pipes in the catalogues, such as the one from the famed Butz-Choquin firm, founded in 1858, which makes more than forty thousand pipes a year. The best pieces are stamped with the "BC" brand in gold. There are several series from the company, among which the most prestigious are the BC Collection and the Maître-Pipier (Master pipe-maker) that are hand-made from the best Corsican briar. They are slightly tinted so that the contrast of the grain is more pronounced, enhancing the beauty of the pipe, but one regrets the very traditional lines and the various plastic bands which are perhaps meant to make these pipes appeal to the younger smoker. It is worth noting, however, that Butz-Choquin produces a special elegant series, Ladies, for women. These pipes have a long mouthpiece like the clay Churchwarden of days gone by.

Another company estab-

lished on an industrial basis in Saint-Claude is the group Cuty Fort, set up in 1987. It unites four established companies: Chacom (founded in 1825), Jeantet (1765), Jean Lacroix (1956) and Vuillard (1850). Between them, these Four Musketeers produce more than two hundred thousand pipes a year, plus a variety of up-market wooden, leather and horn accessories, as a step towards diversification. For Chacom, Yves Grenard designs a new model each year, made in five finishes and in limited editions. Usually classic shapes, the pipes of the year are turned from old Corsican briar, with their fine grain contrasted by a delicate colouring. Jean Lacroix, whose pipes were always traditional, presents every year a collection of no more than ten models, with coloured pieces which highlight the grain (a fine red and a dark grey); they are fitted with hand-made Cumberland mouthpieces. Finally, Cuty Fort markets the original work of Pierre Morel whose freehands are real sculptures; he also specializes in copying old models.

Far from the Jura, in the Gard département, there is another sculptor, but a sculptor in clay – Gérard Prungnaud. In relation to exceptional materials, we have discussed at length the meerschaum work of Philippe Bargiel. In that respect, Gérard Prungnaud is similar. He is an exceptional craftsman, the modest and unique heir to an old tradition. He does not concern himself with business or marketing; he is quite solitary and unknown to most smokers. Nonetheless, Gérard is now one of the rare creators of clay pipes. He first worked in an industrial woodwork firm, then became a wood-carver, and started making white ceramic pipes in his spare time. His passion grew until he became a full-time pipe-maker in 1983. In 1987, he settled in a village with a traditional pottery past: in 1850 Saint-Quentin-la-Poterie had nearly a hundred potters and earthenware workers, and some sixty clay pipe-makers, including the famous Job Clerc. While there were none left in 1983, there are now ten. Gérard Prungnaud makes and sells his pipes from the former village post office, which he bought in 1992 and which still has its postbox. You may find some of his models at the Jean Nicolas pipe-shop in Lyons.

Gérard makes his own moulds, and some fifty of his

Beautiful, functional and extremely well-finished, Gérard Prungnaud's clay pipes renew the traditional craft which was in danger of disappearing. They enhance the flavour of tobacco and may give the smoker additional satisfaction (right).

The pipes made from bog-oak (morta) by Patrice Sébilo are unique. Five thousand years old, this wood is still in the process of fossilization. It is sometimes used in western France to make furniture. In pipes, the wood combines the strength of briar and the sweetness of meerschaum (left).

models are produced in short series. Another sixty are carved by hand, either from a raw piece of clay or from a rough moulded pipe. Gérard Prungnaud produces just under four hundred pipes a year; they are all works of art inspired by traditional clays but they are often stylized. One can admire a gracious feminine hand holding a bowl, a mermaid carrying the bowl on her back, an Oriental with a turban, and a ram's-head. They are extremely well finished, fitted with vulcanite or acrylic mouthpieces or sometimes bamboo. Some are partly tinted in black or grey by "smoking" in the Japanese *raku* tradition which gives a mat finish to tea-cups: as soon as it is out of the kiln, the pipe is placed (while still hot) in a receptacle containing sawdust which is then hermetically closed. In the enclosed space, deprived of oxygen, the sawdust in contact with the hot pipe is consumed, giving off a smoke which sets the carbon on the pipe. The parts destined to stay white have been previously brushed with a mixture of water and salt which forms a protective layer that can be removed later. Gérard Prungnaud's pipes have thick walls which avoid burnt fingers if the pipe is not smoked too fast. These clay pipes by their very nature preserve the authentic taste of the tobacco.

We finish with the rarest and most unique pipes in the world: the morta (bog-oak) pipes of Patrice Sébilo. To the north of the estuary of

the Loire river, the marshes of Brière conceal a treasure which has been immersed in peat for more than five thousand years. Three thousand years before our era, the oak forests of Brittany were invaded by the sea, probably after a landslide. All the trees died and were swallowed by the alluvium. They are now in the process of being fossilized, and they are therefore strong in minerals. They offer Patrice Sébilo a black wood, called morta, which is extremely hard. Something between a plant and a mineral, morta has excellent properties for pipe-making, from a hardness equal to that of briar to a sweetness like meerschaum. Manufacturing differs little from that of briar, but the extraction of morta is a difficult task. It lies deep in the peat, and has to be located with long iron rods. The peat is dug by hand and the tree trunk, sometimes weighing up to a tonne, must be pulled out with hoisting gear. Eight trunks, which have been drying for about two years, will be enough to produce four to five hundred pipes a year, which are sold only from Patrice's workshop at Herbignac.

Patrice Sébilo is therefore the only pipemaker in the world who starts with the raw material and finishes the pipes himself. These black pipes are very beautiful. Each piece is unique and made completely by hand. Morta cracks more than briar while drying and it is therefore more difficult to obtain large blocks.

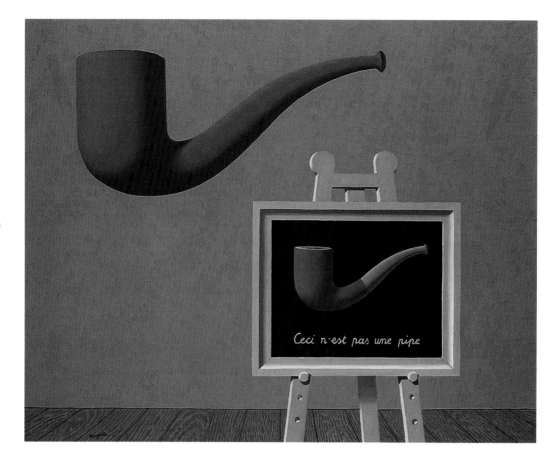

Surrealism in pipes created by the paint-brush of Magritte: *The deception of images,* 1929 (right).

Most of Patrice's pipes have small bowls which go very well with a bent mouthpiece (in vulcanite or occasionally horn obtained from Saint-Claude). But the craftsman knows how to make the best of this constraint. The originality of the bowls is surprising, sometimes with slanted tops and flat bottoms. About half the models have very long mouthpieces, greatly appreciated by women smokers.

Patrice Sébilo started his working life as a tool-fitter in industry, then followed several trades up to the age of thirty. He is now thirty-six. "I became a pipe-maker by accident," he relates, "having decided on the spur of the moment to take over the workshop of an old manufacturer of briar pipes. I learnt the basics of the trade in Saint-Claude and quickly understood that I had at last found my vocation." It is a vocation which does not stop him from producing very fine fountain-pens both in unusual woods and in morta.

Anywhere in the world today, when evoking the future of pipes and their creators, one word recurs: quality. This applies to both design and manufacture. The current decline in pipes is mainly quantitative, while the consumption of tobacco stagnates or diminishes, and fewer smokers take to pipe-smoking. In this context, pipe-makers have two trump-cards: the lesser health risk of pipes as opposed to cigarettes, and the attraction that well-made objects represent for those who have a love of art and craftsmanship. In that respect, the situation of pipe-makers is quite significant: while all industrial enterprises mass produce for a cheaper market, and need to diversify, the most demanding and inventive craftsmen, such as the Ivarssons and Scottis of this world, find an increasing demand for their products. It is as if the pipe was disappearing as a common object, to be gradually replaced by another rarer and more precious object, one which is tasted and admired like a good wine. It is also as if smokers were turning in larger numbers to what used to be a marginal activity, reserved for the privileged few. Tomorrow's collectors will not be short of works of art. In the meantime, if you have not already done so, fill your pipe, light it and, in the blue haze that rises, meditate in peace on that small but promising revolution.

The list of brands given below is not comprehensive, but it suggests a range of pipe brands available.

PIPE BRANDS

ASHTON. Made by one of the new generation English pipe-makers to a very high standard of quality, since the early 1970s, by Bill Ashton-Taylor. His production is fully hand-made in classic shapes and he uses a special process for light sandblast pipes.

ASTLEYS. Established in 1862, originally as manufacturers of meerschaum pipes. Today, the firm has become the symbol of perfection in briar pipes. The pipes are hand-made, and respect the intrinsic beauty of the briar. Great art.

BARLING. Established in the early 1800s, by the Barling family who were originally silversmiths. After changing hands a few times, the company now manufactures in the Isle of Man, both briar and (African) meerschaum.

BBB. One of the longest established London-made brands, founded in the 1850s, now manufactured by Cadogan Investments (formerly Oppenheimer Pipes).

BIG BEN. Range of a Dutch brand.

BLAKEMAR. A small manufacturer of middle-priced pipes who has a factory in Northamptonshire.

BONTEMPS. Brand name of the Berrod-Regad group, situated in Saint-Claude; medium range traditional pipes.

BUTZ-CHOQUIN. Established in Metz in 1818 by Gustave Butz and Etienne Choquin, and leading brand of the Berrod-Regad group since 1951. There are pipes produced in series (the best bear the brand initials BC in gold) and collectors' pipes or freehand pipes, signed by two great pipe-makers, Paul Lanier (who carved the heads on the pipes of the French Premier Smoker of the Year) and Alain Albuisson, young turner/designer.

CASTELLO. Brand founded by Carlo Scotti, responsible for the rebirth of Italian manufacture immediately before the outbreak of the Second World War. Now under the direction of Franco Coppo, the firm of Castello has lost nothing of its quality and creativity. Limited editions.

CHACOM. Saint-Claude brand, which belongs to the Cuty-Fort group, and produces 200,000 pipes a year. The firm was founded in 1825. The renown of Chacom pipes is based on their sweetness, the result of light air-curing of the briar for one to two years, an exclusive process. Chacom also distribute the designs of Pierre Motel.

CHAP. Founded in 1904 at Saint-Claude, this brand leader in the French wholesale market for mass-produced pipes has been part of the Berrod-Regad group since 1988.

CLAUDE ROMAIN. Brand name of the Berrod-Regad group based at Saint-Claude. Made in limited runs, quality and presentation are the byword for this make.

COMOY'S OF LONDON. Established in 1870 by Henri Comoy, this brand has long been the number one English pipe, on account of its briars and its finishes. It now belongs to Cadogan Investments Ltd.

COQUET. Clay pipes made at Puy-Moisson in the Haute-Provence Alps, and at Veinegues (Bouches-du-Rhône).

COURRIEU. Famous firm of Cogolin that uses briar blocks from the Massif des Maures in France. The story goes that in 1802 Charles Courrieu's ancestor, Ulysse Courrieu, alerted by a local shepherd, was the first to manufacture pipes made of briar. Output ranges from 15,000 to 200,000 per year, fifty per cent of which are hand-made (only ten per cent are freehand).

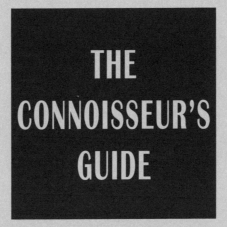

DAVIDOFF. Made of the finest briar, each Davidoff pipe features a flawless, hand-finished bowl and a hand-cut, stain-free stem. The Davidoff pipe is available in fourteen designs and three beautiful finishes: Sandblasted Black, Red Brilliant and Bright Brilliant finish. The Davidoff Giant range offers six designs in the same three finishes.

DR PLUMB'S. Originally introduced in the 1920s, it became the most popular system (gadget) pipe in the world; it was originally made in Saint-Claude, but is now manufactured by Cadogan Investments.

DUNHILL. According to many, the English "must". Forty-five models (each in five different finishes), great classics sold in forty-five countries, partly in twenty-eight Dunhill outlet shops. Elegant styling with its white spot, invented to show which way the stem should be inserted, is known throughout the world. The models are classic, a synthesis of simplicity and perfection.

ELWOOD. *See* Ferndown.

EWA. A Saint-Claude brand, the pipes are produced by the Waille factories, an old-established line of pipe-makers dating back to 1860. Michel Waille revived the tradition of the horn mouthpiece famous in the 1930s.

FALCON. Originally an American invention, Falcon pipes – with the metal stem – have been made in the UK since the mid-1950s. These pipes have the distinction of having the largest volume of sale in Britain. The company recently merged with Merton of London.

FERNDOWN Les Wood runs this small company, L & J S Briars, another of the new generation, and produces top-quality hand-made pipes, also under the brand Elwood. But Les Wood is, above all, a silver- and gold-mounting expert. Some of his pipes are fitted with such adornments, but he also carries out work for other companies.

GBD. Founded in Paris in 1850, GBD pipes became the property of Oppenheimer Pipes early this century. They were made in Saint-Claude and London until the 1970s, and are now manufactured by Cadogan Investments.

GENOD. Saint-Claude master pipe-maker brand, classic and hand-made. The Genod workshops produce special order pipes, and are open to the public. For information telephone: (33) 84 45 00 47.

INVICTA BRIARS. The U.K.'s main pipe repairers who also manufacture a whole range of pipes from the cheapest to the finest hand-mades.

JAMBO. The company, originally London Meerschaum, was set up in South Wales to make meerschaum pipes with African raw material. It passed to Pomeroy & Cooke, in Northamptonshire, after the death of the founder, Alaster Mitchell. It produced classic shapes in meershaum and calabash.

JAMES UPSHALL. Originally created by the late Ken Barnes (Charatan), the company, called Tilshead (from the village where it is situated), is now run by Barry Jones, a very experienced pipe-maker. He has a small team of enthusiastic young operatives and he produces classic freehands which include magnificent straight-grains. His pipes are free of flaws. The lesser grades are stamped Tilshead.

JEAN LACROIX. Traditional pipes from a firm set up in 1956, part of the Cuty Fort group. Quality and attention to detail. Jean Lacroix himself selects the finest grain of the wood and briar. A special feature of the mouthpieces (hand-made in Cumberland) is their modern shape with a gently concave lip, and the high-quality tinting that shows up the briar. Jean Lacroix also designs accessories.

JEANTET. Firm established at Saint-Claude in 1765 and headed by eighth generation director, it belongs to the Cadogan Investments group.

JIMA. A special product, as Jima Pipes have a ceramic bowl – so that the tobacco can be savoured at its purest. Jima has belonged to the Berrod-Regad group since 1988.

LOEWE. Originally made by the company that had a shop in the Haymarket, London, established in 1856, high-quality Loewe pipes always kept a low profile, but were highly appreciated. They are currently made by Cadogan Investments.

MANX. African meerschaum pipes made by Laxey Pipes Ltd on the Isle of Man, which also produces briar pipes.

MERTON & FALCON LTD. U.K. manufacturers and distributors. Makes and sells, worldwide, the Keyser brand. In 1993, Merton bought Falcon and now manufactures these metal-stemmed pipes. The company is U.K. distributor of Amphora, Big Ben, Savinelli and D. B. Mariner. (*See also* Falcon.)

MILLVILLE. Founded in 1983 by Dennis Marshall, former managing director of Charatan. He is also one of the new generation of specialist pipe-makers, producing freehands and series of mid-price fine quality briars.

ORLIK. Established early this century, the Orlik company was taken over by Oppenheimer Pipes (later Cadogan Investments) in the 1970s. Over the years it has produced some high-quality pipes. The brand was famous for its lightweight pipes.

PETERSON DUNCAN. (Incorporating Kapp & Peterson) Classicism, skill and perfect finish. One of the greatest makes of pipe, which owes its success to the innovation of master pipe-maker, Charles Peterson, in 1890, of hollowing out a tube with a large opening at the head of the pipe behind the bowl, to avoid the nuisance of fluid in the pipe. Technique and tasteful design continue to be the hallmark of this firm's production. Kapp & Peterson have reissued a particular model as a tribute to Mark Twain, reproducing the writer's favourite pipe, as well as seven models under the Peterson Sherlock Holmes label, with names associated with the writer, such as Baskerville, Baker Street, etc.

PARKER. A sub-brand of Dunhill, belonging to the Dunhill firm, and a distributor of pipes not licensed to carry the white dot.

POYAT. Brand aimed at the young pipe-smokers' market, launched by the designer Jean-Pierre Vitrac. Two models produced so far – the mini Poyat (plastic and briar, twelve colourways) and the Ace of Poyat in bubinga and briar.

ROPP. Mass-production pipe manufacturers, who were hit by the crisis that affected pipe-makers in 1986, but have since started up again, producing cherrywood pipes for a mild smoke.

SAVINELLI. This make, dating back more than a hundred years, has proved that an Italian firm could compete with Dunhill. Savinelli has a range of forty-eight basic models, some with a choice of finishes. Six exclusive models were produced in 1976 to mark the centenary of the make.

STANWELL. Danish firm set up in 1942 by Poul Nielson who, in collaboration with Sixten Ivarsson and, more recently, Tom Etlang and other talented master pipe-makers, has supplied smokers with a superb briar range.There are fifty-eight models available and certain limited editions. To celebrate the firm's fiftieth anniversary, six of the most famous models have been reissued: No. 32 by Poul Nielsen, Nos. 06 and 70 by Sixten Ivarsson, No. 35 by Anne Julie, No. 169 by Jess Chonowitsch and No. 190 by Tom Etlang.

TILSHEAD. *See* James Upshall.

VAUEN. German make established in 1848, with a current output of a hundred thousand pipes a year. They produce two hundred models, as well as limited editions or freehands such as the Solitaire.

W.Ø. LARSEN. This make has become a standard for stylish and imaginative freehand pipes. Wide range of fine Corsican briars, oval and wide bell-shaped bowls, with narrowing stems. A daring design that works with the texture, brilliance and grain of the wood. Exceptional pipes fetch a high price, such as those with a mouthpiece of reconstituted amber, or with a horn ring, or pipes in precious woods.

WILLMER. A family business established after the Second World War, with a lesser-known brand that has perhaps been underrated. Quality and finish are first class and the sales of the brand are now handled in Britain by a go-ahead wholesale distributor.

MASTER PIPE-MAKERS

Rainer BARBI
im Dorfe 8a, 2077 Brunsbek,
Kronshorst, Germany
Tel: (49) 41 07 96 47
One of the most talented German master pipe-makers based in Hamburg. The sculptor-manufacturer of freehand pipes par excellence. The shape of his pipes is dictated by the raw block of wood, which he works in such a way as to highlight the grain of the wood to maximum advantage. Barbi is a highly original artist who seeks to unite perfect technique and aesthetic appeal.

Philippe BARGIEL, Robert BLATTER, Jean-Pierre FORTON, Gilbert GUYOT, Patrice SEBILO (*see under* SHOPS), .

Karl Heinz JOURA
Schnoor 8, D-28 Bremen, Germany
Tel: (49) 421 32 86 60
This former teacher of physical education came from East Germany and has become one of the best German master pipe-makers. Today based in Bremen, he makes close on two hundred pipes a year, all freehand.

Paul LANIER
Master pipe-maker with Butz-Choquin. He also makes to order (fifty hours' work). For further information contact the workshop on: (33) 84 45 11 11.

Pascal LEONARD
rue Cuvelier 5-7, 5300 Andenne, Belgium
Tel: (32) 85 84 47 64
Grandson of the founder of the Léonard firm of pipe-makers, established at Andenne near Namur. Initially specialized in making pipes for shooting galleries at fairgrounds, Léonard took up production of real pipes in the 1960s. Uses original moulds of clay pipes from the last century.

Jean MASSON
24, route Faucille
39200 Villard-St. Sauveur, France
Tel: (33) 84 45 24 09
A self-taught sculptor from Saint-Claude, Jean Masson works single-handed on portrait pipes, and sculpts all his pipes which are as pleasant to look at as they are to smoke. Produced only in series.

Pierre MOREL
Lieu-dit village Larrivoire
39200 Saint-Claude, France
Tel: (33) 84 42 47 84
An independent-minded master pipe-maker, who works for Cuty Fort. His father was the premier designer of freehand pipes in France.

Gérard PRUNGNAUD
rue Cantonar
30700 St.-Quentin-La-Poterie, France
Tel: (33) 66 22 00 64
Gérard .Prungnaud has gone back to the origins of terracotta and faience. He makes his own plaster moulds – about forty of his models are produced in limited editions, and about sixty are hand-sculpted. Not more than four hundred pipes a year. Perfect finish and close on ninety different pipe models. His favourite subjects are figure-heads and mermaids.

Eyüp SABRI
Talented Turkish sculptor based at Eskisehir, producing meerschaum pipes. Some of his outsize pipes are made as decorations, and all are for sale in Istanbul (*see under* SHOPS, Yerliexport).

Roger VINCENT
2 chemin du Marais
39200 Saint-Claude, France
Tel: (33) 84 45 27 72
Craftsman-sculptor, based at Saint-Claude, following a family tradition of pure style and form.

S H O P S

Where can you buy pipes? And where do you take them for repair, whether they are modern or antique? Where will you find your favourite tobacco, wherever you happen to be – Paris, London, New York or Copenhagen? The shops listed below have been chosen for the selections that they stock and for the quality of service and reception.

AUSTRALIA

MELBOURNE
Benjamins Fine Tobacco
Myer House Arcade, 250 Elizabeth Street
Tel: (61) 3 663 2897

Daniels Fine Tobaccos
300 Lonsdale Street, Melbourne Central
Tel: (61) 3 663 6842

SYDNEY
Alfred Dunhill (Aust) Pty Ltd
Castlereagh Street
Tel: (61) 2 231 5511

TOORAK
J & D of Alexanders
Shop 7, Tok H Centre, 459 Toorak Road
Tel: (61) 3 827 1477

BAHRAIN

MANAMA
Tobacco Road
155 Government Road
Tel: (973) 253 356 or 233 322
Small but trendy shop.

BELGIUM

ANTWERP
Van der Voorde
Lange Koeport Straat, 43–49
Tel: (32) 32 32 0167
A temple to the pleasures of smoking, in the heart of old Antwerp, offering a full range of pipes, cigars and tobaccos.

BRUSSELS
Jean-Pierre Forton
7 rue des Carmes
Tel: (32) 2 502 80 94
Jean-Pierre Forton restores meerschaum and amber pipes, but makes only briar pipes. He produces no more than two hundred pipes a year, in his own unusual style.

Zabia
8–10 Rue Lebeau
Tel: (32) 2.512.94.22
One of the best addresses in Europe, boasting the formidable Mrs Van den Bossche, exceptionally knowledgeable, patient and helpful to all; now owned by Davidoff, but stocks most great brands.

CANADA

CALGARY
Cavendish & Moore
Penny Lane Market
Tel: (1) 403 269-2716
Gourmet tobacconist.

MONTREAL
Robert Blatter
365 President Kennedy
Tel: (1) 514 845–2028
The firm was established in 1907, and is now the fourth generation of master pipe-makers, producing by hand three hundred pieces per year, a small output of unique items, as well as maintaining and repairing Blatter & Blatter pipes.

Davidoff
1425 Sherbrooke Quest
Tel: (1) 514 289 9118
A beautifully decorated shop offering an attractive assortment.

TORONTO
Havana House Cigar & Tobacco Merchant
8 Cumberland Street
Tel: (1) 416 927–7703
87 Avenue Road
Tel: (1) 416 927–9070

VANCOUVER B.C.
R. J. Clark
3 Alexander Street
Tel: (1) 604 687–4136

VICTORIA
Old Morris Tobacconist
1116 Government Street
Tel: (1) 604 382–4811

WINDSOR
Havana House
473 Ouelette Avenue
Tel: (1) 519 254–0017

WINNIPEG
Havana House
185 Carlton Street
Tel: (1) 204 942–0203

CHINA

BEIJING
Davidoff
Teh Palac Hotel Beijing, Lobby Level, 8 Goldfish Lane, Wangfuijing
Tel: (86) 1 512 88 99, ext. 7991

CYPRUS

NICOSIA
Shop Tobacconist Fereos
260–64 Ledra Street
Tel: (357) 2–462168
A large range of pipes for the connoisseur.

Tobacco Boutique Shop
Hilton Hotel
3 Makarios Avenue
Tel: (357) 2–377777
A very large range of pipes for the connoisseur.

DENMARK

COPENHAGEN
W.Ø. Larsen
9 Amagertorv
Tel: (45) 33 12 20 50
The uncontested king of pipe and tobacco brands. This modest retail business was opened by the Larsen family in 1864, and launched its own cigars and tobaccos just before the outbreak of the First World War, and its own pipes during the 1950s, thanks to the skill and inventiveness of Ole Larsen, aided by his son, Niels. The collection of Larsen pipes, the finest pipes in the whole world, are available here as well as four hundred different tobaccos, including forty Larsen brands.

My Own Blend
GL. Mont 4
Tel: (45) 33 32 66 21
Choosing from some forty tobaccos, the pipe-smoker can have an individual blend mixed for him. Range of pipes and smokers' requisites.

EGYPT

CAIRO
Villars
World Trade Centre
Tel: (20) 2 339 4590
Stocks the widest selection of luxury pipes in Egypt.

FRANCE

BORDEAUX
Yves Camus
124, rue des Pilliers-de-Tutelle
Tel: (33) 56 44 47 03
Yves Camus is the only pipe repairer in Bordeaux. His two functions for the past thirty-four years: selling and repairing pipes.

COGOLIN
Charles Courrieu – Les pipes de Cogolin
42 and 58, avenue Clémenceau
Tel: (33) 94 54 63 82
Point of sale and manufacture of Charles Courrieu pipes. As in the Paris shops, Cogolin and other makes of pipe are repaired here.

LILLE
Civette La Tabagie
17 rue Faidherbe
Tel: (33) 20 06 37 56
Unusual place run for the last eight years

by Daniel Marchant. Not only does he offer his customers mixtures that he himself has assembled and tested, but he also repairs new and antique pipes. A large choice of pipes: five hundred items on view.

La Boutique du Fumeur
4, place Béthune
Tel: 33) 20 54 71 36
Classic pipes including Butz-Choquin, Peterson and Chacom, with a predilection for the milder Peterson briars. About fifty brands of tobacco.

LYONS
Jean Nicholas
5, rue Gasparin
Tel: (33) 78 38 09 27
Master pipe-maker chiefly known as a repairer of all kinds of pipes, modern and antique, and as a distributor of numerous brands.

Pierre Vantal
10, rue Emile-Zola
Tel: (33) 78 37 77 77
After running a tobacconist shop for fifteen years, Pierre Vantal has now taken over a shop that dates back over a century. Repairs and sells all brands.

Au Khédive
71 , rue de la République
Tel: (33)78 37 86 95
A classic enterprise offering a vast array of approximately three hundred pipes and more than eighty kinds of named tobaccos.

MARSEILLES
Le Maryland
1 rue de Rome
Tel: (33) 91 54 06 76

NICE
Maison du stylo
18, rue Masséna
Tel: (33) 93 87 77 15

PARIS
A la Civette
157, rue Saint-Honoré
Tel: (33) 142 96 04 99
The oldest tobacconist in France, established at the Palais Royal in 1716. The shop takes its name from the little squirrel-like rodent, whose musk was used to give snuff its aroma. La Civette sells all the Seita products and some others, as well as a fine selection of pipes from the major English, French and other firms, and a range of accessories.

Civette du Palais des Congrès
2 place de la Porte-Maillot
Tel: (33) 140 68 21 41
Pipe-smokers can find five or six different brands here, including Dunhill and Chacom, as well as a wide range of accessories and some twenty classic tobaccos.

Boutique du musée-galerie de la SEITA
12, rue de Surcouf
Tel: (33) 145 56 60 17
On the ground-floor of the Seita office building and next door to the Tobacco Museum.

Boutique 22
22, avenue Victor-Hugo
Tel: (33) 145 01 81 41
This paradise for cigar connoisseurs is also a key address for pipe-smokers.

Alfred Dunhill
15, rue de la Paix
Tel: (33) 142 61 57 58
The best of British style at the heart of Parisian chic in the rue de la Paix. Of the three first Dunhill shops opened before the Second World War (London, Paris, New York), the Paris shop is the only one to have remained intact. Built as a replica of the Duke Street shop on the site of a former eighteenth-century coaching inn, and opened in 1924, it has since been listed as a historic monument.

Flor de Cuba
1, avenue Raymond-Poincaré
Tel: (33) 147 04 90 50
About a hundred tobaccos for pipe-smokers, soon to be stored in a specially humidified cellar, and a range of smokers' accessories.

La Tabagie
10, rue du Départ
centre commercial Maine-Montparnasse
Tel: (33) 145 38 65 18
Set in a light and humidified room, trained staff deal with all smokers' needs. Fine international range of pipes.

La Tabatière Odéon
128, boulevard Saint-Germain
Tel: (33) 146 34 21 89
A shop selling smokers' items, with pipes (Butz Choquin, Chacom, Dunhill and Peterson) and some forty tobaccos.

La Virole
126, boulevard Murat
Tel: (33) 145 27 40 34

Lemaire
59, avenue Victor-Hugo
Tel: ((33) 145 00 75 63
A beautiful shop between the Etoile and the place Victor-Hugo, offering elegant accessories for smokers. The major pipe brands are on sale here as well as the majority of tobaccos available in France.

Le Pot à Tabac
28, rue de la Pépinière
Tel: (33) 145 22 29 14
Classic selection of the most famous pipe brands and about a hundred tobaccos.

Le Tabac du Dôme
108, boulevard du Montparnasse
Tel: (33) 143 34 23 41
Famous for its cigar cellar, as well as for its choice of tobaccos (about fifty brands) and its pipes. The greatest makes are on sale including W. Ø. Larsen.

A la Pipe du Nord
21, boulevard de Magenta
Tel: (33) 142 08 23 47
Pipe manufacture, repair and maintenance.

Au Caïd
24, boulevard Saint-Michel
Tel: (33) 143 26 04 01
The two main concerns of this establishment are the sale of pipes made in Saint-Claude and the restoration of antique pipes – disinfection, repair and adjustment of the mouthpieces.

Gilbert Guyot
7, avenue de Clichy
Tel: (33) 143 87 70 88
Pipe-maker, salesman, manufacturer, repairer, restorer, collector, smoker.

Aux Mines d'Ecume
35, boulevard Saint-Martin
Tel: (33) 142 72 69 19
Most of the pipes sold in the boulevard Saint-Martin are made for the firm by a Saint-Claude craftsman to the order and specification of Maurice Cardon. Any pipe repaired on request, regardless of the material it is made of.

Charles Courrieu – Les pipes de Cogolin
129, rue Saint-Honoré
Tel: (33) 140 28 03 19
This Parisian shop is the most eminent representative in the city of pipes from the Var and has on display the collection of its finest pipes. Sells only Charles Courrieu pipes, freehands and smokers' requisites. Maintenance and repair of pipes on request, whatever the make.

A l'Oriental
Arcades du Palais-Royal
19-22, galerie de Chartres
Tel: (33) 142 96 43 16
The big name pipes are stocked, but the best-selling lines are the ones made in house and marked *A l'Oriental*. Repairs on request, whatever the make and material of pipe.

Naudin Tabac
CNIT La Défense
2, place de la Défense
Tel: (33) 146 98 08 80
Warm welcome extended at this new shop, run by Thierry Naudin. Pipes include Dunhill, Butz-Choquin, Stanwell, Peterson, Chacom and Porsche Design. Wide selection of tobaccos.

Philippe Bargiel
30, rue saint-Lazare
60800 Crépy-en-Valois
Tel: (33) 144 59 00 03 (by appointment)
Master pipe-maker who trained with the firm of Sommer, repairer (whatever the style, make, material and origin of the pipe), qualified sculptor, Philippe Bargiel is one of the last master pipe-makers in the world to manufacture meerschaum pipes in the tradition of the Viennese master pipe-makers.

SAINT-TROPEZ
Charles Courrieu – Les pipes de Cogolin
25, quai Gabriel-Péri
Tel: (33) 94 97 00 91
One of the three sales outlets of the family firm of Courrieu, which has been making pipes – father and son – since 1802, when the firm set up in Cogolin. Sells only Courrieu pipes, mass-produced and freehand. No repairs done on site.

STRASBOURG
Gérard Style et plume
21 rue des Grandes Arcades
Tel: (33) 88 32 12 85
A tobacconist shop also open on Sundays. Choice of tobaccos (more than twenty brands) and pipes (most from Saint-Claude, but others signed Larsen and Peterson). Some meerschaums.

Pip'Cig Maison du Fumeur
14, rue du Vieux-Marché-au-Poisson
Tel: (33) 88 32 60 68
A choice of two thousand pipes; humidified showcase for tobaccos.

HERBIGNAC
Patrice Sébilo
16, avenue de la Monneraye
Tel: (33) 40 88 98 08
Patrice Sébilo is the only master pipe-maker in the world to work morta – oak from Brière, submerged in marshland and saturated with minerals. Patrice Sébilo makes 350 pipes a year (one-off models hand-made) as well as special orders.

───────── **GERMANY** ─────────
MUNICH
Alfred Dunhill
Matteistrasse 3
Tel: (49) 89 22 71 31

───────── **GREECE** ─────────
ATHENS
Balli
1–3 Spyromiliou Street
Tel: (30) 1 322 19 07

───────── **HONG KONG** ─────────
CENTRAL
Davidoff
The Landmark, G12, Ground Floor
Tel: (852) 525 54 28

Davidoff Dépositaire Agrée
Sogo Department Store, Basement 1, Causeway Bay
Tel: (852) 83 18 426

KOWLOON
Davidoff
Peninsula Hotel Lobby, Shop EL3
Tel: (852) 3 721 57. 74
The quintessence of Davidoff style: luxury, sophistication and impeccable product quality.

Davidoff
Regent Hotel, R106
Tel: (852) 721 55 20

───────── **IRELAND** ─────────
DUBLIN
J. J. Fox
119 Grafton Street
Tel: (3531) 700–533

───────── **ITALY** ─────────
ROME
Carmignani
via Colonna Antonina 43
Tel: (39) 6 679 54 19
Examples of English, Danish, French and Italian pipes are stocked, including the 92 Series, in commemoration of the brand's centenary. Not to mention the accessories, in inevitably stylish Italian good taste.

MILAN
Savinelli
via Orifici 2
Tel: (39) 2 345 22 96
This famous brand of Italian pipes has two shops in Milan and one in Genoa. The first has been on the via Orifici since 1876, when a little shop of smokers' items was opened there by Achille Savinelli. The shop sells mass-produced own-brand pipes, as well as top of the range creations, and an array of accessories.

Al Pascia
61 via Torino
Tel: (39) 2 86 45 05 97
More than ten thousand pipes of the best known brands, as well as its own Al Pascia brand (twenty-four models) are sold in this shop, which dates back to 1906. Private collection of eighteenth- and nineteenth-century meerschaums, nineteenth-century Saint-Claude as well as Chinese pipes. Large selection of smokers' requisites from all over the world.

───────── **JAPAN** ─────────
TOKYO
Davidoff
Hotel Okura, Main Lobby, 10-4
Toranomon 2-chome, Minato-ku
Tel: (81) 3 588 85 78

───────── **KUWAIT** ─────────
SAFAT
Jashanmal Department Store
Fahed Al Salem Street
Tel: (965) 2420071–2420072
The smoking department of this huge store has been marvellously redecorated, and stocks a very large choice of beautiful pipes.

───────── **LEBANON** ─────────
BEIRUT
Pour Homme
Mr Zouhair Al Kadi Jazaerli
Bachir Al Kassar Street
Tel: (961) 864 923

───────── **LUXEMBOURG** ─────────
STRASSEN
Terzi Depositaire
exclusif Davidoff, 20, Route d'Arlon
Tel: (352) 45 21 21

───────── **MALAYSIA** ─────────
KUALA LUMPUR
Davidoff
Main Lobby K.L. Hilton Hotel
Jalan P. Ramlee
Tel: (60) 3 238 61 30

───────── **NETHERLANDS** ─────────
AMSTERDAM
Davidoff
Van Baerlestraat 84
Tel: (31) 20 6711042
Beautiful shop with an extensive and varied selection in the museum area; fluent English, French and German spoken.

Hajenius – La Maison du Fumeur
92-96 Rokin
Tel: (31) 20 623 74 94
The emphasis in this Amsterdam institution, founded by Panthaleon Hajenius, is on a large selection of tobaccos, pipes and jars.

───────── **QATAR** ─────────
DOHA
Merch
Salwa Road
Tel: (974) 417317
The smokers' department of this shopping centre stocks a rich assortment of pipes.

───────── **SAUDI ARABIA** ─────────
JEDDAH
Hotel Sands Shop
Al Toubaishi Street, Al Hamra Area
Tel: (966) 2 669202

Hotel Sofitel Shop
Sofitel-Al Hamrah, Palestine Street
Tel: (966) 2 6653873

Randa Trading
Palestine Street, before al Fakeeh Hospital
Tel: (966) 2 6672752
These three shops are decorated with

refined luxury and contain a vast choice of pipes of every price and quality.

SINGAPORE

Davidoff
Hex 01-03 Hilton Intl Hotel, Orchard Road
Tel: (65) 734 23 80

SPAIN

BARCELONA
Gimeno
100 Rambla de las Flores
Tel: (34) 4 302 09 83
Superb – an absolute must – pervaded by the unmistakable smell of fine tobacco and fine cigars.

MADRID
Gonsales De Linares
26 Paseo Habana
Tel: (34) 1 262 22 82

Santiago
18 Calle Alcala
Tel: (34) 1 221 47 16

SWEDEN

GOTHENBURG
Brobergs
Arkaden
Tel: (46) 31 15 12 60

STOCKHOLM
Brobergs Deposit. Davidoff
Sturegallerian 39
Tel: (46) 8 611 69 00

SWITZERLAND

GENEVA
Davidoff
2 Rue de la Rive
Tel: (41) 22 310 90 49

Alfred Dunhill
100 Rue de Rhône
Tel: (41) 22 312 4260

Rhein Tabac
1, rue du Mont-Blanc.
Tel: (41) 22 732 97 64
A shop specializing in tobacco, also stocks all kinds of items for pipe-smokers.

ZURICH
Davidoff
Hotel Savoy, Poststrasse 12
Tel: (41) 1 211 48 00

Durr
Bahnhofplatz 6
Tel: (41) 1 211 63 23

THAILAND

BANGKOK
Davidoff
Lobby Level Hilton Intl, Nal Lert Park, 2 Wireless Road
Tel: (66) 2 253 01 23

Davidoff
Oriental Hotel, Charoen Krong Road
Tel: (66) 2 236 04 00

TURKEY

ISTANBUL
Hakan Cantekin
Turistik Esva, Icbedesten No. 64-65
Kapaliçarsi
Tel: (90) 1 51 20 614
A specialist in Turkish pipes in the land of the meerschaum.

Nursan
Abdl Ipekci Cad No 18/1, Nisantasi
Tel: (90) 212 242 0367

Yerliexport
Istanbul Grand Bazaar
Bedesten Serifaga Sok. 59
Tel: (90) 1 526 2619
Meerschaum pipes from Eyüp Sabri (see p. 93) are sold in this shop in the heart of the Istanbul bazaar.

UNITED ARAB EMIRATES

DUBAI
Le Tabac
Lobby of the Hotel Intercontinental, Deira
Tel: (971) 4 225 008
A small boutique offering beautiful pipes.

UNITED KINGDOM

AYR
T. H. Dalling
5 Burns Statue Square
Tel: 0292 265799

BATH
Frederick Tranter
5 Church Street
Tel: 0255 466197
Small, well-ordered shop behind the cathedral; vast range of pipes, tobaccos and accessories; generous advice from the voluble Mr Richard Tranter.

BIRMINGHAM
John Hollingsworth & Son
5 Temple Row
Tel: 021 236 7768
Bustling city shop with helpful staff; large selection of pipes and tobaccos.

CANTERBURY
Adams & Adams
51 Palace Street
Tel: 0227 786 288
A smoker's emporium, only a minute from the cathedral.

CARDIFF
Lewis Darbey & Co
28-32 Wyndham Arcade, Mill Lane
Tel: 0222 233443
A traditional service and a wide-ranging stock.

The Wellfield
53 Wellfield Road
Tel: 0222 496770
Traditional mahogany interior and unique collection of tobacco signs. An excellent range of pipes and loose tobaccos.

CHELTENHAM
Tobacco World
Regent Arcade
Tel: 0242 222037
Large selection of pipes and tobaccos.

CHESTER
A E Lloyd & Son
Tobacco World, 78 Northgate Street
Tel: 0244 348821
Wide selection of pipes and loose tobaccos.

CHESTERFIELD
Charles Iliffe
2-8 Station Road, Whittington Moor
Tel: 0246 450699
Expert advice and a choice of a hundred briars and meerschaums, and over 120 loose tobaccos.

EDINBURGH
Herbert Love
31 Queensferry Street, Edinburgh
Tel: 031 225 8082
Discreet, narrow shopfront; wide selection.

EXETER
MaGahey The Tobacconist
245 High Street
Tel: 0392 73625
Traditional mahogany interior and unique collection of tobacco signs. An excellent range of pipes and loose tobaccos.

GLASGOW
Tobacco House
9 St Vincent Place
Tel: 041 226 4586
A varied stock of pipes and tobacco. Blending on the premises.

GUERNSEY
Bucktrout
Waterloo House, 20 High Street, St Peter Port
Tel: 0481 724444
A wide range is stocked by this firm, founded in 1830.

HOVE
E Burkitt
117 Church Road, Hove
Tel: 0273 731 351
Family business (opened in 1873) with large range of pipes, tobaccos and lighters.

JERSEY
E Denis & Co Limited
8 York Street
Tel: 0534 24123
Full range of pipe-smoking goods available from this hundred-year-old firm.

LEEDS
C Aston
17 Thorton Arcade
Tel: 0532 347435
A traditional tobacco shop with a full range.

LIVERPOOL
Turmeaus Limited
Oriel Chambers, 16 Water Street
Tel: 051 236 3802
Full range available from this firm with over 170 years' history.

LONDON
Astley's
108-111 Jermyn Street
Tel: 0171 930 1887
Astley's has been a family business since 1862. In his Art Deco shop Paul Bentley is a specialist in Calabria briar pipes (old, clean and light). Not more than three hundred a year. Briar or meerschaum – all shapes at all prices. Second-hand pipes from the beginning of the nineteenth century from all countries with a tradition of pipe-smoking can also be found here.

Alfred Dunhill
30 Duke Street
Tel: 0171 499 9566
Renovated just before the Second World War, the shop in Duke Street remains a traditional British institution. The famous tobacco counter is fitted with twenty-four drawers filled with natural grade tobacco, and covered with a wooden lid. The pipe tobacco blends are prepared here for the individual taste of every customer. In addition to the Dunhill pipes, do not miss the Alfred Dunhill collection of antique pipes (*see under* MUSEUMS).

Harrods
(J.J. Fox)
Knightsbridge
Tel: 0171 730 1234
A quiet resting place from the teeming aisles of the famous store; helpful and knowledgeable assistants. A full range of fine pipes and smoker's requisites.

Jayems
125 Victoria Street
Tel: 0171 828 1472
Full range of pipes, tobacco and lighters. Also do repairs.

Mullins and Westley
Covent Garden
Tel: 0171 836 8345
An address offering a choice of pipes and smokers' requisites, but frequented and famous mainly for its tobacco blends.

Platenchoice
330 Oxford Street
Tel: 0171 493 1025

James J. Fox & Robert Lewis
19 St. James's Street
Tel: 0171 930 3787
An extraordinary emporium with two hundred years of history and experience.

Sahakian–Davidoff
35 St James's Street
Tel: 0171 930 3079
Stocks other well-known makes as well as Davidoff's own brand of pipes.

Selfridges
Oxford Street,
Tel: 0171 629 1234

Shervingtons
337 High Holborn,
Tel: 0171 405 2929
Formerly known as John Brumfit; half-timbered Elizabethan building in legal quarter. Full range of pipes, tobaccos and accessories.

G Smith & Sons
The Snuff Centre, 74 Charing Cross Road
Tel: 0171 836 7422
Full range of pipes and tobaccos. The expert service includes supplying goods by mail order, both at home and for export (duty-free).

Walter Thurgood
London Wall,
Tel: 0171 628 5467
Haunt of City high-fliers, brought up to date by Edward Sahakian and now under the experienced supervision of Barry Coughlan.

G Ward (Tob) Limited
60 Gresham Street
Tel: 0171 606 4318
Full range of pipes, tobaccos and accessories.

MANCHESTER
Astons
Royal Exchange Centre
Tel: 061 832 7895
Neat, well-ordered shop with full range of pipes and accessories.

MARLOW ON THAMES
Coster & Son Limited
52 High Street
Tel: 0628 482045

MIDDLESBROUGH
Forshaws Limited
107 Albert Road, Cleveland Centre
Tel: 0642 242307

NOTTINGHAM
T F Gauntley
4 High Street
Tel: 0602 417973
Over a thousand pipes and lighters.

OTLEY
James Barber
33 Kirkgate
Tel: 0943 462603
Over a thousand pipes in stock in this shop.

PENZANCE
West Cornwall Cigar Co
Abbey Street
Tel: 0736 51257
Traditional shop selling pipes, tobaccos and accessories.

SOLIHULL
John Hollingsworth
97 High Street
Tel: 021 705 4549
Wide range of pipes and accessories.

ST. ANDREWS
Janetta
Westport, 209 South Street
Tel: 0334 77723
Full range of pipes and loose tobaccos.

STOKE ON TRENT
J M Edwards
24 Fountain Square, Hanley
Tel: 0782 281416

STRATFORD ON AVON
Lands
29 Central Chambers
Tel: 0789 292508
Over two thousand pipes in stock.

WORTHING
Macmillans
2a Portland Square
Tel: 0903 200881

YORK
Choice Select
6 Coppergate
Tel: 0904 656156
Wide range of pipes, tobaccos and accessories in "olde worlde" setting.

──────── **UNITED STATES** ────────

ARIZONA
Ford & Haig
7076 Fifth Avenue, Scottsdale
Tel: (1) 602–946–0608

Stag Tobacconist
9627 A Metro Parkway West, Phoenix
Tel: (1) 602–943–8519

CALIFORNIA
Barney & Linda Squires
The Pipe Squire, 346 Coddington Centre, Santa Rosa
Tel: (1) 707–573–8544

Century City Tobacco
10250 Sta. Monica Blvd. #27,
Los Angeles
Tel: (1) 310–277–0760

Davidoff of Geneva Inc.
232 North Rodeo Drive, Beverly Hills
Tel: (1) 310–278–4888
Offers everything a smoker can dream of.

Alfred Dunhill
290 Post Street, San Francisco
Tel: (1) 415 781 3368

Tinder Box
2729 Wilshire Blvd, Santa Monica
Tel: (1) 310–828–4511
Established in 1928, pipe, cigar and gift
shop; walk–in humidor.

Tobacco Trader
4722 Admiralty Way, Marina Del Rey
Tel: (1) 310–823–5831

COLORADO
Jerri's Tobacco Shop
1616 Glenarn Place, Denver
Tel: (1) 303–825–3522

CONNECTICUT
Greenwich Tobacconist
8 Havemeyer Place, Greenwich
Tel: (1) 203–869–5401

The Owl Shop
268 College Street, New Haven
Tel: (1) 203–624–3250

FLORIDA
Bennington Tobacco
Royal Palm Plaza 80, 501 S.E. Mizner Blvd,
Boca Raton
Tel: (1) 470–391–1372

Edward's Pipe and Tobacco
3235 Henderson Blvd, Tampa
Tel: (1) 813–872–0723

King's Treasure Tobacco Co.
Bayside Market Place, 401 Biscayene Blvd,
Miami
Tel: (1) 305–374–5593

Smoker's Gallery
Galleria Mall, 2366 E. Sunrise Blvd,
Ft-Lauderdale
Tel: (1) 305–561–0002

Smoker's Gallery
801 N Congress Avenue,
Boynton Beach Mall, Boynton Beach
Tel: (1) 407–736–5533

Smoker's Gallery
12801 W Sunrise Blvd., Sawgrass Mills,
Sunrise
Tel: (1) 305–846–2631

GEORGIA
Tinder Box (Lenox Square)
3393 Peachtree Road, Atlanta
Tel: (1) 404–231–9852

Tinder Box # 153
1246–A Cumberland Mall, Atlanta
Tel: (1) 404–432–0028

ILLINOIS
Alfred Dunhill
Water Tower Place,
835 North Michigan Avenue, Chicago
Tel: (1) 312 467 4455

Iwan Ries & Company
19 South Wabash, Chicago
Tel: (1) 213–372–1308

Rubovits Cigar
320 South Lasalle Street, Chicago
Tel: (1) 312–939–3780

Jack Schwartz Cigar
175 W. Jackson, Chicago
Tel: (10 312–782–7898

Up Down Shop
1550 N. Wells, Chicago
Tel: (1) 312–337–8505

MARYLAND
Fader & Sons
107E Baltimore Street,
Baltimore
Tel: (1) 301–685–5511

Fader's Tobacconist
9173 Reistertown Rd., Ownings Mills
Tel: (1) 410–363–7799

Fader's Tobacconist
25 W Allenghey Avenue, Towson
Tel: (1) 410–828–4555

MASSACHUSETTS
David P. Erlich & Co.
32 Tremont Street, Boston
Tel: (1) 617–227–1720

The Pipe Rack
(Larry Gilman)
1247–49 Centre St., Newton Center
Tel: (1) 617–969–3734

MICHIGAN
Churchills
1301 W. Long Lake Road, Troy
Tel: (1) 313–641–0740

MISSOURI
Diebels Gallery
426 Ward Parkway, Kansas City
Tel: (1) 816–931–2988

NEW JERSEY
Brick Church
Short Hills Mall, Shorthills
Tel: (1) 201–379–6921

NEW YORK
Arnold's Tobacco Shop
323 Madison Avenue, New York
Tel: (1) 212–697–1477

Barclay–Rex Pipe Shop
7 Maiden Lane, New York
Tel: (1) 212–692–9680

Barclay–Rex
70E 42nd St., New York
Tel: (1) 212–692–9680

Davidoff of Geneva Inc.
535 Madison Avenue, New York
Tel: (1) 212–751–9060

De La Concha
1390 Avenue of the Americas,
New York
Tel: (1) 212–757–3167

Alfred Dunhill
450 Park Avenue, New York
Tel: (1) 212–753– 9292

Nat Sherman International
500 Fifth Avenue, New York
Tel: (1) 212–246–8639

NORTH CAROLINA
Tinder Box
Hancs Mall, 3323 Silas Creek Parkway,
Suite 208, Winston Salem
Tel: (1) 919–765–9511

Tinder Box (South Park)
4400 Sharon Road, Charlotte
Tel: (1) 704–366–5164

OHIO
Cousins Cigar Company
1828 Euclid Ave., Cleveland
Tel: (1) 216–781–9390

Straus Tobacconist
410 Walnut Street, Cincinnati
Tel: (1) 513–621–3388

OREGON
Rich's Cigar Store
801 SW Alder, Portland
Tel: (1) 800–669–1527

PENNSYLVANIA
Holt's Cigar
114 South 16th Street, Philadelphia
Tel: (1) 215–563–0763

TENNESSEE
Uptown's Pipe & Tobacco
3900 Hillsborough Road, Nashville
Tel: (1) 615–292–6866

TEXAS
The Humidor at River Center
849 East Commerce, Ste. 393, San Antonio
Tel: (1) 210–222–0501

The Humidor
6900 San Pedro, Suite 111, San Antonio
Tel: (1) 210–824–1209

The Humidor at North Star Mall
Loop 410, Ste 112, San Antonio
Tel: (1) 512–308–8545

Jeffrey Stone Ltd
9694 Westheimer, Houston
Tel: (1) 713–783–3555

Pipe World Inc.
2160 Highland Mall, Austin
Tel: (1) 512–451–3713

Up In Smoke
2315 Galleria Mall, Dallas
Tel: (1) 214–458–7501

VIRGINIA
Georgetown Tobacco & Pipe Store Inc.
Tysons Corner Center, McClean
Tel: (1) 703–893–3366

John B Hayes
11755 L Fair Oaks Mall, Fairfax,
Tel: (1) 703–385–3033

Tobacco Barn
6201 Arlington Blvd, 7 Corners Center,
Falls Church
Tel: (10 703–536–5588

Tobacco Barn
6568 Springfield, Springfield
Tel: (1) 703–971–1933

Tobacco Barn
1100 S Hayes Street, Store #2004,
Arlington
Tel: (1) 703–415–5554

WASHINGTON DC
Georgetown Tobacco
3144 M – Street, Washington
Tel: (1) 202–338–5100

W Curtis Draper
640–14th Street N.W
Tel: (1) 202–638–2555

A N T I Q U E   D E A L E R S

The intrinsic beauty, rarity and perfection of a pipe, a tobacco jar, a snuff box or a pipe-rack establish the commercial value of these antique pieces just as much as public demand, which is ever on the increase. Antique-dealers are a happy breed whose own passion can bring joy to the collector.

Denise CORBIER
3, rue de l'Odéon
75006 Paris
Tel: (33) 143 26 03 20
The only woman expert in antique pipes. Denise Corbier began in the profession thirty years ago. Tobacco jars, snuff-boxes, cigar- and cigarette-holders, carved moulds, clay and wooden pipes, meerschaum and porcelain pipes – her shop traces the history and origins of the golden age of the pipe in the nineteenth century. Denise Corbier's favourite period is 1850-1930. Her main assets are great experience and friendliness

Dominique DELALANDE
2, place du Palais-Royale
Louvre des Antiquaires
75001 Paris
Tel: (33) 142 60 19 35
An expert known worldwide in the field of antique pipes. What appeals to Dominique Delalande is the very rare and the very beautiful – he responds to the demands of the public without yielding to extremes of fashion. This pipe-lover has built up one of the most varied collections in the world in terms of materials, origins and quality of workmanship. His ambition is to exhibit them and set up a museum to house them.

ANTIQUARIUS – THE PIPE SHOP
135 King's Road
London SW3 4PW
Tel: 0171 352 33 15
This Chelsea shop has a huge range of antique pipes for the connoisseur dating up to the Edwardian period (with some 300 in stock at any one time). It opened in 1970. Brian Tipping – collector and antique-dealer – is one of the most knowledgeable specialists in meerschaum pipes. No pipe-smoker should miss this lively London spot. The prices cover a wide range and there are a variety of smokers' accessories including jars and cabinets.

T O B A C C O   B R A N D S

ALSBO (Danish brand)
   Resolution With an American Virginia and African Malawi base, this is the jewel in the crown of the Danish firm of Stokkebye. A mild, cool tobacco with aroma of rum, bourbon and vanilla.
   Black Aroma of vanilla, hazel and undergrowth in this tobacco with a base of black Cavendish, Burley and Virginia.
   Gold A light tobacco with a Cavendish and Virginia base and vanilla and pistachio aroma.
   Premium Slightly fruity, with vanilla and caramel aromas, and based on Virginia, Burley and Cavendish.

   Danish de Luxe White American and African Virginia based, a mild, sweet tobacco with an aroma of honey.
   Danish de Luxe Yellow Mild, sweet, with a hint of vanilla, Virginia and Burley-based tobacco.

AMPHORA (Dutch brand)
   Cesare Borgia a different kind of "Amphora" with a detectable dash of Latakia. Strongly perfumed and smoky tobacco.
   Regular An aromatic elegant classic.
   Ultra Mild An aromatic blend modelled on Regular but more complex.
   Ultra Light Modelled on Ultra Mild, but with a less pronounced saucing or flavouring.
   Vintage Malt Whisky An aromatic tobacco with a flavour of whisky and cherry.
   Rich Aroma One of the recent Dutch specialities – flavours worked on the classic base of Virginia and Burley, presented in the form of Cavendish ready-rubbed.
   Full Aroma In the same series of tobacco with strong aromas, one of the more perfumed.
   Golden For smokers fond of the old blends. A classic with a light aroma, milder than the black, listed next.

Black Another great classic which has become a standard. Light subtle aroma.

ASHTON

Tobacco made for the pipe brand of the same name; it is available in three mixtures of various cuts.

CLAN (Dutch brand)

Aromatic A mild, light, sweet Virginia- and Burley-based tobacco with little aroma.

Light Aromatic Even lighter than the previous one.

Mild Cavendish Light and natural, a satisfyingly coarse cut-tobacco.

DAVIDOFF (Swiss brand)

Scottish Mixture An extremely mild tobacco, light and aromatic, based on Virginia, Burley and Kentucky.

Danish Mixture Virginia-, Burley- and black Cavendish-based, a mild, light and aromatic tobacco.

Royalty A fairly potent tobacco, Virginia-, Burley- and Latakia-based.

English Mixture A mild, Virginia-based tobacco with a distinct smoky flavour. Heavy and sweet.

DUNHILL (English brand)

Standard Mixture Medium Fairly strong tobacco. Owes its distinct aroma to the large proportion of Latakia.

Early Morning Pipe. One of the best-known English blends in the tradition of Standard Mixture Medium, but even lighter.

Mild Blend Blend of different Virginias. A great broad-cut English classic.

Black Aromatic Honey flavour and mildly perceptible *saucing* in this balanced Dunhill 92 Virginia-based blend.

FOUR SQUARE (Originally British, now made in Denmark). Available in a number of variations: Dark Blue, Dark Blue mixture, Green, Purple, Red, Yellow labels.

GALLAHER

Benson & Hedges Mellow Virginia One of the leading traditional U.K. brands available in flake, ready-rubbed and mild blends; a slow-burning Virginia blend of medium cut with full flavour.

Bondman A full-flavour Virginia blend of light and dark tobacco, medium strength and medium cut.

Escudu Navy de Luxe This is a curly-cut blend to which has been added a touch of Perique; medium cut.

Condor One of the two top British tobaccos, available in long-cut flake, ready rubbed and also in a light blend; a full strength slow-burning tobacco with positive characteristics.

John Cotton Mixture A traditional medium strength English mixture with a touch of Latakia.

Balkan Sobranie This is available in the well-established Virginia No 10, a broken flake, the 759 Mixture with Oriental and Latakia, and Smoking Mixture, also enhanced with Oriental.

Sobranie Reserve A fairly modern addition to the Sobranie "house" in two variants, Virginia Mixture, complemented with red and black Cavendish and a ready-rubbed Virginia.

War Horse A strong traditional English tobacco available in sliced flake bars and rolls.

GAWITH, HOGGARTH & Co

Bobs Flake A medium strength, cool smoke, brown in colour, sweetened with chocolate.

Broken Cake A half-rubbed broad-cut mild and cool tobacco.

Kendal Black Cherry A special mixture, introduced a few years ago, with a smooth flavour of cherries.

Kendal Twist The company produces a number of authentic traditional English tobaccos known as twist, sold in pieces or in "ropes".

HALF & HALF (American brand)

Light American Vanilla-flavoured, mild. A stronger aroma and a lasting flavour.

Burley & Bright A renowned Virginia- and Burley-based classic, like all the Half & Halfs. Fine rich flavour, despite the light, mild blend.

IMPERIAL TOBACCO

Capstan Medium Old-established blend of mild Virginia flake.

Digger Flake A Latakia mixture, broad-cut, but of medium strength.

Dutch Blend A recently introduced aromatic tobacco as an answer to the growing popularity of aromatic tobaccos.

Gold Black A mixture of Virginia, Cavendish and other choice tobaccos, sweetened by a secret process; one of the top brands in the U.K.

St Bruno Available in flake and ready-rubbed; St Bruno is one of the two top-selling pipe tobaccos in Britain; it has a Virginia base to which other choice tobaccos have been added.

Three Nuns A popular curly-cut medium blend.

Walnut Flake A flake "plug" tobacco, full strength.

Whiskey Ready Rubbed A blend of Virginia tobaccos with a special flavour, in medium cut.

JOHN BRUMFIT'S (British brand, made in Germany)

Cherry Cream Distinct taste of cherry in this Virginia and Burley blend. Mild and slightly spicy.

Orange Virginian Reminiscent of Old Radford's and Davidoff's Scottish blend. Mild and orange-flavoured

ROTHMANS

Craven This old brand was re-introduced some years ago as a popularly priced pipe tobacco, broad cut and available in aromatic mixture, mild ready-rubbed and mild flake, suitable for beginners.

Erinmore One of the top popular tobaccos in the U.K., sold in full-flavoured flake and ready-rubbed forms and also in the milder, sweeter mixture with Latakia.

Murrays Mellow Mixture A medium-cut, medium strength with a fine bouquet produced by a touch of Latakia.

Yachtsman A Continental-type Cavendish mixture, enriched with honey.

TROOST (Dutch brand)

Aromatic Same type of tobacco as the Amphora collection. In the tradition of recent aromatic Dutch tobaccos. Good broad cut.

Black Cavendish On the same model as the Aromatic. Mild and rich, sweet aroma.

OTHER TOBACCOS

Flying Dutchman Mild tobacco, fine cut, aromatic, balanced and elegant.

Indian Summer Rather perfumed, this tobacco is made according to a Mormon recipe, in Holland.

Radford's In a variety of flavours.

Cavas Made in Holland by Oldencott, a so-called Irish blend, with a distinct aroma.

Kentucky Bird This Burley- and Virginia-based tobacco has little perfume, but is extremely mild and fine and includes a few rose petals.

Caledonian Red Not as strong as Caledonian Green, with a Virginia, Burley and Black Cavendish base, this mild tobacco makes some people think of maple syrup.

Caledonian Green Stronger than the previous one, this is a non-aromatic tobacco with a base of Virginia, Latakia and smoky Oriental tobaccos.

Premier Cru Light, balanced and elegant tobacco with a base of Virginia, Périque and Oriental tobaccos.

Irish Mead Ideal for new smokers, light and faintly aromatic, mild and mellow, a tobacco based on Virginia, Burley and honey-flavoured Oriental tobaccos.

Mac Baren International tobacco brand which comes in a variety of aromas available worldwide.

MILD FRENCH TOBACCOS

Amsterdamer The regular and the mild, both highly aromatic are a Swiss brand, for which the tobaccos are manufactured in France under licence. Aromatic.

Narval Limited sale today, with an aromatic Virginia and an aromatic blend, less rich and less elegant than the others.

Saint-Claude Two mild tobaccos from the Saint-Claude brand – the aromatic Nordic Confrérie and the more classic and discreet Old Style Confrérie

FRENCH TRADITIONAL TOBACCOS

Saint-Claude The Qualité Tradition is a strong tobacco, equivalent to that of Gitanes and other Gauloises. Earthy tang which feels rough, with no great finesse.

Caporal Blend of French tobaccos and Oriental tobaccos for Caporal Export (similar to Saint-Claude, but even stronger); the plain Caporal is what is known as "grey" tobacco (even plainer than the Export), the Scaferlati Supérieur Caporal has a stronger taste; the Scaferlati Doux Caporal is lighter, because it is "washed" to remove surplus tar and nicotine. Scaferlati pipe tobacco, coarse cut, is the cheapest tobacco. Within this group of strong dark tobaccos, the Bergerac (scaferlati blend Caporal) is the lightest of the Caporals.

M U S E U M S

AUSTRIA

Vienna – Tobacco Museum of Austria
Oesterreichisches Museum
7 Messepalast (entrance Mariahilfer Straße 2)
Tel: (43) 1 526 17 16
A collection without equal in the world. Tribute to the history of tobacco and associated artifacts. The museum seeks to tell the story of tobacco on two levels – cultural and sociological. Launched in 1873 with an array of meerschaums and other smokers' articles made to mark the International Fair in Vienna, the museum took on a new lease of life in the 1930s, and then again in 1949 following damage and thefts during the Second World War. Set up in the form of a ticket kiosk, it is a faithful reproduction of a tobacconist in the time of the Austrian monarchy. It has a fine range of snuff-boxes, clay pipes, porcelain pipes, and African and American pipes.The more unusual objects include a pipe in the shape of a rose, made for the Duke of Brunswick (one of the oldest European pipes, dating from 1602), the giant carved wooden pipe presented to the Emperor Franz Joseph, and an imposing meerschaum in the Gothic style. The museum also has on display a fair number of documents on the Austrian Tobacco Company.

BELGIUM

Werwick – Taback Museum Brikkenmolen
Musée du tabac, domaine de Brikkenmolen
63 Koestraat
Tel: (32) 56 31 49 29/10 41/47 31
15 km. from Courtrai, in the outbuildings of the late eighteenth-century Brikkenmolen mill, a tobacco museum was opened in 1987 with a collection of 2,500 objects on the cultivation of tobacco, assembled from 1977 onwards, thanks to the Amis du Tabac association. At the entrance there is a pre-war tobacconist, while the first floor has been set out as a small factory with tobacco-processing machines. As far as actual pipes are concerned, there is the full panoply – Dutch, Austrian, Italian, Swiss, Belgian, and French. Further, eighteenth-century earthenware tobacco-jars, carved snuff-boxes and ivory rasps. Important archive of advertisements. Worth noting is the education section on the history of tobacco.

Andenne – Musée communal de la céramique à Andenne
29, rue Charles-Lapierre
Tel: (32) 85 84 11 50
Situated in the Namur region, a museum of ceramics, that traces the history of Andenne ceramics from Roman times to the twentieth century: the development of the clay pipe, the glorious days of Andenne clay, a white and creamy deposit, whose plasticity was first noted by a pipe-maker from Coblenz. The tradition was continued until 1930. Look out for the two kilns (one medieval, the other from the last century), a model workshop (based on Pascal Léonard's) and a foundry.

Vresse-sur-Sémois – Musée du tabac et du folklore
(Tourist and Cultural Centre of Vresse)
rue Albert-Raty
Tel: (32) 61 50 08 27
In a region at the heart of Belgian tobacco production, a museum with a collection of over five hundred pipes from the fifteenth to the nineteenth century, in clay, ceramic and meerschaum. The story of tobacco is presented by a variety of objects such as snuff-boxes and cutters. Twentieth-century pictures provide excellent illustrations.

DENMARK

Copenhagen – Pipe Museum W.Ø. Larsen
9 Amagertorv
Tel: (45) 33 12 20 50
The most popular museum in Denmark on the subject of pipes and tobacco. Adjacent to the Larsen shop, in the centre of Copenhagen, it is a place dedicated to smokers down the centuries – snuff-boxes, pipes from every continent, made of every kind of material, tobacco jars and containers. Look out for antique silver pipe-cleaners on which the modern versions are based. Impressive tobacco library, which can be visited by appointment.

ENGLAND

London – Dunhill Museum
Burlington Arcade
Tel: 0171 493 6369
Off Piccadilly, not far from the Dunhill shop in Duke Street (*see under* SHOPS), is this museum shop, no bigger than a dolls' house, opened in 1990. Ian MacOmish, the Archives Manager, had the commission of buying back antique pieces for the famous British firm. These include the Shield (with a wind-screen for use in an open-top car). He has now retired and has been succeeded by Howard Smith.

Brighton – The Royal Pavilion
Old Stein, East Sussex
Tel: 273 60 30 05
Rebuilt from 1817 onwards, the Royal Pavilion is an architectural fantasy in the Moghul style dedicated to oriental art. Set in the gardens is the Brighton Museum and Art Gallery, where the Willett Collection has an interesting collection of terracotta pipes from 1790 -1800, as well as pipes from the nineteenth century.

FRANCE

Grasse – Collection Alice de Rothschild
Bibliothèque municipale,
boulevard Antoine-Maure
Tel: (33) 93 36 26 85
This collection can be seen by appointment only. Born in Frankfurt in 1847, Alice de Rothschild, was a strong and mysterious personality, the owner of a villa on the Côte d'Azur, which Queen Victoria was in the habit of visiting. There are 450 prize items here (very few of wood), which have been in the ownership of the Grasse municipal library since 1927. Yet the value of the collection is in its eighteenth-century meerschaum pipes, Venetian clay pipes, impressive polychrome porcelain bowls from Saxony, and Staffordshire clay pipes.

Dieppe–Musée municipal Vieux Château
rue de Chastes
Tel: (33) 35 84 19 76
A collection of fragments of eighteenth- and

nineteenth-century clay pipes (265 bowls and 186 mouthpieces), which can be seen by appointment.

Paris – Musée de la Seita
rue de Surcouf
Tel: (33) 145 56 60 17
A permanent tobacco exhibition installed in a gallery on the ground floor of the Seita building. Tobacco scales, various kinds of pipes, including opium pipes, with panels explaining the manufacture and production of tobacco. Bookshop adjacent to the museum (see under SHOPS).

Saint-Claude – Pipe Museum
1 bis, rue Gambetta
Tel: (33) 84 45 17 00
The epic of the pipe as centred in Saint-Claude: working with wood (a craft dating back to the seventh century), manufacturing processes, the development of the pipe throughout the world, and the museum's private collections. Beech, cherry, boxwood and, since 1854, briar root – from wood-turning to carving, the entire history of the skill of the master pipe-makers of the Jura region. What is also shown is how a city that was a major stopping-point on the pilgrim roads to Santiago de Compostella exchanged religious artifacts for pipe mouthpieces and bowls, hornwork, amber and ivory.

Saint-Omer – Musée Sandelin
14 rue Carnot
Tel: (33) 21 38 00 94
Installed in an eighteenth-century mansion, the property of Madame Sandelin, the present museum is furnished throughout in the style of the period and exhibits art objects and paintings – including Flemish and Dutch – as well as a collection of clay pipes. Two thousand items from the firm of Duméril, which was one of the two most famous – the other being Fiolet – at the time when St. Omer was known for tobacco and pipe production. Without question the finest collection of French clay pipes with figures of Christ and of famous individuals, from antiquity to the present day.

Bergerac – Musée du tabac
Maison Peyrarède, place du Feu
Tel: (33) 53 63 04 13
The museum was set up by Georges-Henri Rivière in 1950 and relaunched in 1982 by Bernard Clergeot. Together with the Institute of Tobacco and the Training Centre it is one of the three antennae of the French tobacco capital. Housed in an early seventeenth-century mansion, Bergerac's tobacco museum has an anthropological slant. In other words, it presents civilizations in terms of tobacco in its natural environment. The collection consists of thousands of objects of which three hundred are pipes – all the most important types are represented.

This region boasts some 200-300 dark tobacco growers, so take the opportunity to visit the research laboratory of the Institute of Tobacco (itinerary signposted with arrows available free on request) to see growing methods, and the use and varieties of Nicotiana.
Institut du Tabac (The Institute of Tobacco) is at Domaine de la Tour, 24100 Bergerac
Tel: (33) 53 63 66 00.

GERMANY

Hamburg –
Tabakhistorische Sammlung Reemtsma
Parkstrasse 51
Tel: (49) 40 82 00 / 20 54
(Open by appointment)
This 1930s brick-built former residence of P.F. Reemtsma, industrialist and cigar manufacturer, houses six thousand documents relating to the use of tobacco. There are also some rare items, inlcuding some of the first clay pipes, packet wrappers from Russian and Turkish cigarettes, and smokers' accessories from North America, Africa and Asia.

Bremen –
Bremer Landesmuseum – Focke Museum
Schwachhauser Heerstrasse 240
Tel: (49) 421 361 35 75
In the setting of a museum devoted to the history of Bremen and the surrounding area, an important collection dealing with pipes and tobacco cultivation.

Bremen Überseemuseum
Bahnhofsplatz 13
Tel: (49) 421 397 83 57
Historic facts on the history of tobacco in the framework of a complete overview of Oceanic, African, American and Pre-Columbian civilizations, with an emphasis on the environment, economy and religion.

Husum – Tabakmuseum in Husum
Wasserreihe 52,
Tel: (49) 48 41 61 276
Private museum run by Helmut Schwermer, who displays accessories, posters and books on the subject of tobacco in a building that is over one hundred years old.

ITALY

Gavirate – Pipe Museum
Via de Chiostro 1/3
Tel: 332 74 77 50 (by appointment)
In Lombardy, near Varese, at the northernmost tip of the lake of the same name, Alberto Paronelli, president of the Pipe Academy, has installed one of the most comprehensive pipe museums in a house that belonged to his grandfather. No less than one thousand pipes from all over the world,

six wood lathes from Saint-Claude (still in working order), three hundred wooden and briar tools dating from the last century and a collection of three thousand steel awls as well as old pipe-factory registers and catalogues, books and posters. The library contains over a thousand works in different languages on the subject of the pipe. There are two rooms given over to the restoration of pipes.

NETHERLANDS

Gouda – Moriaan
Blackmoor, Westhaven 29
Tel: (31) 182 088 444
50 km from Amsterdam, Gouda is an old mercantile town famous for its cheeses and its pipes – the Guild of Master Pipe-Makers was established here in 1661. The Moriaan Museum is set in a former sugar refinery, whose Renaissance facade dates from 1617. Since 1938 it has been combined with a shop (which sold tea, coffee and spices in the eighteenth-century) conveying the opulent atmosphere of eighteenth-century luxury enterprises in Holland with a range of smokers' requisites. Ceramics, tiles decorated with tobacco-based designs from 1600-1850, an important collection of ceramic and clay pipes, snuffboxes, and a machine for shredding tobacco, as well as a video which shows pipe-making in Gouda's heyday.

Leiden – Leiden Clay Pipe Museum
Oude Vest 159a
Tel: (31) 71 12 13 40
Leiden, former centre of the clothing industry and historic showpiece, famous for its university which was the first in the Netherlands, has one of the finest collections of clay pipes. The museum incorporates a research centre for the study of pipes, and offers a complete overview of clay pipes – from Pre-Columbian to ceramic pipes, not to mention Turkish pipes and hookahs, personalized French pipes (1880) and engraved copper moulds. There is also typographical material dating from 1870, belonging to a Gouda pipe-maker.

Groningen – Niemeyer Museum
Brugstraat 24
Tel: (31) 50 12 22 02
A fourteenth-century residence in Groningen, the major northern city of the Netherlands, houses the Maritime Museum of the North and the Tobacco Museum. Objects related to tobacco-smoking in Pre-Columbian America, American-Indian pipes, clay Gouda long pipes, copper moulds, splendid meerschaum pipes with silver covers, porcelain pipes (note the pipe with the figure of Madame de Staël) and horn and porcelain pipes are on display. Be sure to see the reconstruction of a seventeenth-century tobacconist shop.

Stockholm – Nordiska Museet
Djurgardsvagen 6 -16.
Tel: (39) 46 8 666 46 00
The Nordic Museum on the island of Djurgarden was founded in 1872 by Artur Hazelius, who set up the open-air museum at Skansen. It holds over a hundred pipes – mostly clay, some meerschaum and briar with silver lips. The theme of the museum is the life and work of the Swedish people.

Lausanne –
Musée de la pipe et des objets du tabac
Galerie de Coq-Muet
7 rue de l'Académie
Tel: (41) 21 23 43 23
An antique dealer specializing in antique art and sculpture, Jacques Schmied is also a pipe collector. His pieces are on display in showcases in the basement of his shop in Lausanne, between the cathedral and the castle. He has over 2,500 pieces, chosen for their rarity and historical value rather than for their beauty. The most spectacular include eighteenth- and nineteenth-century glass pipes from Murano, silver pipes, and Swiss seventeenth-century boxwood pipes. Also on show are tobacco jars and boxes and other accessories, and engravings. A private museum worth a visit.

C L U B S & A S S O C I A T I O N S

Pipe Club of London
40 Crescent Drive, Petts Wood
Orpington, Kent BR5 1BD

The Sweet Briars
c/o The Rosemary Tavern
Rosemary Road, Norwich, Norfolk

The Cotswold Pipe Club
Regent Arcade, Cheltenham, Glos.

In France there are about forty pipe clubs that organize regional meetings, debates, conferences, and competitions including the endurance exercises known as pipe-smokers' championships.

Pipe Club de France
9, rue Saint-Fiacre, 75002 Paris, France
Tel: (33) 142 36 51 02
Founded by André-Paul Bastien in 1969, member of the International Committee of Pipe Clubs, which covers nineteen countries in Europe, Asia and America, the current president of the Pipe Club de France is Roger Almerge.

Euro-Pipe Club of Brussels
Le Poechenellekelder, rue de Chène 5
B-1000 Brussels, Belgium
Founded by Jean-Pierre Forton and Michel Ringnoir, with Roger Van Tournhout as its president, the Euro-Pipe Club will send out a list of all pipe clubs in Belgium.

Quebec Pipe Smokers Club
CP 910 Succursale Desjardins, Montreal, Quebec, H5B 1C1, Canada
Founded in 1992, this club has a membership of ninety, organizes demonstrations and meetings, with an annual competition, and five dinners each year. The club publishes a newsletter six times a year.

ASSOCIATIONS

The Pipesmokers' Council
19 Elrington Road, London E8 3BJ
Tel: 0171 241 6950

International Pipe Academy
Via de Chiostro 1/6 , 21026 Gavirate, Italy
Tel: (39) 332 74 77 50
Founded in 1984 by André-Paul Bastien, Alberto Paronelli and seven international pipe experts. It now has twenty-two members from fourteen countries, under the aegis of its great master, Pierre Schiltz.

Association du calumet de la paix
(Pipe of Peace Association)
22, avenue Emile-Zola, 750l5 Paris, France
Tel: (33) 145 77 70 64
Founded in 1991, when the first anti-smoking measures were introduced, this association has more than 23,000 members, of whom one quarter are non-smokers. It operates in harmony with smokers and non-smokers alike, and intercedes in cases of litigation. Its slogan is: tolerance, dialogue, and good humour.

Association of Master Pipe-makers of Saint-Claude
42, rue du Pré
BP 32, 39200 Saint-Claude, France
Tel: (33) 84 45 04 02 (9 a.m. to 12 p.m.)
On the commercial level, this is an umbrella association for twelve Saint-Claude brands (Bontemps, Butz-Choquin, Chacom, Chap, Ewa, Ropp, Vuillard, Genod, Graco, Jeantet, Jean Lacroix and Claude Romain), which manufacture and distribute 700,000 pipes per year. On the social level, the association owes much to Edgar Faure, the parliamentary deputy for the Jura region and great tobacco enthusiast, who was responsible for bringing it to life again in 1966. That same year, he was declared Premier Pipe Smoker of France. Further, the association has over seven hundred members. In order to become a member of the association, and experience the magical and secret induction ceremony, it is essential to be an unmitigated pipe-fanatic, and preferably to be sponsored by one of the members when submitting an application for membership to the association.

International Committee of Pipe Clubs
CIPC, M. Geert Derske, Krommeniestraat 55,Tilburg 5045 RT, Holland.
Contacts with pipe clubs of member countries can be obtained from this committee. The general secretariat is headed by Roger Almerge (*see under* "Pipe Club de France").

U.S. Pipe Tobacco Council
1100 17th Street N.W.
Suite 504, Washington D.C. 20036, U.S.A.
Tel: (1) 202 223 8207

MAGAZINES AND BULLETINS

Pipesmokers Welcome Guide. The Pipesmokers' Council, 19 Elrington Road, London E8 3BJ.

Tobacco. Editor: Jacques Cole, Queensway House, 2 Queensway, Redhill, Surrey RH1 1QS (a second publication which does not appear regularly: Pipe Line).

La revue du tabac. International Tobacco Review, 18, rue Saint-Fiacre, 75002 Paris. Fortnightly publication of the Pipe Club de France intended primarily for tobacco professionals, a source of valuable information.

La lettre de la confrérie des maîtres-pipiers de Saint-Claude (*see under* ASSOCIATIONS). Every January the association informs its members of cultural and media events that have taken place during the year, and lists the names of new members.

Le grenier du collectionneur (The Collector's Attic). 88A avenue du Polo, 1150 Brussels, Belgium. Quarterly bulletin published by Jean Léo, specialist in clay pipes. For bibliophiles and collectors, see issues devoted to the pipe: Nos. 43, 57, 67, 75.

A : top briar pipe quality, rich in grain, including bird's-eye.

AB : well-grained pipe quality without flaws.

AC : less well-grained than AB, a few flaws are tolerated.

Amber : fossil resin from prehistoric forests used for making mouthpieces; originally found on the shores of the Baltic Sea, it is very difficult to obtain and is very expensive.

Ambrolith : (also known by other similar names) a synthetic product imitating amber.

Angoulmoisine : name originally given by André Thevet to the flower of the tobacco plant.

Apooke : original name (now unused) given to Virginia tobacco by the early settlers.

Apple : straight round model that looks like an apple; also made in bent.

Bale : unit for packing briar *ébauchons* (100 kilos); half bales are now common. Also applied to a set quantity of tobacco leaves.

Band or **Mount** : decorative metal band sometimes fitted to the most vulnerable part of the pipe-stem. Can also be made from precious metals. On "army" pipes, they are sometimes called "olive" mounts.

Base : or "basic", tobacco which is the main component of a blend.

Beater : worker who mixes the clay for pipes in a tub, with a large metal bar.

Bent : classic shape explained by its name; it is less heavy on the teeth than a straight pipe.

Bent Albert : a special bent shape with slanted bowl.

Bent Army : bent pipe fitted with an "olive" fitting; the mouthpiece can easily be removed for safety.

Bent Rhodesian : a bent version of the Rhodesian shape which has a very thick stem.

Billiard : the most popular straight pipe with an upright slightly rounded bowl.

Bird's-eye : type of grain on a briar pipe which looks like a series of birds' eyes; it is rare, but is actually the cross-section of straight-grains.

Blend : the mixing of a number of tobaccos, that can vary from six to thirty.

Blender : the tobacco expert who buys tobacco and creates the blends.

Blond : light tobacco with high sugar content and which is dried artificially.

Blowing : air jet under pressure that cleans the draught bore of pipes. Sometimes called "blow through".

Boring : drilling of the bowl with hand-tools.

Bouffarde : French expression for an ordinary pipe, supposedly from the name of a Napoleonic army corporal who died at the battle of Friedland, pipe in hand.

Bowl : the pipe without a mouthpiece; made from briar, meerschaum, clay or other material.

Bowl turning : the operation that shapes the bowl and its inside.

Broussin : French term for a briar root, the bulge (or burl) that forms between the actual roots and the trunk of the briar.

Briar : *Erica arborea*, which grows mainly around the Mediterranean Sea, the burl of which (commonly known as the root) produces a very hard wood suitable for pipe-making; it is heat resistant and retains the aroma of tobacco.

Briar root : the "growth" (burl) between the actual root of the briar, and the trunk.

Buffing : last process of finishing a briar pipe on a cloth-covered wheel.

Bulldog : sturdy briar pipe model with a diamond-shaped stem and a rounded top to the bowl; also available in bents.

Burley : type of light tobacco.

Burning : some colours are fixed to the briar by burning or flaming.

Calabash : pipe made from the gourd or outer casing of the calabash fruit, a native of South Africa; generally fitted with a meerschaum cup.

Carbonizing : the layer of tobacco residue that adheres to the inside of pipe bowls.

Canadian : model of pipe with a long "flat" (actually oval) stem and a short mouthpiece.

Chipparde : another French term for an ordinary pipe.

Chuck : a tool fixed on a lathe; it holds a briar block in its two "jaws".

Churchwarden : long clay pipe named after the members of Parish councils in England.

Clay (pipe) : clay has been used to make pipes since the sixteenth century; the main producers have been Holland, Belgium, France and Great Britain. They are still made and often used for tobacco testing, since they do not affect the taste of the tobacco.

Colour : also called tint, which is used on briar.

Combustion hole : the bored part of the bowl which takes the tobacco.

Corncob : a pipe invented by a Missouri farmer in 1869. The bowl is made from the dried cob of maize, treated with plaster and honey. It smokes well, but has a short life. Sometimes called Missouri meerschaum, hybrid corn has been specially developed for pipe-making. Corncob pipes are very cheap.

Crimp cut : a special type of cut obtained by shredding tobacco leaves in short and curly strands which then undergo a special drying process.

Culotteur : French name for the semi-"professional" smoker who used to carbonize pipes for others in the nineteenth century. There was no known title in English for this.

Cumberland : a type of high-quality vulcanite mouthpiece, generally dark brown with light streaks. Originally fitted to the Dunhill series of the same name.

Curly cut : type of tobacco cut introduced in the nineteenth century; it is a twisted tobacco, like a cord, which is then cut in thin slices and looks like a curl.

Cut : the width of strands of tobacco, from fine to coarse, via medium and large.

Dark : strong tobacco generally air-dried and cured.

Dark air-cured : dark tobacco dried and cured naturally.

Desiccation : second stage in the quick drying of light (bright) tobaccos; oxidation starts once the leaves have turned yellow.

Doorooker : Dutch term for enamelled clay pipes; the designs remained white while the rest of the pipe darkened.

Draught : the bore through the pipe which allows the passage of the smoke; a good draught ensures good smoking.

Drilling : boring into a briar pipe-stem, either for the draught bore, or for fitting the mouthpiece.

Dublin : a pipe shape which originated from clay designs; the bowl is slightly laid-back and wider at the top.

Ébauchon : briar block; this French term is normally used in English in the industry.

Enamel worker : woman who applied enamel colours with a brush between the two firings of clay pipes; she would have been called a slip-worker in a pottery.

Etched (wood) : a bowl surface carved by the etching method, with small cutters or special tools.

Etching : method used to imitate sandblast; sometimes called "surface carving".

Filling : the action of filling a pipe with tobacco, which needs to be done properly to obtain a good smoke.

Filling : also called puttying. This operation consists of filling small flaws in the briar with putty (also called mastic by some manufacturers) with a special spatula.

Filter : device which absorbs tar and nicotine when placed into the stem of a pipe It is cylindrical and made of paper or filled with filtering material such as charcoal or meerschaum dust. (*see also* System).

Finishers : women workers who polished clay pipes with an agate stone.

Fitting : operation that "marries" the stem of the bowl to the mouthpiece.

Flake cut : generic term for pressed tobaccos.

Flake : thin slices obtained from pressed tobaccos.

Flame : generally used to describe the nature of the grain in briar. "Grain" is more often used than "flame" in English, unless referring to flame-grain which is not as perfect as straight-grain.

Flavouring : the addition of an "agent" (spirit or extract of fruit, etc.) to modify the taste of tobacco.

Floc : this is the French name for the push or peg of a mouthpiece; the French name is often used by British manufacturers.

Fleurs (pipe) : a French name given to pipes which still show the outer crust of the briar at the top of the bowl. There is no generally used English term, although the most common is "crusted top".

Flue-cured : method of artificial drying used for the majority of basic tobaccos around the world.

Fraising : in briar bowl turning, the operation that clears the excess wood round the bottom.

Freehand : pipes made entirely by hand without use of machines or even holding-chucks.

Gouwenaar : a long clay pipe made in Gouda.

Grades : quality standard of tobacco leaves according to their position on the plant. Each level is also subdivided according to development, texture and other potentials.

Grain or **Graining** : the natural pattern of briar. When coloured (or tinted) the soft parts absorb the colour and show the grain.

Granulated : type of smoking tobacco, pressed and cut into small cubes.

Gris : traditional French pipe-tobacco – there is no English equivalent.

Horsetail : a plant with hollow rush-type stems used for polishing meerschaum pipes.

Humidifier : this is perhaps the nearest name that can be given to a slice of potato or apple, orange or lemon peel placed in a pouch to keep the tobacco fresh. It is hardly ever used in Britain, except occasionally in tobacco jars that may not have a good seal.

Juice : the liquid residue from tar and condensation that occurs in pipes; commonly called "goo".

Kentucky : a dark tobacco, generally fire-cured, which grows in Kentucky and Tennessee, but is also cultivated in Canada, Italy and Malawi.

Latakia : a very dark tobacco grown in Syria which gives a special flavour in mixtures.

Levelling : papering (sanding) operation to align (or level) the stem of a pipe with the mouthpiece.

Light air-cured : light or bright tobaccos naturally dried such as the Burley and Maryland.

Lip : part of the mouthpiece held in the teeth.

Liverpool : long-stemmed Billiard shape of pipe with a short mouthpiece.

Loose leaf-cut : name given to tobacco mixtures that contain some tobacco that has been neither shredded nor pressed.

Lovat : pipe shape similar to the Liverpool, but fitted with a short "saddle" mouthpiece; named after Henry Fraser, Lord Lovat, of First World War fame.

Marseillaise : a size of briar block (*ébauchon*); the French term is used in English, but more often referred to as "M" size.

Maryland : light (bright) tobacco used occasionally in mixtures to soften the strength of another tobacco.

Meerschaum : a silicate of magnesia; it is a fragile and solid mineral suitable for pipe-making and generally found in the region of Anatolia in Turkey. The name comes from the German and it was thought originally to have been created by sea-foam – it actually floats on water. It was probably first used in the seventeenth century.

Mixte A : the quality below the AC, which admits a few sand-spots and other very minor flaws. Often called English Mixte in Britain.

Mixte ordinaire : a slightly lower quality than Mixte A, referred to in Britain as Mixte O or French Mixte.

Mixtures : ready blended tobaccos which are put together without further process.

Mount : *see* Band.

Mousquetaires : French name given to metal pipes made by army blacksmiths in the seventeenth century. No English name has been traced, but slavers used metal pipes called "Trait [trade] pipes" after the French *pipe de traite* when negotiating for slaves in Africa.

Mouthpiece : the part fitted to a pipe that is held in the mouth (or teeth); can be made of cherrywood, horn, bone, amber or plastic material, but vulcanite is now most frequently used.

Nicotiana tabacum : name give by the French botanist Jean Liebaut to the tobacco plant brought back from Portugal by Jean Nicot; it has red or pink flowers.

Nicotiana rustica : this type of tobacco plant bears yellow flowers and the leaves are used for smoking in narghiles (hookahs).

Nicotine : a strong and toxic alkaloid, deadly in its pure state.

Orient or **Oriental** : tobacco grown in Greece, Bulgaria, Turkey, Syria, the former Yugoslavia, Albania, Romania and southern Russia, and in parts of Italy, Lebanon, Iran, Iraq and Israel; generally has small leaves.

Panels : flat surfaces cut on the sides of briar bowls. They vary in number to produce pipes such as panel-Billiards, panel-Apples, etc.

Patina : yellow to brown colour which develops on a meerschaum pipe; caused by absorbed tar and the beeswax used on the pipes.

Perique : very special type of tobacco grown only in the parish of St James in Louisiana, USA. It is prepared by a unique process which has been in use since the fourteenth century. Ideal in small quantity in mixtures.

Petun : original name used in France for tobacco, which originated from the South American name. The verb "to petun" was used in England for "to smoke" in the early days.

Pipe : from the Latin *pipa*, meaning reed or tube, given to smoking instruments made from wood, briar, clay, meerschaum and other materials.

Pipe cleaner : cotton wound around a metal core for cleaning the draught holes of stems and mouthpieces.

Pipe-maker : 1. craftsman who makes complete pipes with the aid of a lathe; 2. craftsman who makes pipes without mechanical aid and can be called a Master pipe-maker.

Pipe-rack : small rack made to hold pipes when not in use, varying from those which accommodate one or two to those with space for a dozen or more.

Pipe-tamper : generally, a short metal rod with a flat round piece at one end to tamp down the lit tobacco; can be part of a pipe-tool or a single item. Tampers were made decorated with figures of personalities or literary characters.

Pipe-tool : a three-pronged instrument consisting of a "prodder" (thin rod), a blade and a flat metal part to act as tamper.

Plateaux : "slices" cut across a briar root, used for making freehand briars.

Plug : small plug placed in the open combustion hole of a clay pipe.

Poker : *see* Stand-up-Poker.

Polishing : operation to smooth out the surface of briar bowls and mouthpieces to produce a perfect surface for colouring and finishing.

Polishing peg : tool used to polish the interior of briar bowls.

Porcelain : porcelain pipes were mostly made in Germany; they were heavy and fragile and could sometimes make the tobacco taste somewhat acrid. They are highly-prized as collectors' pieces.

Pot : shape of pipe with vertical sides, based on Hungarian pipe bowls.

Pouch : soft container made of leather or cloth to carry tobacco in the pocket, usually lined with rubber or rubber-based material.

Pressed (tobacco) : method of tobacco preparation by which various tobaccos are pressed under steam, then sliced to produce flake.

Priming : gathering or thinning out the lower leaves on a tobacco plant.

Prince : pipe shape with the bottom wider than the top.

Pumicing : the operation in briar pipe-making that polishes an already coloured bowl to obtain a uniform colour; it is also used on the mouthpiece.

Pyrolite : very tough material, also called carbon graphite (99.995 per cent pure carbon) evolved in aeronautical research. Used for a short time to produce pipes.

Race : the lowest quality of briar block (*ébauchons*) and turned bowls.

Rasping : sometimes called "shaping"; an operation carried out on a wheel, or by hand with a rasp, to eliminate extra briar after bowl turning.

Ready rubbed : pressed tobacco which has been broken up; eliminates the need for smokers to rub in the hand.

Reamer : tool used to clean excess carbon from the inside of a pipe bowl.

Reaming : an operation to enlarge the bore of the briar stem to fit the mouthpiece.

Relevée : type of *ébauchon* (briar block) – usually called simply "R" in English – for the turning of bent shapes.

Roller : worker (in clay-pipe making) in charge of rolling the clay to be placed in the metal moulds.

Rough bowl : state of a bowl when it has been turned but not completely shaped.

Sandblasting : operation to eliminate the soft parts of the briar, leaving the harder parts. It is carried out using a jet of sand (more normally now metal or glass grit) under pressure.

Sandblast (pipe) : pipe bowl that has been sandblasted; it gives a rough appearance, but is light in weight.

Sawing : first operation in briar pipe-making, cutting the *ébauchon* block to fit the turning machine's chuck.

Sauce : various additives used to modify the taste of tobacco.

Scaferlati : French name for cut-tobacco.

Scraper : the instrument used in scraping, which can also be a reamer.

Scraping : cleaning, by scraping or reaming the inside of a bowl, to eliminate excess carbon.

Smoking parties : very popular at the end of the sixteenth century in London, where smoking was taught; "ancestors" of the modern Pipe Clubs.

Stamping : last operation in pipe-making, when the manufacturer stamps the brand of the pipe, series number, shape number and other relevant markings.

Stand-up-Poker : derived from the Billiard shape, this model has a flat round bottom and can be put on a table without it falling over.

Stearin : greasy material used instead of beeswax by Turkish makers of meerschaum pipes.

Stem : the thinner part of the bowl (at right angles on a straight) into which the mouthpiece is fitted; also called "shank".

Stem-turning : operation of turning the stem with fast-turning cutters, called a "varlope" (the French term) by older pipe-workers in Britain.

Straight : one of the two basic types of pipes, the other being bent.

Straight-grain : highest quality of briar pipes: the grain runs upward on the bowl.

Strips : tobacco leaves before shredding.

Sun-curing : method of curing Oriental tobaccos.

System : also called "fitment" or "gadget" and occasionally "filter", this is a metal anti-nicotine device; very popular between the two World Wars, but considered superfluous by purists.

Tabakscollegium : name given by Emperor Frederick I in 1740 to the tobacco "college" at the Prussian court; its meetings followed the pipe evenings started by his father Frederick William I.

Tapping : any operation requiring the cutting of a screw thread; for example, when a metal system needs to be screw-fitted.

Tobaco : according to sixteenth-century Spanish sailors, it was the name given by the Indian natives of Hispaniola to the rolled leaves which they smoked.

Tobacco : plant belonging to the Solanaceae family, called *Nicotiana* in honour of Jean Nicot, who introduced it into France. There are at least sixty varieties.

Tobago : the island in the West Indies which may have given tobacco its name.

Tubing : fitting the system or filter in a pipe.

Vienna meerschaum : reconstituted meerschaum from offcuts of solid blocks. It can be moulded or carved.

Virginia : state of the United States where Virginia tobacco was originally grown. This variety is now grown all over the world.

"V" Reservoir : the part of a porcelain pipe which gathers humidity and tar, to counteract the lack of porosity of the material.

Vulcanite : the name used for a vulcanized rubber mouthpiece.

Whale oil : grease obtained from the frontal bulge of the sperm whale used to treat meerschaum pipes.

B I B L I O G R A P H Y

The bibliography that follows is not a compilation of literary works, but of technical works on pipes and tobacco. It is not complete, but does at least take into account the diversity of subjects and their specialized nature.

THE PIPE – GENERAL WORKS
The Pipe Book, Alfred Henry Dunhill, Arthur Barker Limited 1969

The Pipe, Georges Herment 1954
The Ultimate Pipe Book, Rick Hacker
The Christmas Pipe, Rick Hacker
The Global Guide to Tobacco Literature, Benjamin Rapaport, published under the aegis of the International Pipe Academy.

DIFFERENT TYPES OF PIPE
The Clay Tobacco Pipe, D. Helme 1978

A Complete Guide to Collecting Antique Pipes, Benjamin Rapaport, 1979

THE ART OF PIPE-SMOKING
The Gentle Art of Smoking, Alfred Henry Dunhill, Max Reinhardt Ltd. London 1981

TOBACCO
All About Tobacco, M.M. Sherman, New York 1970